ANNA

This book was published with the aid of the AMOS FUND –
Office of the President of Israel

ANNA

A Teenager on the Run

Anna Podgajecki

Translated from the Hebrew by Sandy Bloom

AMBERLEY YAD VASHEM

Academic Editor: Tikva Fatal-Knaani
Language Editor: Ora Cummings
Production Editor: Gayle Green

© First published in Hebrew 2002 and in English 2011 by Yad Vashem
This edition published 2016

Amberley Publishing
The Hill, Stroud
Gloucestershire, GL5 4EP

www.amberley-books.com

British Library Cataloguing in Publication Data.
A catalogue record for this book is available from the British Library.

ISBN 978 1 4456 5877 3 (print)
ISBN 978 1 4456 5878 0 (ebook)

Typeset in 10.5pt on 13.5pt Sabon.
Typesetting and Origination by Amberley Publishing.
Printed in the UK.

In memory of my parents, Idit and Wolf Rubinstein; my brother Efi; my sisters, Nina, Raya, Liuba and Batya; and all my relatives who were murdered by the Germans in 1942. This book is a monument in their honor.

Contents

Introduction

I am here in this world, having endured and survived the Holocaust and remain alive purely by chance. To this day I suffer from the terrible consequences of the absolute destruction wrought upon us by the Germans—one blow, followed by another and another, seemingly without end.

From an early age I have possessed a phenomenal memory. Many of my schoolmates envied the ease with which I excelled in my studies, due to my amazing memory. But the German occupation turned this aptitude into a curse, as I am not able to free myself of my horrendous recollections. My memory takes revenge on me and abuses me powerfully. Suffering has no mercy. My mind's eye is constantly full of appalling mental pictures, giving me no respite, both by day and by night.

It is unpleasant to have to admit that sometimes I regret having stayed alive. I ask myself: Was it worthwhile fighting so hard for a life full of misery, suffering and tears? But in those black days, when death was an integral part of our very existence, I thought otherwise. For some reason it was important to me to prove to the Germans and their henchmen that it was impossible to kill all the Jews, that there is no perfect crime, because witnesses to their actions are still alive!

Many years have passed since then but I am still unable to calm my inner turmoil. It is impossible to run away from such horrific death and destruction. After all, the Holocaust was not about armed soldiers dying in battle while carrying out their duty; it was not about death in fatal accidents due to human error. My sisters and brother were killed when they were children or just infants, when they did not even understand what they were accused of and why they were condemned to die. Their only 'sin' was that they were born Jews.

CHAPTER I

Before the Storm

I am Anna, daughter of Wolf and Idit Rubinstein who lived in the village of Korzec (Korets) in the Volhynia region. I am grateful to God that I was lucky to be born to such good-hearted and young, beautiful people, both inside and out. I was a happy, much loved, child and my entire world was marvelous.

Something strange happened to me when I reached an age when a child begins to remember early events. It was the first *Seder* of Passover and our apartment wore a festive air of joyous anticipation. I must have been tired because I fell asleep in Father's strong arms, and that's when I experienced my first dream—a dream, or rather a nightmare, that frightened me almost to death. It was about my uncle Michael Weiner, my mother's youngest brother, who I was very close to. In my dream I saw terrifying things that had no connection to reality. In my dream I saw my uncle lying under my bed in a strange uniform that I had never seen before; he was covered with blood, and he had only one foot. He looked as if he were dead. This dream came true many years later.

I awoke sobbing and shouted hysterically that I did not want to stay in our house any longer. No one could calm me down and my parents had no choice: in the middle of the night, they brought me to my maternal grandparents. I was terrified of the dream repeating itself and I was in a terrible temper.

My grandmother claimed that dreams have no meaning and in general she felt that one mustn't believe in things that cannot be substantiated rationally. In fact, none of my relatives placed any stock in dreams. They had never heard of a dream actually foretelling the future and as a child, I could not know that I belonged to that small group of people who could foresee the future and the unknown. Now, in my old age, I can verify that this same uncanny ability has accompanied me throughout my life and I cannot rid myself of it.

I lived with my grandparents for about three years, and they indulged me as if I was their only child. Nothing in the world could induce me to visit my parents. Older grandchildren also lived with me during that time; of course my grandparents loved all their grandchildren—but they reserved a special place in their hearts for me. Also, my mother's younger sister was still living at home with her parents and she was like a little mother to me; she was my favorite aunt. Yes, for me, the time I lived with my grandparents was unforgettable and exceptional.

There was great love between my grandparents. In many ways, Grandfather and Grandmother resembled each other as they both had pale, ash blonde hair and blue eyes. Everyone in our large family was tall and very handsome, on the inside as well as the outside. All their lives my grandparents loved animals and even though they were city dwellers they kept a small farmstead with two horses, two Dutch cows, a cat and lots of small kittens with colored ribbons around their necks. There was a special corner for geese and turkeys in the yard, as well as several fruit trees with early-ripening fruit. The cows produced milk that was in such great demand—people were willing to pay any price—that my grandparents never allowed themselves to consume their own milk products.

Grandmother was a quiet woman, not the type to engage in long-winded philosophical discussions, and because she was always busy she never had time for idle chatter either.

Whenever I went with her to take the cows out to pasture, she would search for special plants from which to extract medicine. She always had bottles full of all kinds of homemade remedies. Appearances were important to Grandmother and everything she had or did was in good taste. Even the clothes she wore, that she received from her sister in Boston, were lovely.

Grandfather, who loved horses, was employed in those days as a veterinarian. He was a tall, proud man, with a well-groomed moustache and penetrating blue eyes that missed nothing. I suspected that Grandfather might have enjoyed alcohol on the sly, but I never saw him drunk or even tipsy.

From the stories I heard, it seemed that Grandfather had been quite an adventurer in his youth. He had traveled a great deal in his Russian homeland, as well as in Poland, Germany and who knew where else. In fact, he had lived for some time in the United States, in Boston, and sent official papers back to Czarist Russia in order to arrange for his wife and small children to join him. Grandfather was very busy in Boston getting things ready for his family when he developed some unfortunate medical problems. The physicians who attended him advised him to have his leg amputated before it was too late. Grandfather was very worried and understood that his life was in danger. His family in Russia was preparing for the trip to America, to be with him and he was afraid that if he were not to recover, his family would be unable to manage on their own as immigrants in a foreign country. He felt that he had no choice but to return to his family and undergo surgery there, in Russia, his own country.

Grandfather traveled home and his leg recovered completely. But then, in 1917, the communist revolution took place. Grandfather was arrested immediately and accused of espionage, of having been sent by American capitalists to spy on Russia. He was tried and the judges sentenced him to death.

Grandfather's large family moved heaven and earth to save him. Grandmother contacted a Pole who dealt with smuggling people and merchandise over the Russian-Polish border. The man agreed—for a handsome sum of money—to organize a group of his friends to help Grandfather escape from jail and cross the border to Poland. The escape was successful; Grandfather, Grandmother and the children found themselves safe and sound—but penniless—in Poland. They remained, for lack of choice, in the village of Korzec on the Polish-Russian border, and it was there that they lost two of their children to hunger and cold. Eventually, however, they succeeded in building a home for themselves with a small farmstead that provided them with a livelihood. They raised horses and cows, grew fruit trees and sold their produce to the neighbors. Grandmother and Grandfather were gratified with the fruits of their labors and had started to plan to enlarge their small farm when one night it was all burned to the ground. Again, my grandparents were left with nothing, but they took comfort in the fact that they and their children had survived the deadly flames. My grandparents were upstanding, proud citizens who succeeded in rebuilding everything from scratch with honest hard work. I discovered all this from the stories one of my mother's brothers used to tell.

I remember vividly my trips with Grandfather; how I loved those outings! Grandfather used to sit me down in front of him on his horse. He took care to make me feel so secure and protected that I was confident enough to hold the reins and pet the horse's head and neck. Harnessed to a wagon, the horses were cheerfully decorated and had small bells hanging from their necks. When I sat in a sled I felt like a princess. Grandfather covered me with sheepskins and we traveled far and wide. I wanted those trips to last forever.

I shall never forget my grandparents' house. At first glance, it looked like the home of wealthy people; all the furniture in that house had been lovingly handmade. My grandparents were both sociable people; Grandfather had many acquaintances in the local villages and he and Grandmother often entertained groups of people in their beautiful home. Important guests could frequently be seen sitting at their dining table. During the Christian holidays. Grandfather was also often invited to visit his non-Jewish neighbors and was treated as a distinguished and welcome guest. Still, although my grandparents had many friends and acquaintances in Korzec, they felt lonely; for some reason, they felt like strangers in Poland and longed for Russia. As a young child, I wasn't capable of understanding the significance of all this.

I have some wonderful childhood memories. As time goes by, I can recall more and more incidents. For example, the loving care with which my Grandmother treated her Dutch cows. She always tried to take me with her when she went to tend the cows and I gradually learned to help her and did as much as I could. This was evidently Grandmother's purpose in taking me along, although at first I caused more trouble than I was worth because I always came home covered in mud and dirt!

I remember how I used to run barefoot through the green grass, which was damp with morning dew, enjoying the sensation on the soles of my feet. I was like a blissful kid and my grandparents loved to hear me laugh—a childish gurgling chuckle that could be heard from a great distance. What city child could ever know the utter bliss of the freedom I experienced in those far off days?

Time passed quickly and my grandparents enrolled me in a local Polish school. I now needed special conditions; for example, I had to have a space of my own in which to do my homework. New school friends started to visit me, children who also wanted to play with the house pets. I seemed to have become something of a nuisance, but my grandparents continued to indulge me. I wanted to stay with them forever— but something unexpected happened that affected my position in my grandparents' home. The wife of one of my mother's brothers died during childbirth, leaving two orphaned children. These two little girls were brought immediately to my grandparents' and all at once their immaculate home became crowded and unpleasant. This selfless act—the adoption of two little orphan girls—was one of the many acts of extraordinary altruism and dedication on the part of my grandparents.

It was not long after when Grandfather and Grandmother sat me down one day and informed me that it was time for me to return to my parents' house. As a result, I became very sick. My poor Grandmother tended to me with great devotion day and night until, slowly but surely, I began to recover. My grandparents were sorry for the pressure they had placed on me to leave them; they were sure that this was the main reason for my illness and blamed themselves for my suffering. They said that they would never try to force me to return to my parents. Wonder of wonders, I made a miraculous recovery from my mysterious illness!

Although they never mentioned the matter again, after I recovered, I did not stay much longer with my grandparents. One day, a beautiful wagon drawn by decorated horses pulled up next to the house and my mother's youngest brother, Michael Weiner, and his friends walked in. They appeared to be in high spirits and asked me to join them on a trip. I jumped up and down with excitement and we left the house together. We took a spin around the outskirts of our town until, eventually, the wagon came to a halt in an unfamiliar neighborhood. The young men asked me if I would like to go in and visit some acquaintances of theirs. I agreed. The house seemed strange to me and I didn't see a soul. We entered a small, glass-walled porch and turned into a charming large room, empty of furniture and smelling of new paint. There was a door there that led into another room. Suddenly I noticed a magnificent, high-wheeled baby carriage standing not far from me. In the carriage was an angelic-looking child with blue eyes and a very high forehead. He had straight, thick hair that was an ash blonde color. I couldn't take my eyes off him. I walked up to the carriage and let the little boy grab my long hair. At that moment, without even knowing who he was, I fell in love with him. The child diverted my attention and I continued to play with him. We had a good time together, and we laughed.

Suddenly I realized that I was alone with the little boy in the big room. I became confused and ran into the adjacent room to look for my uncle and his friends. Instead of the young men I was very surprised to find my parents and my younger sister. Their eyes followed me anxiously, to see how I would react. And it was at that minute that the penny dropped and in a flash I understood that my parents were moving into a new apartment so that I would come back to live with them.

But their stories and explanations had no effect: I wanted nothing to do with any excuses for what they had done. I felt that I had been set up and deceived and that the 'outing' with my uncle was an act of deception. I felt unwanted by my grandparents and cried bitterly at the pain of the sudden, abrupt move. It took me a long time to adjust to my new home and I mourned the end of those wonderful days when I lived with my grandparents. I spent a lot of time alone, thinking and remembering my magical past.

During my three years with my grandparents I had distanced myself from my family; I didn't even know that I had a new baby brother until I was tricked into entering my parent's new apartment. My parents were, of course, overjoyed at the birth of their son Efraim after two girls. As a young girl, I knew some sad moments in which I cried, but most of the time I was happy and could never have imagined what a wretched childhood awaited my younger siblings. I must say that those poor children endured the difficult times better than many adults. It's hard to believe, but during the German occupation, the children suffered in silence.

I loved Korzec and everything in it; I thought it was the most beautiful place in the world. My family was with me and my parents created healthy, stable living conditions for us all. My life was without worry, so that when I look back on it, my early childhood seems like paradise.

Until 1939, the town of Korzec was on the Polish-Russian border. The part my family lived in was on the Polish side. Korzec was very clean and green; in its immediate vicinity there were cultivated fields and broad woodlands. The Korczyk River flowed near the town; its deep, wide waters surrounded Korzec and all its residents enjoyed the river's crystal-clear waters.

Korzec boasted a number of monasteries and churches. The Jewish community, too, owned elegant, well-organized synagogues, of which one was the Central Synagogue, with its exquisite architecture on the outside and fabulously valuable decorations inside. This holy site was the pride and joy of every local Jew. When the Germans occupied Korzec, they burned down this magnificent synagogue and demolished it to its very foundations. Then they systematically desecrated and destroyed all the other synagogues in the town.

Where we lived there were Poles, Ukrainians, Germans, Czechs and Jews. The Jewish families were large, united and loyal, which gave us all a sense of security, stability and hope for the future. Since everyone in Korzec knew every one else personally, people tended to contend with their day-to-day existential struggles in a decent, respectable and honest fashion. It was for this reason that our town was virtually crime-free. In my opinion, it was a situation that created interdependence among the residents, Jews and non-Jews alike, and most of the local inhabitants had Jewish friends. This was the way it had been for generations. True, there were several ardent antisemites among the townspeople, who believed that Jews belonged in Palestine and should go and live in their own country; some of them even hung seditious anti-Semitic posters in their shop windows. At times, the average Jew would feel like an alien in his own homeland, even though the Jews were loyal citizens. However, although anti-Semitic views were sometimes aired quite openly, there was no real physical violence against the Jews. Other minority groups in Korzec also had problems; the Ukrainians would frequently quarrel among themselves and quarrels would sometimes lead to acts of revenge. On occasion, one of the warring sides would ask the Jews to arbitrate.

My father was born in Korzec and many of his relatives had lived in the Volhynia region for several generations. Some of them owned property and valuables that had been passed down from father to son, over many generations. My father's mother and oldest brother lived in the United States and his two older sisters lived with their families in Argentina. Until 1939 my father had had the opportunity to emigrate and join his relatives—either in Argentina or the United States; he was a skilled mechanic and could have made a living anywhere. But as a Jew, he yearned for a Jewish homeland and the only place he was willing to emigrate to was Israel. Father was active in the Jewish Worker's Union and envied those people who had been able to secure the coveted 'certificate' that would have allowed him and his family to settle in the Land of Israel. Immigration to Palestine was limited in those days by the British Mandatory authorities and many Jews were denied the necessary permission. Father was still young in those years, he was healthy and full of vigor and had high hopes that one day, he, too, would be allowed to go to the Land of Israel—especially since his skills were so crucial to the young state-in-making.

He loved his job, was outstanding at it and worked all his life as a mechanic. He invented numerous devices and would proudly hang the official patent certificates on his workshop walls. His workshop and adjoining store were on Stalina Street, right beside the large Nikolaevska church. Standing in front of the church were a row of Jewish-owned red brick stores which, following the German occupation, were all reduced to rubble and disappeared from the face of the earth, because they hid the church behind them.

My father was a vain man. I well remember his fashionable suits, all in fashionable colors. The local photographers used to ask my father for permission to take his photograph, so as to display it in their shop windows, because he was rather a handsome man.

Due to my father's excellent workmanship and sterling reputation, many a door was opened to him that was not open to other Jews. Even the local antisemites would come to my father because there was no one else who could do the kind of work that he could. They would come to him in person and tell him that they would never harm a Jew like him. Truly—there was no work he could not do.

Father worked hard and sometimes helped members of our extended family as well, but he bore his heavy responsibilities and never complained. Also, we were proud of the fact that almost everything in our house was homemade; we always baked our own bread, made our own noodles and prepared our own preserves and jams for the whole year. For the winter months, we'd prepare large quantities of pickled vegetables that tasted heavenly—we even knew how to preserve apples.

People who knew my mother testify to the fact that she was a beauty. Her eyes were a blue-green and her ash blonde hair was very long. People used to say that my mother looked like a model. It was a fact that everyone in our family was good looking. As people would often say, "the apple doesn't fall far from the tree."

My mother was born after her parents had produced five sons. She was a princess, always the center of attention, and used to love telling us stories of her wonderful childhood.

She went to a Russian school, where she learned ballet. But something happened in her childhood that put an end to her dreams—the communist revolution. Her family lost everything in the revolution and they arrived in Poland as penniless refugees. My mother remembered it as a time of hunger and great suffering. I believe that this first crisis in her life affected her personality and behavior later on.

Although my parents got married very young their marriage was a very successful one. Their decision to have a large family was based on the belief that big families provide their members with their own support and aid. They brought eight children into the world, five daughters and three sons. I was the oldest and was followed by my sister Nina and my brother Efi (Efraim), then there was Leon and my sisters Raya and Liuba. Another child—a beautiful blonde baby girl named Batya—was born on the verge of the German occupation. Who could have known that this baby would never see a happy day in her life! There was another boy who died in infancy. All the children were wanted and loved; all were healthy, handsome and successful. Leon and Raya were dark like Father, while all the other children took after Mother, with her blonde hair, blue eyes and black eyelashes and eyebrows. Yes, all my parents' children were distinctive in many ways.

My parents were very conscientious in the way they raised their children and they expected us to do our share and help around the house as much as we could. They were deeply devoted to their children and we were devoted to their welfare in return—both in good times and in bad.

Women envied my mother and would often ask her for her secret in rearing such delightful, well-behaved children. My mother would only mention 'grandma's recipe', which stressed the importance of investing in the first-born; the rest would follow of its own accord.

I was proud of my parents and wanted to be just like them in every way. They knew how to unite the family and to create a warm atmosphere of mutual love. Truth and honesty were the foundations of their existence. Today, I yearn for those wonderful years; I had no idea then that my childhood would prove to be the happiest period of my life, even though I am pained by my childhood memories, because of what happened afterwards.

Even though our family was a large one, we always made room for two young men from Lithuania, students in the local *yeshiva* (rabbinical academy). As soon as the two completed their studies and left, we would immediately 'adopt' two others to replace them. I never understood how my parents were able to assume responsibility for these young men. Apparently, the young men were orphans and it was a big mitzvah (a good deed) to open one's home to orphans, and my parents believed that by virtue of their kind-heartedness, their own children would never become orphans. Whenever a stranger from out of town visited our synagogue, he would always be directed to our home. Father didn't know how to refuse a hungry person and always welcomed unexpected guests.

As children we always enjoyed equality, until at some point I, as the first-born in the family, began to receive more clothing and shoes than my siblings. The change was not only in quantity, but quality, too. Mother began to worry about my future and my tendency to sacrifice my own needs for the sake of others. She made time to talk to me and told me that I must think of myself, too; she encouraged me to limit my generosity and self-sacrifice. I think she was concerned that I might be underprivileged and discriminated against all my life. I didn't appreciate at the time how special Mother really was. She made a point of reminding me that my brothers and sisters were *her* children, not mine and responsibility for their upbringing was hers and not mine. I sensed a slightly apologetic tone in her voice for having allowed herself to become so dependent on my help with the younger children. But I never changed; perhaps Mother's lectures had been too late; or perhaps self-sacrifice was just my nature. Who knows?

In 1937, my parents came to the conclusion that they had to make a special effort to become homeowners. They had their eye on a piece of land in the middle of town, on the corner of Monasterska and Stalina Streets, surrounded by a high fence. The plot contained three ramshackle houses, neglected and unfit for human habitation. Although several people were interested in purchasing that plot of land, no one knew whom to approach. My father decided to take the initiative and seek out the owner. In the end, he traveled to Warsaw to meet the owner and seal the deal.

My parents were overjoyed and began pulling down the dilapidated houses on their newly purchased plot of land. The houses were decorated with a lot of intricately designed, old-fashioned copper artefacts that several art dealers came to look at. But when they tried to persuade my father to sell he refused. The art dealers later admitted that all the artwork was priceless, as were the large chandeliers that hung from the ceilings. We later discovered that the houses had once belonged to Polish aristocrats.

The next few years turned out to be very difficult for our family because, once they had paid for the land, my parents had no money left over for day-to-day necessities. As a family, therefore, we paid a high price for this building project and the children often had to share in the backbreaking construction work when there was not enough food to eat. Our financial situation was so bad that one of the children would sometimes collapse from hunger and hard work. Father refused to approach our extended family or let them know how bad the situation really was, especially since he already owed them money. And the construction lasted for years, because we didn't have the money to complete it. Still, eventually, a two-family house was built, one for the family and the other for the children, in the future. One of the houses consisted of five enormous rooms, a kitchen and a long hall that separated the two apartments. It was beautiful, and we were all very proud of our new home. Who could have known that our beloved home would one day turn into a dangerous trap that would bring catastrophe to us all?

Very early one morning in the summer of 1939 we heard the drone of airplanes. This was unusual in our town, so we dressed quickly and rushed out to join our father who was already outside. It was still dark. We saw airplanes in the sky and they did not leave. Our neighbors were standing nervously beside the walls of their houses, trembling with fear. Everyone knew that Father had once served in the army, so they asked him, "What's going on here? Why are the airplanes here—are they going to bomb us?"

Suddenly we heard another unfamiliar sound—that of approaching vehicles, which Father thought sounded like tanks. The noise intensified as the vehicles came closer. Father ran towards the main street that was close to our home and I followed him despite his objections. I always felt safe and secure near Father and no shots were fired. We stood on the sidewalk next to the road and that's when we saw a military vehicle approaching from the Soviet border. Many of the local people also rushed over to see for themselves.

The Russian soldiers were very friendly and greeted us warmly, asking if Warsaw, the Polish capital, was close to our town. It might have seemed as if Russia wanted to take over all of Poland. Slowly and gradually, numerous army units passed by and continued on their way. It looked like a giant military procession; it was impressive and it was also full of joy, everything appeared to be well organized and shining. Yes, it transpired that this was the Russian occupation of some of Poland's territory in 1939; an occupation that would last for only two years, until the Nazis arrived.

The atmosphere was friendly and genial and the local residents were relaxed and in a good mood. For the first time, people started to talk about relatives who lived in Russia. Throughout the day, the town gradually filled with military personnel who regaled us all with stories of the 'communist paradise'. Suddenly we were important people in an important town and there was a palpable feeling of relief in the very air we breathed; the transition from one regime to another was taking place without bloodshed and without war. It was as if the doors of a prison were opening. The new local municipal administration acted quickly to install its essential health, educational and cultural institutions. A free municipal library opened its doors; all of a sudden our town boasted a magnificent culture hall, where there was dancing accompanied by the military orchestra. The streets were filled with soldiers all day and all night and our sleepy, quiet town became bustling and lively.

The Soviet administration opened new schools. Previously, children had finished their education after only seven grades, but the new regime decided to add extra grades. It seemed that we would now be given the chance to obtain further state-funded education and we were very happy. My mother, who had studied ballet as a girl, decided that the time had come for me to learn how to dance. Under the Polish regime I had completed my elementary school education; most of my teachers came from central Poland. Under the Russian occupation we received new teachers. From 1939 until 1941 I attended evening classes where lessons were in Russian; we were also taught German. I never had time to do my homework and worried that I wouldn't be able to keep up my grades, but luckily my excellent memory came to my rescue. In those days, everything came easily to me; I excelled in languages and had a special talent for picking up the right accents. This discovery, that I had a talent for languages, brought about a great change in my life. My brothers and sisters also did well in school.

The fact that Father no longer had to worry about earning a livelihood constituted a significant change in our lives. Local municipal clerks visited our home and filled in registration forms for all the children. They explained that, according to Soviet law large families were entitled to government funded financial support. Thus, we and many other families began receiving a monthly child allowance. Also, my parents enlisted the help of some old friends to arrange for me to get some professional training in the telephone-telegraph department of the central post office. I began working by day and studying by night and in that way I managed to provide the family with some additional income.

Now that my parents had more money at their disposal, they went overboard on a shopping spree. They rushed out to buy beautiful new furniture and a large wall clock and to lay porcelain tiles. They chose some attractive new curtains to hang at all the windows. But, most important of all, they bought several imported musical instruments. It seemed that their dream had finally come true and each of their children was able to choose his or her own musical instrument.

Although my mother encouraged me to dress nicely and take care of my skin and hair, I was still forbidden to walk down the street with any of my male classmates. Father had eyes in the back of his head and it made no difference how far behind me the boy walked, my father would always notice. He would then go up to the boy and say, "You're wasting your time. Anna's not the one for you!" Having always been accustomed to obeying my parents, I did not get angry with them. I wasn't even allowed to go out alone in the evenings. My parents believed that children achieved their independence and self-confidence by working on things they were able to do on their own and not through wasting their childhood on frivolity and empty entertainment. I didn't even dare ask for permission to go dancing at the cultural center. Admittedly, I was too young for such things, but I did love music and longed to hear the orchestra. So I was never able to become friendly with any of the boys, though there was many a mother who tried to make friends with me in order to introduce me to her sons.

Looking back, I feel sad that I didn't know how to enjoy every moment of my childhood and early teen years. It hurts me to think that I wasn't able to appreciate life in my big happy family, though I do remember the blissful feeling I had when I played in wet sand on a rainy day. Like everyone else, I too have pleasant memories that I hold on to and I always think back to happy events that I can dwell on, without feeling pain.

How well I remember Sioma Dreizer, that irritating boy I was forced to share a school bench with for years. Sioma was good-looking and blonde, with gray-blue eyes. He was a habitual troublemaker, daring and full of self-confidence; everything came too easily to him. The problem was that he wanted to have fun and to entertain the other children at my expense. He went out of his way to invent new pranks with which to torment me and wouldn't miss an opportunity to take advantage of the fact that he sat next to me. His favorite game was to tie my braids to the school bench, or to anything else within reach. Then, when the teacher asked me to stand up, my long braids would be pulled back and look like a pair of clotheslines with all kinds of things hanging from them. My classmates would burst out laughing and even the teacher struggled to hide his smile. The whole thing was so embarrassing that I wished the ground would open up and swallow me. In fact, I suffered so much that I actually dreaded going to school.

I wasn't the only girl to be teased in school. The principal's only daughter was also in our class and she, too, had long braids. During recess, when all the children were in the huge schoolyard that was closed on all sides, Sioma would hide behind me, quickly grab at my braids and shout at the top of his voice, "Gallop, horsy!" Unfortunately, I always seemed to get caught out, because as soon as Sioma grabbed my hair, I'd try to run off as fast as possible, and he, of course would run after me, holding both my braids. He was thrilled to bits at

Anna

having managed to fool me again and I couldn't understand how I always fell into his trap. In any case, the result was inevitably the same, all my classmates laughed their heads off, while I suffered in silence and wept inside. I hated that boy with a passion and wished he would disappear off the face of the earth.

But the teachers never seemed to notice my distress and continued to seat us next to each other, despite all my protests. I clearly remember the annual school 'photograph day'. Once we had all taken our places according to plan, excited at having our photograph taken, the teachers suddenly moved a table into our midst. They called me to sit at the table and who did they place right next to me? That awful Sioma! The teachers were delighted to see us side by side and forced us to sit as close together as possible and even made us lean our heads against each other. I was so mortified that I wept in front of the whole school and that is how the photograph was taken!

A few years later, when I was a little older, Mrs. Dreizer began to plan little 'surprise' meetings with me. Sioma's mother was a tall, elegant woman, still young looking and pretty. I'd be walking out of school to find Mrs. Dreizer waiting for me, hoping for a little chat with me. She used all kinds of excuses to get me to visit their home. Her husband and her eldest daughter welcomed me as if I were an important guest. Their daughter was three years older than me, but she treated me as if I were the same age and a good friend of hers.

But every time I stepped foot in that house I was terrified of meeting Sioma, so I was never able to relax. Fortunately, I didn't ever run into him there; his family tried very hard to make me feel as if I was one of them, which I found extremely strange at the time.

I talked to my mother about these strange visits that I was forced to make and asked her for advice. My mother stared at some spot above my head and then answered me quietly, as if she was talking to herself, "Too soon, much too soon." After a long silence she started stroking my head and said, "You don't need to consult with me, dear; after all, these people were once our neighbors."

It was obvious that the Dreizer family were making plans for the future and not for the present. They never dreamed that a war would break out which would destroy us all. Not a single member of the Dreizer family survived; they were among the innocent victims murdered in our town in 1942.

After Germany and Russia decided to divide Poland between themselves,[1] our town began to receive many refugees from central Poland who were fearful of the anticipated Nazi occupation. From day to day the stream of refugees grew stronger and we were exposed to the appalling stories about the horrors these people had witnessed. Still, in my family we were certain that nothing bad would happen to us; after all, we were living under Russian rule and Russia was a big and powerful country.

Refugees began to settle in our region. There seemed to be no families with children among the refugee population and I was curious as to the reason. I was told that families with children were unable to escape from German-occupied territory. It was rumored that all the refugees were Jews because the Jewish population was under greatest threat from the Nazi regime. They described the terrible difficulties they had had to endure in order to cross the border onto the Russian side.

We welcomed four young, Warsaw-born Jewish men into our home, who told us that their families had stayed behind to guard their property. Our guests were tall, handsome,

---

1   Molotov-Ribbentrop Pact—a Nazi-Soviet pact entered into between Nazi Germany and the Soviet Union on August 23, 1939. This pact involved the division of parts of Europe, and especially Poland, into German and Soviet spheres of influence.

energetic and self-confident. They had high hopes that all this would blow over and they would be able to return home. But it was obvious by their behavior that they were under great stress; they were restless and spent much of their time outside on the street, listening to the latest news. They were among the first to leave for Russia even before the outbreak of war.

Meanwhile, life in Korzec continued as usual and many people, including us, still hoped that no foreign conqueror would set foot there. Nonetheless, all the townspeople attacked the local stores with a vengeance, buying up and stockpiling basic necessities, especially edibles. Our neighbors all spoke about the need to store food in case war broke out. It was no wonder, then, that my parents spent all their money on foodstuffs; they had a large family and a lot of mouths to feed. Food was a basic necessity, after all.

How were we to know then that we would never benefit from any of the food we had stored?

CHAPTER 2

The Germans Are Coming

On June 22, 1941, Nazi Germany invaded the USSR. Everywhere the streets were filled with young people trying to get the latest news from better-informed adults. Only a few homes possessed a radio. The uncertainty bred palpable stress. Day and night heavy traffic moved along the main road, as young Soviet soldiers made their way west to the battle-front. They left just as they had first entered Korzec two years before, their uniforms crisp and neat and tidy, as if they were about to join a festive parade. Sometimes the large numbers of vehicles on the road formed bottlenecks in the traffic and when this happened the soldiers were quick to take advantage of the reprieve by trying to strike up conversations with the local girls, so as to have someone to write them letters and correspond with from the frontlines. This behavior was unorthodox, but was now acceptable, due to the unique conditions of the times we were living in; everyone felt sorry for the Russian soldiers on their way to join the fierce fighting in the battlefields. The fact was that even the top military ranks had no idea what was really happening and no one could have foreseen Russia's crushing defeat.

As usual, the Jews were most concerned as it is they who are always the ones to bear the brunt of political upheavals. As children, we were confident that our parents would protect us from harm, although we also absorbed the atmosphere of stress and concern. We watched as the refugees left our town and made their way towards Russia. These people had no transport; they walked, pushing before them, with their last strength, small, very primitive wagons.

It was a tragic sight, one that left a great impression on me. There was something to it that was more powerful than sadness or fear. I, too, wanted to quickly make our escape to Russia. I rebelled against my parents and demanded that we evacuate our family, immediately, while we still had the chance. On the other hand, there were seeds of doubt in my heart; I wasn't certain that I was right. Over and over again, I asked myself if I really understood the situation better than my experienced parents? I was fraught and wrestled with myself day and night. I simply didn't know what to do.

Deeply distressed, I found a sympathetic ear in Eli Dunaevsky, a former schoolmate. A quiet, shy boy. Eli had tried very hard to befriend me when we were at school together. He would wait in the yard until I left the classroom and tried to escort me home, but he was afraid of my father and never dared approach my house. I don't know why my parents were so opposed to my having a boyfriend, maybe it was because they had never known any other kind of upbringing. When the war started. Eli often tried to 'bump into' me on the street even though we lived in different neighborhoods. I would never have dared invite a boy to my home. I think my parents were afraid of my becoming accustomed to someone who was unsuitable, which would ruin the rest of my life.

I was quite happy, therefore, when Eli wanted to discuss his own misgivings with me over the current situation. He was particularly interested in hearing what my parents thought about the total evacuation of our town. I told Eli that the war had given me the courage to offer my father advice and to tell him what I thought he should do, even though I was still dependent on him. Eli knew my parents well; he knew that they were people who were not easily persuaded. Still, he said I should try to use subterfuge in order to achieve the desired results; to pretend I was leaving on my own to join the refugees. He was sure that my parents would soon follow. For some reason, I thought so, too. It seemed that I had found a solution to my dilemma and confidently carried out my plan. Sadly, however, I wasn't able to save my family.

Things were different with the Dunaevsky family, who managed to get away in time. While they were living in Russia, Eli volunteered for the Red Army. After the war, I learned that he had been a pilot and he had been killed in battle.

It was common knowledge in our town that Father was a veteran soldier. Before the war even began Father received an order from the local office of the War Ministry to train youngsters and even some who were older. Of course it was all done in accordance with a list he had been supplied with. Father's military training regime was carried out in the enormous grounds of an old castle, a site that had been the object of many scary legends. Although no one else was surprised that Father had been chosen for this work, I was quite worried. I was concerned that Father might be drafted into the army and asked my mother, "Don't they have professional soldiers to do this kind of work? Why did they have to pick Father?"

Soon after Father began training soldiers, war was officially declared between Russia and Germany. Admittedly, the atmosphere had been tense for some time, but the official declaration still came as a bombshell for the Jewish community. A massive recruitment drive was launched immediately after the official announcement. All over town homes were filled with tears and suffering; families worried about the fate of their menfolk who were called to the frontlines. The recruits had no way of knowing at the time that the fate of the small children they had left at home would be worse than that of the soldiers at the front.

The German invasion was imminent and panic and alarm reigned, especially among the Jews. Panic shopping gripped the population as people tried to stockpile basic commodities and the shelves were soon stripped bare. In the belief that money loses its value during political upheaval and wartime, my parents decided to spend theirs. Not only did they stockpile on foodstuffs, but they also bought expensive household items; they felt that these could be exchanged for food, if necessity arose. But this, as it turned out, was a fatal mistake. Refugees cannot take large items with them, and leaving our home would have meant leaving behind all the fruits of our labors. Although we couldn't have known that in advance, our lovely home, and all it contained, become a death trap.

Meanwhile, the stream of refugees turned into a flood of panic-stricken people, racing to distance themselves from the advancing German monster. Everyone was going in the same direction—toward Russia.

Like many of the town's youngsters, I too stood on the main street watching the frenzied spectacle. A group of Ukrainians sniggered and joked at the tops of their voices that the powerful German army was capable of overtaking anyone who was trying to escape them. The Russian soldiers all looked so young. It was easy enough to guess what their fate would be and I grieved at the thought that many of them were going to their death in battle. I had no way of knowing then about the Holocaust that awaited the Jewish people, or the kind of horrors the Germans were capable of committing. As I stood there with people from my neighborhood, I could not, of course, foresee that these same people would soon turn their backs on us, their Jewish neighbors; they would not even spare our babies. At that time I was still a naïve child. Still, I became more determined than ever to convince my father that we had to join the stream of refugees. Quickly I ran home.

Again I confronted Father with painfully harsh arguments. I cried, I screamed, I stood in front of my father and demanded: We must flee, now!

My father responded with his usual excuses. How could we leave behind so much food and expensive property and march off with seven children? We had no car and the train station was 35 kilometers away. The younger children were too small to walk on their own, and Grandmother was too old to walk so far. How could we carry the children, as well as the food necessary for so many people? Also, there was my mother's younger sister and her baby; her husband had been drafted to the front. How could we abandon her in these difficult times?

At last, Father began making plans, albeit belated, to acquire a horse-drawn carriage, which he would pay for with stored merchandise or with the house. But the people he approached turned him away with vague promises that were never kept. What was happening? It was too late, too late. Others had made such plans a long time ago.

Still we could not pull our eyes away from the human tragedy that was unfolding in front of our very eyes. The massive human river continued on its way towards Russia, day and night, exhaustion evident on the faces of many of the refugees who lacked basic necessities. Our hearts went out to them.

So I tried to argue with Father, but in truth I had no answer to the logistical problems he raised. Mother was shocked at my impertinence, and scolded me, "How dare you speak to your father like this! How dare you attempt to tell him what to do! You are the one who is dependent on him, not the opposite."

My mother always said that Father was right. She was willing to follow him anywhere, even to Hell itself. She never made demands on him, never argued with him. And now, when he needed her to urge him to leave, to take my side against his inaction, she was silent.

It was a terrible, painful dilemma.

During one of those turbulent days, several young men from our neighborhood paid me a visit. They told me that they had left their families with the objective of getting away as fast as they could. They asked about our family; wanted to know what we had decided. It was an opportunity for me to raise my argument yet again; and again, I cried and shouted, "We must leave, now! Now, before it's too late!" And then something totally unexpected happened.

I was sitting on the porch, refusing to enter the house, when I saw my parents coming toward me pushing a bicycle and carrying a large package of clothes and food for me. "You are right, Anna," they said. "It's time for you to leave us. You must join the young people who are fleeing the town." I was dumbfounded. "You are very talented," my parents told me. "You know how to work; you know how to get along with people. You can take care of yourself, you can support yourself."

But, to my eternal regret, I did not interpret their actions correctly. Who could believe that my over-protective parents, who wouldn't even allow me to invite home a boy from school, would send me out with strangers to manage on my own?

Instead of understanding, compassion and gratitude, even sorrow, I burned with anger. And then I remembered Eli Dunaevsky's suggestion. Yes, I would pretend to leave, and they would come running after me. "I'll show them," I thought. "They'll run after me barefoot in the middle of the night!" That would convince them to bring the whole family along.

I rode off slowly on my bicycle, hoping against hope that Father would try to catch up with me. My mind raced furiously. Could I really be sure that I, a thirteen-year-old, was cleverer than the adults I had trusted my entire life? After all, everything I valued and held dear was in that house—my parents, my brothers and sisters. Now I was alone, totally alone, for the first time in my life. My legs automatically led me to the old pre-1939 border. I looked around and asked myself, "Where is Father?" He could easily have caught up with me on his own bicycle!

I felt sad and hopeless. But then I noticed large numbers of refugees, sitting on either side of the road. The road was blocked off by Ukrainians who claimed they were acting on German orders. The Ukrainian thugs bellowed threats at us but the refugees just ignored them and waited for a Red Army vehicle to chase away the Ukrainians and let us cross the border. The Ukrainians continued talking among themselves, and I was horrified to overhear them talking about what the Germans were planning to do to the Jews once they occupied the city.

This was worse than I feared. I had to do something, to at least take the older children with me, to get them out of town as fast as possible. We were wasting precious time. So I turned around and rode home.

At home, I ran into Father who was doubling his efforts to obtain a horse and carriage in order to flee the country. Yet everywhere he turned, he received only vague, empty, promises. Only later did we understand why the locals wouldn't sell us anything as valuable as a horse and carriage, when they could steal from us freely once the Germans were in charge. One thing was obvious—Father had waited far too long. It was too late.

My heart was racing; I wanted to gather up the older children and take some clothing; I wanted my parents' blessing. We were still on the porch, talking, when we were shaken by bombs going off right above our heads. Our house was in the center of town next to a courthouse, a hotel and a restaurant. The first bomb hit the hotel and the air was soon filled with the screams of wounded and dying people. Our own roof was punctured by shrapnel from exploding bombs. We were in the middle of an unexpected air raid that heralded the real beginning of the war for us and chaos reigned. My parents and I grabbed the smaller children and we raced, together with everyone else, towards the gardens and fields beside the river.

The battlefront had reached our town. For the first time, my father emerged from the state in which he had been denying the severity of the situation. We were trapped and our last avenue of rescue had been blocked.

We realized that it was dangerous to stay near the river, which was exposed to shelling from above, but it was equally dangerous to return home, because our house stood in a very prominent location and was exposed on all four sides. A battle was raging in one of the cemeteries at the entrance to Korzec—a lost battle, as we soon realized. We took shelter in the garden of some Polish acquaintances, a family by the name of Lizewski who owned a grocery store in the center of town. Meanwhile, the children had not eaten all day. They were barefoot and almost naked and so exhausted they fell asleep on the ground under a tree in one of the far corners of the garden. We let them sleep where they were and did not disturb the Lizewski family who lived there. My parents, of course, were very worried as they sat next to their children.

I can remember this as if it all happened yesterday. It was my first real experience of war. I moved some distance away from the family and sat alone under a large tree in the garden. The thick foliage cut me off from everyone else and I felt truly alone. It was a night of fire and death and everything had happened so quickly and so close to where we had been standing on our own porch. Yet frightening as the night was, I dreaded the morning even more. Who knew what tomorrow would bring? I recalled the threats I had heard recently from the neighbors, especially the Ukrainian nationalists, threats we had never heard before. And I remembered the shocking stories I had heard whispered about Jews in nearby villages.

Mother came to sit next to me and we talked about the children and the events of the past day. Yet Mother's biggest problem was Father and how to alleviate his emotional suffering. "Your father is suffering terribly," she said sadly, "and I want you to understand how badly his conscience is troubling him for not having listened to you and leaving when we still had the chance. He looks at our helpless children and dies a thousand deaths for not taking them away from here in time." We sat quietly for a few minutes. Mother continued, "You know your father, Anna. I think that you'll agree with me that it's best if you stay away from him now. It's painful for him to look you in the eye." Mother was even afraid that Father might consider committing suicide. She begged me repeatedly to never, ever mention the quarrel we had. Then she left me. So now, in the worst moments of my life, the parents I loved so much could not face me. I was alone.

The aerial explosions subsided, but we could still hear the sounds of shots being fired. I approached the fence and strained my eyes to see what was happening on the other side of the river. Finally, I was able to make out a long line of Soviet soldiers on the far bank, right opposite me. They did not have weapons or hats, their clothes were torn and many didn't even have boots. The wounded ones had makeshift bandages from pieces of clothing. Some of the wounded soldiers were supported by their comrades and they were all barely able to drag their feet. There was not a single local person in sight. Where had they all disappeared to? I knew that all this was happening in a residential area, an area where well-off people lived, with fields and fruit trees. Why didn't anyone offer the defeated soldiers some fruit from their trees? Why did no one bring some old piece of clothing or even a rag to use as a bandage? I thought it was awful.

The children woke up and were hungry and shivering from the cold. Our neighborhood appeared deserted. Mother and Father argued over who would go home to bring some food and clothing. In the end Mother agreed to go and take me with her.

We tiptoed quietly down our lifeless street and carefully entered our house. Inside, we immediately covered all the windows with various old blankets, closed all the doors and sealed the entrances. As quickly as we could, we went around hiding all our valuables. Finally, we quickly packed baskets with food and clothing and were prepared to leave when we heard a series of terrible shrieks. We ran to the attic overlooking the road and saw two crying children hiding behind their house on the corner of Stalina-Monasterska, almost opposite us. We were horrified to see some cheerful young German soldiers in leather uniforms coming out of the house, cursing and swearing loudly. They joined some other soldiers and appeared to be the first group of Germans to reach our town. Together they goose-stepped down the main street toward the old Russian border, in a threatening display of power.

From the attic we kept our eyes on the children who had hidden near a wall outside our house. They started to crawl closer to our house and Mother and I waited behind a closed door until we had a chance to whisk them inside. We recognized them as Dr. Shlugileit's children and they were trembling with fear. They described how the Germans stormed into their home and threatened their parents at knifepoint, demanding gold, cash and jewelry. Although the soldiers were given everything they asked for they still killed the children's parents and grandmother. Distraught, the poor children managed to slip away, narrowly avoiding their own death. Mother and I took the unfortunate orphans over to the home of other neighbors, the Werniks, who took them in.

We were shaken as we rushed back to our own children in the Lizewski garden, where we had left them with Father. Father told Mother that he had visually tracked the route of the defeated Russian army, hoping that there might still be a chance of following them over the old border. He didn't know that the Germans had already occupied our town. "But when I saw them at the sugar factory close to the border," Father explained, "I saw the German soldiers rounding up the Russians and taking them prisoner."

I decided to take a run through the side streets to the sugar factory. The Russian prisoners, including many who were wounded, were sitting far from the main road. All of a sudden, people started pouring in from the nearby villages, all dressed in their Sunday clothes. They took their positions on both sides of the main road, cracking sunflower seeds and telling jokes, as they watched horrible events unfolding. What on earth was happening? I noticed that there were no Jews among these people; everyone knew how dangerous it was for Jews to cross the main road.

But one brave soul was willing to risk his life in order to help others. I watched as Dr. Wallach ran in carrying his doctor's bag, with a white bandage with a big red star on his arm. An older woman I didn't recognize was with him, carrying a suitcase; she, too, sported a bandage with a red star, although hers was tied around her forehead. Everyone in Korzec and its surroundings recognized Dr. Wallach as the Jewish doctor who treated anyone who needed treating, be they rich or poor, with the greatest devotion. The people wanted to see how the Germans would react to the audacious Jew. But Dr. Wallach marched courageously into the middle of the road, allowing the German occupiers to see him clearly. The Germans, who didn't know he was a Jew, were furious and hurled threats and curses at him. Raising their rifles threateningly, they pushed the doctor out of their way. I found out later that the Germans had locked up some of their prisoners of war in a Jewish home on the main street, turning it into a makeshift prisoner camp. Sometimes I used to walk past the house and heard that Dr. Wallach had paid the Germans a hefty sum of money in exchange for the right to treat the prisoners. In fact, the kind doctor was the only person who extended any kind of help to the Russian prisoners of war.

The Germans then managed to ferret out the Jews and communists among the prisoners and, to my absolute horror, shot them to death on the spot. All this took place in front of a large crowd of people who agreed, "We knew that one day the Day of Judgment would come and the Jews and communists would be exterminated!" The air was full of curses and insults towards the Soviet regime.

The Germans commanded the prisoners to stand up and organize themselves into rows. And then another tragedy unfolded before our very eyes. The German brutes started beating to death all the wounded prisoners who were unable to stand. The rows of prisoners shrank as the Germans continued to beat those who supported their comrades. The entire area looked like a battleground, as more and more dead prisoners dropped to the ground and the road was filled with bodies. The Germans then encircled the remaining group of prisoners to check that no further wounded prisoners were hiding among their comrades.

It was my first encounter with death, let alone the brutal murders I had just witnessed. For the first time in my life I, who had been raised by loving parents who did their best to protect me from all evil, had seen the vicious cruelty that humans are capable of.

I felt the sky was falling in on me and bit my lip to keep from screaming. How could those villagers in their Sunday best remain indifferent? As this bloodbath took place, I heard the locals defend the Germans for having acted in self-defense against a mob of violent Russian prisoners. I had no idea on that horrendous day that our fate as Jews would be even worse than that of the Russian prisoners.

Anti-Jewish laws were quick to come. According to the first decree, every Jew was to wear a yellow star in two prominent places—on his chest and back. This was designed to distinguish between Jews and non-Jews, to make things easier for the German murderers. Jews were forbidden from walking on sidewalks or even at the sides of the road and were permitted to walk only in the middle of the road, to make it easy for German and Ukrainian murderers to see their Jewish victims from afar. A walk in the middle of the road meant taking one's life in one's hands; woe betide any Jew unfortunate enough to encounter a group of Ukrainians or Germans!

My mother had befriended a Russian woman who had moved to Korzec in 1939, following the Russian occupation of our town. My mother had moved to Korzec in her youth, as a refugee from Russia, which is probably why she was inclined to help this woman get acclimatized to her new life in Korzec. The woman soon met a local man and they began visiting my parents together, especially when they were in need of some help. Even though the young couple had no intention of getting married, my parents never objected to their visits. Although things under the German occupation had changed, some Soviet citizens chose to remain, even though their relatives remained in Russia, and they had no qualms about becoming traitors.

Only a few days after the Germans moved into town, we were delighted to have our Russian friend and her boyfriend visit us. But there was something odd about this 'visit.' I was standing in front of the house and was the first to notice that the young man insisted on remaining outside. I ran to greet him but he looked embarrassed, standing rooted to the spot. The young man was a neighbor who had known my parents for years, but all he could do now was stand staring down at the ground. We soon discovered why. The Russian woman stepped onto our porch and ordered him into the house immediately. He said nothing but just did as he was told. My mother still didn't understand and ran to greet her guests, in spite of their decidedly peculiar behavior. Mother's Russian friend did not so much as throw us a look. She acted as if she was the mistress of the home and marched straight up to the windows, but she could not reach the curtains. So she commanded her boyfriend to climb up on the table and take down the curtains. Our house had many large windows and our thieving 'friends' managed to steal all the curtains before taking down our large, new clock. They were able to work quickly because they had visited our house so frequently and knew exactly where everything was. They then packed up their booty in a flash.

My parents were astonished at this *chutzpah* and deeply wounded by this ugly display of greed from so-called 'friends'. "After all we've done for you," Mother said, "you dare to come here and steal from us? We thought you'd come to help us! You convinced us that you were true friends and we believed you. What happened? How could we have been so wrong?" And then the Russian lady, who had pretended to be our friend, came very close to Mother and hissed, "Idit, why are you crying? It's time for you to wake up from your innocence. What are you complaining about? After all, they will kill you and your children too. Your family will disappear without a trace. You should be happy that it is your 'friend' who is taking these things, instead of common thieves from far away. This way, too. I'll have a souvenir from my 'friends'!"

They ran out of the house and my parents had no time to recuperate from that blow before neighbors raced in with the news that our store was being burgled. At that time Jews tended to stay inside their homes in order to avoid contact with the German occupiers; nonetheless, my parents decided to make their way to the store, perhaps in the hope of salvaging some of the merchandise. I knew how futile and very dangerous this was so I followed them in an attempt to stop them. All my life, I had been the good daughter, the one who helped and obeyed my parents, but everything had changed. I said, "Keep away from the thieves; they will kill anyone who dares to get in their way!" But my parents wouldn't listen. I wasn't aware at the time that I am blessed with an innate instinctive ability to analyses a situation and come to a quick decision. But who was going to listen to a young girl who still lived under her parents' roof?

We could hear from a distance the shouting and arguing of the rioters who had descended upon our store on the main street. Yet my parents continued to run. Our store was the first of a row of Jewish stores, all of which had a number of steep stairs leading up to their entrances. At our store a crowd of people was pushing itself up the stairs and through the door. They were squeezed so tightly together that some were even standing on one foot; inside, the store was packed with thugs. I kept my eyes on my unfortunate parents, who were still unable to understand that this no longer belonged to them. I even saw a tragic-comic element in the situation; it was clear that all was lost. But my parents still tried to talk to the crowd—neighbors who had once been their friends—to appeal to their better nature and plead for mercy. The response was crude, vulgar, raucous laughter. Outside, women waiting for their husbands to emerge with the spoils responded with, "Why should we suffer too just because we were once your friends? You no longer need any of these things anyway; the Germans are saying that your days are numbered!" Some Ukrainians said, "Do you think we're stupid enough to fight for you? Our church leaders tell us that all Jews are communists and should be wiped off the face of the earth; otherwise you'll bring the Russians back!" Others said, "Your property belongs to us, the local people, and not to the Germans. We have to take advantage of our rights, because you lived with us, not with the Germans." Only now did my parents understand that they had to disappear before it was too late.

Our beautiful home was next on their list. Criminals burst into our house and our cellar, ignoring the fact that the doors were locked and we were at home. Here, too, thieves fought among themselves for the loot. Our cries and appeals for mercy fell on deaf ears; we begged them to leave us some food, but our neighbors walked off with our entire food stores: six sacks of flour, large quantities of honey, jams and vegetables and much more.

We were not the only victims; the same happened to all the other Jews. The thieves became beasts of prey, turning their backs on the sick, the old and the babies. They took every last crumb of food, leaving us, and all the other Jewish families, hungry.

Anyone who did not experience all this won't be able to understand the terrible fear and stress we were under as a result of the rampages on Jewish homes during the Nazi occupation. We were never safe in our own homes, day or night. Worst of all were the German soldiers who burst into Jewish houses in the middle of the night looking for girls. The brutal rapes that took place in our neighborhoods every night were terrible; the shrieks of the victims were blood-curdling. We were utterly helpless; there was no one to come to our aid and there was nothing we could do, because anyone who left their house during curfew would be shot on the spot. My younger sister Nina was only ten years old, but she was a beautiful girl and looked older than her years. My whole family joined the effort to hide her. Although I was older than Nina, I was still innocent and did not really understand why. My sister and I spent our nights either in the cellar or the attic, joined by other Jewish girls from the neighborhood. It was hard to sleep and our nights were filled with fear and insomnia.

We had a lovely wooden fence around our house that provided some measure of protection, but all too soon the local Ukrainians took it away. They stood outside our house discussing how to remove the fence, as if we were totally uninvolved and the fence belonged only to them. One day a horse-drawn wagon drew up outside our house and three Ukrainians dismantled the enormous wooden fence, together with its iron chain that served as a kind of protective barrier. Father stood watching at the window, but this time he did not try to stop them.

After the theft we realized the importance of the fence and its disappearance caused us great distress. Anyone walking by on the street could now look straight into the house; at night, the only ones walking by were German soldiers and Ukrainian policemen and we could hear the frightening thud of their hobnailed boots on the flagstone road just below our windows. To this very day I shudder when I recall that sound. The soldiers spent much of their time walking round and round Jewish houses and broke in whenever they felt like it. One morning some Germans broke into our house and demanded that Father turn over all our copper ornaments. Thus, we were not only hungry, but also very tired because of the fear that prevented us from getting much sleep at night.

One day the local Ukrainian rulers ordered the Jews to collect all the copper from their homes and bring it to them. The Jews hurried to do as they were told and brought in a large quantity of copper items, some of which had been handed down in their families for generations. The Ukrainians jeered at the Jews and said, "Don't worry, we'll give the copper back to you in a different form." They told us that the copper was being sent to Germany, where it would be melted down and made into bullets with which to kill Jews. I, too, took our remaining copper utensils to the designated warehouse, where policemen forced me to spend many hours sorting it all by type.

From the very beginning of the occupation, German officers began arriving in Korzec even though they had no official connection to our town. It later transpired that German officers, passing through on their way to the Russian front, would notice Jewish houses on the main road and stop off in the town to find ways to steal from them.

Thus, from all directions thieves and intruders made our lives unbearable: Germans, Ukrainians, and our neighbors. Jews were beset on from all sides and we were more than willing to relinquish our possessions in exchange for our lives. We had no rest, by day or by night; no sooner had we finished collecting valuables for one group of Germans pointing their weapons at us, than another group would arrive with a different set of demands. There was no end in sight.

We were tormented not only by German soldiers and local Ukrainian officials but also by the intelligentsia, the elected representatives of the German government, all puffed up with arrogance and conceit. The local rulers enjoyed themselves at the expense of Jewish valuables and possessions, Jewish money and Jewish forced labor. The Bavarian-born German mayor held large parties and invited relatives and acquaintances to celebrate. We Jews were the only ones who knew the cost of one such night as it was us who were forced to 'donate' the valuable gifts the mayor presented to all his guests. This, after all, was the whole objective of the parties.

One day, a group of high-ranking German officers arrived in Korzec and announced that they wanted to evaluate the size of the town's Jewish community. They ordered the local rabbis to report to one of their commandeered houses and spared no effort in humiliating the religious leaders. German thugs personally cut off the rabbis' beards and forced them, mostly older men, to crawl on their hands and knees and bark like dogs. The drunken Germans crowed and jeered as they mercilessly mocked and humiliated the rabbis.

The Germans offered the Jews to 'exchange' their wealth for their lives.

They produced a detailed list of items belonging to Jews, including diamonds, furs and other valuables and demanded that this 'order' be filled within 24 hours. The Jewish community was under terrible stress and a group of its men undertook the extremely dangerous task of visiting neighboring communities in order to raise the necessary ransom.

Several days after the German invasion, Ukrainian and Polish families started to appear in Korzec, even though these people had traditionally lived outside Polish borders. Meanwhile, some of the newly arrived fascists from Germany joined the local Ukrainians in controlling the local municipality and talked about building a 'bridge of a friendship' between the Germans and the Ukrainians. At all their joint meetings, they were quick to rubber-stamp all the new German edicts against the Jews. We followed these proceedings carefully as we were dependent on the local Ukrainian rulers as well as the Germans.

Immediately after the German invasion, Ukrainian policemen appeared in the Jewish neighborhoods dressed in special new uniforms. They told us that they had prepared these even before the arrival of the Germans. The problem was that these policemen were locals and knew everyone. They were the ones who went into every Jewish house and rounded up hungry children for forced labor, knowing which houses had children.

I was one of those children who were escorted to work in the tobacco fields under guard of Ukrainian policemen. They told us what to do and exactly how much time was allotted for each task. We were terrified of them and worked like little slaves so that they would not beat us. We had to tie the tobacco plants to pillars from bottom to top and the plants grew as high as electric poles. When we were forced to climb on rotting, rickety pillars, we cried out of fear while the Ukrainian policemen laughed and cursed at us hysterically. We older children got together and came to the decision that we would undertake all the difficult and dangerous work. So I climbed up tall, rotting pillars in spite of the fear and in spite of the danger, so that a smaller, younger child wouldn't have to.

And we were forced to clean the city. Small children were put to work collecting rocks left behind by the German air attack that had preceded the invasion, in order to improve the general appearance of Korzec. We then had to build walls in accordance with the orders we received.

Jewish men were taken for forced labor. They were divided into groups and sent to all kinds of places according to the demands of the Germans or Ukrainians and given jobs that ranged from repairing the main road to working in the sugar factory. A large group was employed as porters for the Germans, loading and unloading cargo onto trucks. In order to abuse and humiliate, the Germans would sometimes harness Jewish men to heavily laden wagons, instead of horses, which they then forced them to pull.

This was the hell they created for the Jews and only the Jews. It seemed to us then that the whole world was hostile and wanted only to torment us. It is difficult today, even impossible, to translate into dry, simple words the terrible suffering, hunger and fear that engulfed us from morning to night. But much worse was yet to come.

Father was put to work building roads and unloading huge barrels of beer. He was subjected to murderous beatings; it was hell for him, but he did his best to keep his spirits up for the sake of the other Jews with him.

After the German invasion the Jews had good reason to be depressed; the Germans' firepower made a very forceful, threatening impression. My father was extremely worried but did not talk about his fears. He'd listen patiently to the bitter words of other Jews and then say, "Don't be so quick to bury the Soviet Union and its army. Don't forget that Russia still has General Winter and General Mud, in other words, our unbearably cold, muddy winters and impassable forests. What we are seeing now, all this German display of military power on the main road, is merely a magnificent military parade."

CHAPTER 3
Hunger

Our neighbors, the Zickman family, owned a grand house on our street. During the occupation, Germans lived in their house and Mrs. Zickman was happy for these 'guests' to allow her to serve them. For a while, two young German officers were billeted in the Zickman house; both Vienna-born, it was their job to scour the area and to acquire potatoes for the German army. For this purpose they employed Jewish labor and used the enormous cellars on the main street. I was one of the Jewish youngsters who was brought to these cellars and forced to work at sorting the potatoes according to type and size. Many of the potatoes were rotten and frozen, causing a revolting, almost unbearable stench in the cellar and it was our job to pick out the rotten ones and remove them from the others. We all worked very hard, way beyond our physical capabilities, carrying the heavy potato sacks, which were then shipped to Germany, from one cellar to another. I was put to work with a girl called Rosa Broder who was a few years older and, despite our age difference, we were bound by our common situation and became very close friends, doing our best to stay together.

Rosa had a sickly mother and needed someone stronger than herself to lean on; in my large family she found loving support, especially from my parents. I would occasionally visit Rosa's mother, who was very grateful to my parents for taking Rosa under their wing. Rosa also had a married brother, an educated young man who worked for the Jewish Community. However, for some reason, which I never discovered, Rosa avoided her brother and sought my parents' company instead.

Rosa and I soon realized that we had been given a golden opportunity to steal frozen potatoes that had been discarded outside the cellars, even though they were not fit for human consumption. We were very hungry and decided to go ahead, although we knew that the Germans had threatened to punish anyone who dared to touch these potatoes. It was part of their cruel system to starve and weaken us, so that we would be unable to rise up against them. But the hunger that plagued us was stronger than our fear of being caught and punished. The hungry children at home were thrilled to be able to eat a stinking, mud-covered, rotten potato and they couldn't even wait another second for it to be cleaned. The truth was that none of us was capable of waiting until the potatoes defrosted; we were so hungry that those frozen potatoes were a real treat. I looked at my family and thought: No punishment can frighten or stop me from bringing them food. So I continued to steal the frozen potatoes.

One day I was summoned unexpectedly by the German officers to their office. Certain that they had discovered my terrible secret, that I was stealing frozen rotten potatoes for my starving family, my head filled with all kinds of frightening thoughts and I resigned myself to my fate and walked into the office. Two German officers looked at each other, in no hurry to speak to me. I was very tense, sure that they knew everything there was to know about my heinous 'crime'. My imagination went into overdrive and I saw myself standing in the dark in one of the cellars while the Germans pointed their weapons and shot me. Suddenly, both officers started talking at the same time. They talked about death and asked me if I was afraid of dying. "Soon," they said, "not a single Jew will have survived here; all the Jews will be killed. Meanwhile, we are being posted elsewhere where there are no longer any Jews left. We would like you to come with us, to continue working for us." I felt as if burning coals were being thrust into my throat, before the scalding heat turned into freezing cold. I could not utter a word and the Germans must have sensed something of what I was thinking by the expression on my face. "You have nothing to worry about," they reassured me. "We know that you and Rosa are very close, we plan to take you both; we have no intention of separating you." I turned into stone and at that moment, Rosa walked in. The Germans started to convince her that this was her only hope of remaining alive. Rosa acted normally at first, but at a certain point she collapsed in tears. "I will go anywhere," she said, "as long as Anna is with me."

It was a response I had not expected and I was alarmed by the realization that another person's life depended on me. I felt bitter, but decided to keep my focus and ask some questions. Yes, I was dependable, hard-working, did not collapse under pressure and suffering; but I was a young girl, who had always relied on her parents and had never lived alone. I was willing to sacrifice everything for the sake of my family; I could not conceive of abandoning them when their lives were in danger, to save myself. If they wanted to murder my brothers and sisters, whom I had helped to raise, I would rather die first. What kind of a life would I have, all alone?

I suspected the real intentions of these Germans. They were army men, frequently relocated from place to place; how could they possibly be able to save two Jewish girls from death? I didn't like the fact that they had not prepared any kind of documents for us. This was the first time I had ever met Germans who took pity on Jews or offered them any help. What were their real motives? Here I was, a young, innocent girl in my teens; still, their offer struck me as dubious. Although I did not wish to portray myself as a pathetic person in need of their mercy, I was careful not to insult or anger them. Without thanking them for their offer, I merely told the Germans that I had to get my father's permission first.

Since the German invasion, I had always obeyed my mother's request to keep out of my father's way in order to spare him any additional suffering. My father was a very sensitive man and he blamed himself for his family's plight, for not having taken my advice and escaped from Korzec when there was still the chance to do so. Now, however, I needed to consult with him.

The Germans agreed, but insisted on accompanying me and talking to Father themselves. I knew my father wouldn't be pleased, but I had no choice and I received a whole loaf of bread as a gift. Together, Rosa and I walked toward my home, followed by the two young German officers. We stepped into the house and they got right to the point. "The authorities plan to kill all the Jews," they told my parents bluntly. "Soon, there will be no Jews left alive. We are giving you the opportunity to save one child, your daughter Anna. You would be wise to appreciate this opportunity."

This visit and the offer came as a shock to my parents. My mother remained silent, as usual, allowing my father to speak for them both. She never intervened in Father's conversations; to her, he was the final arbiter even when she disagreed with his opinion. Father said, "You can see how many children I have; they are all beautiful. Look at how they have suffered; look at the state they are in. Now you come and tell me that the Germans want to kill us all. Why? And if you really want to save the life of a Jewish child, why did you pick my oldest daughter, of all the children?" The Germans walked out of the house and we never saw them again.

My father didn't believe them and their promises and it was thus that I passed over the only opportunity I had to save myself. Rosa Broder did not go with the German rescuers either because she respected my father's decision. She didn't want to go on her own to an unknown destination.

Some German soldiers had established a mobile kitchen in our yard. My parents warned us constantly to keep away from the Germans, so as not to provide them with some excuse to accuse us of something. The soldiers used to bring us their laundry—for free, of course. I had to carry heavy sacks of dirty laundry to the river, which was located at a distance from us in a valley, on the other side of the steep hill on which the town was situated. I had no choice but to drag the sacks to the river and wash the clothes there. I then had to climb back up the steep incline to the top of the hill, while hanging on for dear life to small protrusions in the ground. I had always been a hard and industrious worker but this task was both grueling and dangerous. By the time I finished, it was late at night and I was drenched in sweat and water. Suddenly, I realized that I was completely alone, not far from the bridge above the main road. I stopped for a moment to look at the river: it was broad and deep and the water was clear as a mirror.

I knew that Jews had once lived in this valley and that there used to be large, well-tended gardens on the riverbank, rich with vegetables and fruit trees. I started thinking that there might be some kind of food in the vicinity that we could eat. We never received any kind of food from the local authorities and were always hungry; as far as I knew, this was true for all the Jews.

Before the German occupation, one of the houses on the riverbank had belonged to my uncle, Ben Zion Rubinstein. Father, who was the youngest son in his family, had grown up in this area. Now I trembled with anticipation as I noticed a large number of white cabbages in the garden that had once belonged to my uncle. With my hands shaking with fear, I picked off a few cabbage leaves and ran to the water to rinse them, hoping no one would see me. I was very hungry, but after eating that cabbage my fear was slightly alleviated. Coming out of the water, I looked in all directions before picking a whole cabbage and eating it. Although I was still hungry, I couldn't stop thinking about my permanently hungry brothers and sisters and knew I had to find a way to bring them a delicious fresh cabbage. This thought infused me with courage. There was some room left in my laundry sack because I had dried and folded the clean clothes during the day and it now took up less space. I stuffed as many cabbages as I could into the sack and did not allow myself to think for a minute about the punishment I would face if someone noticed me. My main worry was technical: how was I going to climb up that steep hill with such a heavy load? I searched around and found an old metal screen nearby that had once been part of a gate. I placed my heavy sack on the screen and then focused all my strength on pulling it up the steep hill. The physical effort was staggering, as was my tension level—I doubted if I would survive a fall down that hill. But the real danger loomed when I finally reached the top, because now I was in plain view of houses belonging to the Ukrainians, who kept dogs. I used the last of my strength to drag myself and my burden down the long street to my home. I had made it.

It was after nine o 'clock and my worried parents and brothers and sisters were very happy to see me back, safe and sound. No Jew dared to be outside at such a late hour. But I was home safe and had even brought some food.

The children fell on the cabbage ravenously. I realized that it would not take long for word to spread about the stolen cabbage and then everyone would make sure to carefully guard his or her vegetable patch. I watched the starving children eat and asked myself, "What have I to lose?" I grabbed the now-empty laundry sack and my mother immediately understood my intentions. She hugged me and begged me not to go. "You are asking to die, Anna," she cried. "You have done enough, more than enough. I don't want you to be the first victim in our family." I don't know how I managed it, but the result of my foray was that I brought back a real prize—a full sack of cabbages.

Yes, hunger was our all-consuming problem. There were still many valuables in the house that my parents had managed to hide; we hoped to exchange these valuables for food. Unfortunately, however, in our own town or even in the nearby village we couldn't sell any of our valuables for food because the locals already had plenty of valuables that they had plundered from the

Jews. So we tried to reach villages that were further away and risked our lives to get there. We knew that if we were discovered, any small child could hand us over to the Germans. Any Jew that was found on a Christian street would be robbed of his merchandise and beaten up. In any case, despite all our efforts we never had success in trying to exchange merchandise for food. In that time period, we failed in all our efforts and eventually Father said it was better to die of hunger and let all our possessions rot.

Every day, the Ukrainian police organized the Jews into different forced labor units. Our Ukrainian neighbors knew the exact size of every Jewish household, the children's ages and their capacity to work, which made it extremely difficult to escape being sent on hard-labor assignments. Occasionally, however, I managed to do so and took advantage of every spare moment to look for work in neighboring villages and to get food for my family. When I did this I wasn't wearing the yellow star and knew what kind of punishment I could expect if I was discovered, even once, outside my own neighborhood. When I arrived at the villages I tried to appear full of self-confidence and presented myself as a hard worker, who could carry out any kind of physical labor. Of course, most people knew my father and were well aware that I was Jewish. In a small town like Korzec, it was almost impossible to go anywhere without people knowing who you were.

Growing up, I had always seen my parents as strong, wise and enterprising people. I often listened to their words of wisdom; I was proud of them, and tried to be like them. My parents never complained of discrimination or accused people of taking advantage of them; instead they talked about honesty and justice and told us that the human race was good and merciful. My parents had always demanded absolute truth from their children, but we had been thrust into a completely different reality. In order to survive we were obliged to lie and cheat and we had to contend with the cruel brutality of others, including people who had once been our friends. I used to ask myself, "What planet did my parents come from? What kind of education did they give us, which so contradicts our own reality? What type of children did they hope to bring up?" Inside I was angry with them for trusting others when they had no rational basis for doing so. My parents taught us to love humankind and they paid dearly for it. They had brought us to the verge of an abyss from which there was no way back.

I worked in the villages at different times and during different seasons and usually asked for a few cups of grain as payment. I remember once, in winter, having to use an axe to dig a hole in the frozen river. I needed to reach the freezing water below the ice in order to wash linen yarn, which was then used to weave fabric. Sometimes I also had to wash dirty clothes in the same icy water. I wondered why they washed linen yarn in the middle of winter and was told by some locals, "We no longer have poor people among us who are willing to take on work for others. It's very difficult nowadays to find agriculture laborers, especially in the high season." There was nothing new in this. The wealth and plenty of our Ukrainian 'neighbors' had come at our expense—after robbing us blind, they had no need to work hard themselves. I myself had to walk barefoot over ice and snow to wash dirty laundry in a hole in the ice. At first, it felt as if I was walking on needles, but after a while the sensation passed. But I was never sick. I didn't even think about illness at that time. Even under those difficult circumstances, I was able to appreciate the humorous aspect of my situation; when Ukrainian farmers walked past me and noticed that I was walking barefoot in the snow, they stopped and crossed themselves!

When I worked in the villages, the Ukrainian families ignored me as they would an inanimate object, or as if I was dead. My status was not even that of a lowly domestic workhorse, although sometimes this served me in good stead, because it put me in a position that enabled me to overhear their conversations, as when we worked in the fields or treated the tobacco and the Ukrainians in the vicinity talked among themselves as if they were alone. That's when I discovered that they hated the Germans just as they had looked down on the Poles in their time; what they really wanted was their own, independent country and this time they felt sure that they would get rid of the Russians for good. The Germans, on the other hand, looked down on their Ukrainian cohorts; indeed we had heard the Germans refer to them as 'Ukrainian pigs' and suchlike. I can't explain why, even after having been told that 'they' were going to kill all the Jews, we retained a shred of optimism. We could neither swallow such a bitter pill, nor could we believe it. How could 'they' kill an entire nation? It just didn't seem possible, however much they hated us.

The Jews who were employed by the Germans in hard physical labor were issued documents so that Ukrainian policemen would be unable to stop them on their way to or from work and transfer them elsewhere. However, even such German-issued documents gave no real security to the Jewish laborer. Sometimes, entire groups of workers did not return home after work and simply disappeared. The uncertainty of not knowing which of the laborers would come back from a day's work created unbearable tension and stress in the community. The children, therefore, formed a kind of spy ring to try and discover the fate of the workers and then transmit the news from house to house. But in spite of everything, we hoped that those Jews who had disappeared were still alive and working somewhere on a road, as the Ukrainian policemen had told us. After all, which of us is capable of living without hope for even one day of a miserable existence?

I recall one beautiful summer day in 1941; it was the Ukrainians' Preczysta holiday celebrating the day that Mary rose to the heavens. Early in the morning two Germans, accompanied by Ukrainian policemen, stormed into our house and ordered my father to go with them. This was nothing new; things like that happened all the time. They quickly disappeared into a tarpaulin-covered truck; we couldn't see if there was anyone else in the truck. As they drove off, I remained on the street to try to find out where the truck had gone and who else was being taken that morning. I then contacted some other children who, as usual, were trying to track down the whereabouts of Jewish laborers. When we were involved in this kind of spying we would walk in the side streets, close to the walls; we were stealthy, careful not to be seen, not to give away our very existence. But suddenly something unusual happened; something that changed all the rules of the game.

A terrible rumor started flying in all directions, people were shouting and crying and the news spread like wildfire. "The Germans and Ukrainians are setting up roadblocks!" someone shouted; and another, "The Ukrainians are rounding up all the Jewish males!" and a third, "The Germans are coming—we're finished!"

I felt the blood boiling in my head, as if a thousand hammers were pounding at my brain. I thought of Father, who might have been one of the first to fall into the murderers' hands. Then I thought of my beloved uncle Menashe Weiner, my mother's brother, who worked in the sugar factory; he was one of those who had been issued a certificate by the Germans, stating that his work was essential. My other uncle, with the similar name, Michael Weiner, was also my mother's brother. I was unable to control myself and ran through the main street, towards the sugar factory. Large numbers of Ukrainian policemen appeared suddenly out of nowhere and used ropes to tie the hands of the Jewish males. But something was different in this scene: now the work was being done by young Ukrainian 'volunteers' who were not policemen. Their cruel blows were aimed to kill; nothing was worse than falling into their hands. It all happened on the main street that led from Russia to Poland. I managed to make my way to the pharmacy on the corner of Stalina and Berezdowa. From some distance, I spotted my beloved uncle among the Jewish men who were surrounded, their hands tied, by numerous policemen. The policemen and Ukrainians directed the victims towards an alleyway. Jewish children crowded around me, trying to follow their loved ones. We decided take a roundabout route in an attempt to see where the men were being led and what was being done to them.

We soon discovered that they were being led along the main street towards a house that had belonged to a wealthy Jew called Mahler, where a Ukrainian police unit (not the central police) was now stationed. The yard contained a huge granary warehouse and it was to this building that all the victims were taken. With all the other children I circled the warehouse looking for holes in the walls, to peek inside, but found none. I squeezed myself next to the wall and asked loudly if anyone had seen my father inside. There were many voices all saying the same thing at the same, but the message was clear: "It's so crowded in here that we are suffocating and can't even see each other." Mahler's house stood a short distance from where we were.

Suddenly, we were attacked by a group of policemen, who captured two children, aged twelve and thirteen, from the group near me and marched them into the warehouse to join the others. I was the only girl in the group and it transpired that I was spared not because I was more agile than the others but because, on that particular day, they were not interested in catching girls. I ran and hid in the cellar under the big pharmacy to witness with my own eyes what was going to happen to the Jewish men trapped in the warehouse.

Suddenly, I noticed that the Jewish men were being led from the alley in which the police station was located, directly onto the main road. I was able to keep my eyes on them as I stared through a low, small window facing the main street, literally opposite the victims. Numerous Germans and their Ukrainian sidekicks organized the Jews into rows, as if they were organizing a procession. Hands tied, the Jews, including children, were arranged in rows. I saw my mother's brother in the first row and will always remember him as he looked then: tall, handsome, athletic and statuesque. All the men in the first rows were tall and muscular. I looked around wildly for my father, my eyes full of tears. The terrified children had been placed in the back rows and were weeping bitterly. Was my father among them?

I decided impulsively to run after them; I went out into the middle of the road; I wanted to be beside my father at this terrible time. I watched the Ukrainians, not the uniformed policemen, busily beating the tied-up Jews with clubs, all the time looking around for new victims. The Ukrainian policemen were occupied in endless discussions. A crazed, bloodthirsty crowd was whipping those defenseless Jews mercilessly, as if those Jewish men and boys, exhausted from forced labor and near starvation, could have put up a fight! Later in the ghetto I learned that their number had been five hundred and fifty—exhausted and weak Jewish men, against a wild, ferocious crowd.

They were under close guard and surrounded by a circle of murderers, which made it impossible to get very close to them. A young Ukrainian man, aged around twenty, was first to notice me. He was an old acquaintance and a frequent customer in Father's store. I remembered that he even used to borrow Father's bicycle. Before the war, he had been a post office messenger. I was shocked to see him now among the murderers, wielding an enormous club usually used to separate horses harnessed to wagons.

Things started happening quickly and unexpectedly: the first blow knocked me down on my face. The man continued to beat me until I lost consciousness. People must have thought I was dead and just left me there. I don't know how long I lay there; I was unable to see or hear anything.

I discovered later what had happened. The murderers left the site once the Jewish men had been taken away. I remained lying in the middle of the road, abandoned for dead. My maternal grandmother lived nearby on Berezdowa Street; someone ran to tell her that I had been killed and that she should bring a sheet and take me to her house. To everyone's welcome surprise, I awoke after a few hours and recovered from the terrible pain. After a while I was even able to stand up. Everywhere I went, people exclaimed that that I'd returned from the dead. In truth, I have suffered all my life from that brutal beating and later even became disabled.

Most of the town's Jews hid in their houses as all this was happening and had no way of knowing what happened to the captured men and boys who disappeared as if they had never existed. Of course the community tried to extract information and bribed a Ukrainian to search for the missing Jews. The information he provided was that all our men were working under tight German security on repairing the main road to Kiev. In fact, he said, he had even managed to speak to them from a distance and they asked him to pass on their regards to their families. He told us that the men were suffering from the cold at night and asked for warm clothes. That same Ukrainian arrived with a wagon to collect clothing packages, which he claimed he would take to the Jewish men.

This liar managed to deceive everyone because of past incidents when Ukrainian policemen were bribed into providing information. Moreover, this particular Ukrainian was selected because of a long-standing acquaintance with the Jews and they trusted him. Still, when I check my memories, I find it really hard to understand the naïveté of my fellow Jews, among whom I lived and was raised. As a child myself, at the time, I try not to pass judgment, but it does seem to me that those Jews must have been as innocent as children. It was not the first time that men had failed to return from work, but in this case the number of people involved was larger than usual and the group included children. Every time something similar happened, the authorities provided the same reason: Jewish men had been taken to work on road repairs and would return home when the job was done. And we were supposed to believe that the faster our men worked, the sooner they would be allowed to return home.

I could not have known at the time, but exactly one year later, I took a wrong turn and stumbled across the mass grave in which those same Jews had been buried. When I discovered the truth about the missing men we had all searched for but never found, there was no one left to mourn them because by then their families had all been murdered, too.

Later that morning of the Ukrainian festival I discovered that my father's work detail had been among those that fell into the murderers' snare. He and the others were being forced to carry heavy rocks from one place to another for no apparent purpose and my father's sixth sense led him to believe that something very bad was about to happen. He saw that his group was thoroughly guarded by the German murderers and their Ukrainian henchmen and he was completely unable to exchange even a few words with the other Jews, to warn them. He decided to save himself. As a soldier, my father had been very courageous and knew how to use his wits when faced with danger; this time, he succeeded in escaping from the death trap and made his way home. There was a makeshift hiding place in our house and, although not enough to ensure his long-term survival, it was better than nothing. On that day of the Ukrainian festival in 1941, Father was able to slip through the fingers of the German murderers and save himself from certain death. The fact is that all the Jews who were working with him were killed that same day. Thus, he managed to extend his life for a while, but the question is whether all that suffering was worth it, for a little while longer in this world.

During the German occupation, all Jews were obliged to work every day and sometimes at night, too. The Germans did not consider people who were too ill, however, although I had sustained a spinal cord injury from an earlier beating and was in great pain, I was still taken, together with other women, to the German canteen and ordered to sweep the area clean. My body ached terribly, tears poured like rain down my face but I was afraid of a further beating; after all, we Jews had no human rights.

After completing that job, I was one of several women who were pulled out of the group. We were sent to the canteen's huge courtyard and informed that we were to come every morning to clean it and to pay special attention to the lavatories. On that day, I worked alongside my good friend Rosa Broder.

The Germans ordered the Jewish males to build a long row of lavatory stalls in the canteen courtyard. The canteen was located next to the main Poland-to-Russia highway and German soldiers traveling along it would stop at the canteen and use the stalls in the yard. Rosa Broder and I were in charge of cleaning those stalls.

A woman called Staniszewska, a cheerful divorcee of about forty five, ran the canteen. Staniszewska's family had lived for many years in a Jewish-owned house in Korzec's Jewish neighborhood, under Polish rule. She was the manager of a pastry shop and almost all her customers had been Jews; her three sons all had Jewish friends. After the occupation, Staniszewska took to amusing herself with the German soldiers on their way to the front. Sometimes they were the same age as her sons. Some of her German friends arranged for her to be given the job of managing the canteen from the villa that had once belonged to a Jew. That villa became the site of endless parties and entertainment. Two Jewish girls were employed as maids under Staniszewska; they worked hard and did their best to please her because they were terrified of her sons. These boys, who had previously been considered cowards, had suddenly become vicious thugs who went out of their way to harm the Jews who had once been their friends. As they robbed Jews and informed on them, these three thugs would jeer, "Why should we be afraid of you; everyone knows that the Germans are going to kill all the Jews; you won't be needing any of your valuables anymore!"

One day, a large group of German women walked into the canteen dressed in what appeared to be a costume of some sort that consisted of loose, long gray dresses with white cuffs and collars and long white aprons; on their heads they wore a kind of white hat. Someone introduced them as 'nurses' (*schwester*) but there was nothing about them that hinted at a connection to medicine. The women were accompanied by some quite elderly soldiers and they all spoke at once, laughing wildly and screeching hysterically. It's hard to describe the commotion, their modest outfits completely belying their outrageous behavior. They looked into all the nearby rooms and were impressed by the magnificent halls. After a thorough examination the group left the building, boarded the bus outside and drove off in a flurry. Only two of the German women stayed behind to mingle with the permanent work staff, trying to learn everyone's names. Once they knew who everyone was, Staniszewska pointed to Rosa and me and said we were Jews, employed temporarily to clean the bathrooms in the yard. Turning to us, the German women ordered us to swab down the floors every day, but from now on this would have to be done after two a.m., the time when the drunken soldiers left the place. Drunken German soldiers would hold loud discussions in the canteen before leaving for the battlefront and were inevitably full of anger and dread; sometimes they even fell asleep on a chair. Rosa and I always worked under pressure and fear. During the day, we worked in the kitchen and were the personal slaves of the German women; although at first our tasks had only involved cleaning, we later 'graduated' to peeling potatoes.

There were now three women in the house: the Polish Staniszewska and the two Germans, who told us they came from Bratislavia (today Wrocław in Poland). Each woman wanted to establish her own rules, each had her own German male 'protectors' and each felt strong and invincible. Power struggles among the three became inevitable, as did reciprocal spying and each plotting against the others, while manipulating us Jewish girls. Although the German women were hardly young, it was their job to entertain the German men who visited the canteen; they held conversations with all the guests, as if it were a private event between friends. Rosa and I were young and unsophisticated; we had never been exposed to the big world and had grown up in the shadow of protective parents. To us this situation was shocking. The German women entertained men in their rooms, completely indifferent to our presence; because we were like corpses to them.

In those dark days of Nazi occupation, Jews were treated like beasts of burden—except that beasts are fed and treated better than we were. We were considered expendable, our lives had no value and no one had mercy on us. I still don't understand how I could have done the hard work demanded of me, work that was beyond my strength. We worked almost around the clock in the German canteen and were not allowed to sleep; we were not even allowed a short break. They say that young people find it easier to overcome hardship and Rosa and I supported each other as we worked side by side. Sometimes we would seek out a remote corner of the house, close our eyes for a few minutes and then return to our tasks.

Right opposite, on the other side of the road, stood my family home. My family, who could watch me from their windows, was very worried about me; even the younger ones understood the complex and tragic circumstances in which I was trapped. They would stand at the windows peering into the darkness, hoping against hope for me to come home for an occasional few hours. They had good reason to worry'. A Jewish girl like me had no protection whatsoever, not from the law and certainly not from any ethical considerations on the part of our oppressors. At night my mother used to climb on the pillars of the porch in order to peer through the window of the kitchen, to see if I was still alive. She knew she was risking her life doing this.

My family suffered from hunger. Every day, one or more of the children would faint. My sister Nina had terrible backache and cried incessantly. Ukraine winters are always cold but those of 1941 and 1942 were especially harsh and there was no heating at all. The children would wrap themselves up in everything they could and looked beseechingly at their parents, but the wretched parents were just as helpless.

But it was food, or lack of it, that was the major problem. Anyone daring to slip away to some other village in an attempt to find food knew he risked being attacked by thieves and beaten to death. Some of our neighbors, who managed to obtain a small quantity of grain, asked Father to create a primitive contraption for grinding the grain into flour. Father had no tools left, everything had been stolen, but necessity being the mother of invention, he used a nail and a stone to create two round, primitive grinders the size of a liter jar. It took an entire day to grind approximately three cups of flour. Since the grownups were forced to work for the Germans or the local police, the task of wheat grinding was carried out by younger, hungry children, who worked beyond their strength, so as not to die of hunger. For every cup of flour that Father produced, he would set aside a few of grains of wheat for his own family. During the winter, my parents managed to amass a priceless six cups of flour. They decided to put the flour in our hiding place until the spring *Shavuot* festival; meanwhile, we were sustained by faith and patience. But fate had its own cruel rules: all our hopes were later shattered and that precious store of flour was stolen on that disastrous day of the *Shavuot* festival.[2]

Somehow our family survived the winter in spite of these inhuman conditions.

And all the time Father worked fervently to find a way to rescue me. He visited old friends and acquaintances who owed him favors, but they turned their backs on him, even the most respectable and decent of them. Disillusion burned like salt on an open wound, as people who once had been close friends abandoned us in our time of need.

Father visited a Polish shoemaker he respected whose family promised him a rescue plan for me, according to which they would send me, with a new Polish identity, to their relatives in Polesye to work as a housemaid. I spoke fluent Polish and, with my blonde hair and fair complexion, I looked 'Aryan'. The shoemaker set a

---

2   The *Shavuot* festival is celebrated on the sixth day of the Hebrew month of Sivan (May–June). It traditionally commemorates the giving of the Tablets of the Law on Mount Sinai.

date for me to go to his house and collect from him everything I would need to start a new life. My naïve parents believed that the man really wanted to help them and believed we had nothing to lose. I was reluctant to leave my little brothers and sisters in order to save myself and my mother had to work very hard to persuade me that it was the only way. I was afraid of living on my own, far from my family. My mother gave me plenty of advice on how to act among strangers and all the conversations in our house focused on the forthcoming changes in my life.

My parents waited impatiently for the agreed-upon date. On the designated day, they wiped their tears and ordered me to walk with them to the shoemaker who would provide me with the address of his relatives and a letter of recommendation. But it became apparent that the shoemaker had had a change of heart, which had a devastating effect on my parents, who had lost precious time in their search for another way out for me.

In the spring of 1942, rumors were afoot that the Germans were planning to liquidate us very soon. The alarm and panic were intense; we had nowhere to go, no place to hide. Jews enlisted people to discover what was really happening and we learned that the Germans had started to recruit Ukrainian men from the nearby villages to dig three enormous pits in a forest next to the Kozak village. We were told the exact size and depth of these pits, and received daily updates regarding their progress. After about two weeks we heard that the pits were ready and the workers had left the site. After a feverish search, some Jews found a way to approach the German rulers of our fate. They asked directly, "Are you really planning to liquidate us all, as we are led to believe?"

To their surprise the Jewish emissaries were received quite graciously by several high-ranking German officers. Such treatment was new to them and they were suspicious. The Germans tried to convince the Jews that there was no connection between them and the pits that had been dug in Kozak Forest. They explained that the pits had been dug in order to provide the earth necessary for paving the road. Needless to say, it later transpired that it was just one of the tricks used by the Germans to reassure the Jewish population and to keep the whole incident as quiet as possible.

Children were privy to everything that happened in the Jewish arena and were always the first to disseminate and spread any kind of news. In those dark times children tried very hard not to bother their parents who were occupied with the endless concerns of basic existence. Children were no longer playing games; their faces were sad and very serious and they talked about death and other weighty subjects, just like their parents.

It was thus that the children warned each other to be on the alert for German murderers who could break into their houses at night. The neighborhood children decided to stay dressed at night and to sleep under their beds. But many children were terrified to fall asleep and were permanently tired, their faces sallow and sick-looking. Even when they did sleep, their sleep was tense; they'd shout in their sleep or wake up frightened and burst into tears. Then they'd run around examining every corner of the house for intruders.

I was one of the very few Jews from Korzec to survive the Holocaust, but I am still unable to accurately describe myself. Can I really say, "I am lucky to be alive?" Or would the opposite be true? From personal experience I know that many Holocaust survivors are like fruit, whose skin is the only thing to have remained whole. Those who happened to have stayed alive feel as if they are aliens in this world. It has not been easy for me to live alone, without my family; I have always been extremely sad. All my life my fear of people has remained engraved in my soul. My experience remains embedded deep within me; I am unable to overcome it or free myself of it. I continue to relive my memories of the past; and it is for this reason that I sentenced myself to this painful seclusion.

This is my last opportunity to muster my strength and, through my writing, create a memorial to the children I loved so much.

CHAPTER 4

They Passed By and Disappeared

The Germans, who had not prepared their army for the harsh winter of 1942, suffered huge losses in their war with the Soviet Union. The Jews knew of the German failures on the battlefield and tended—in order to hold on to some vestige of hope—to exaggerate the problems encountered by the German army. The Jews searched for any possible glimmer of hope, which they then spread quickly throughout the community; they supported each other, trying to keep their hopes up and survive one day at a time. However miserable and broken we were, we did not allow 'them' to destroy our hopes for a better future. We tried at first to hold on to the belief that despite it all, there was a chance we might survive the hatred and animosity that surrounded us. Such thoughts were as essential to us as the air we breathed, in order to stay alive. Without them, we would have lost our minds or killed ourselves. But then we reached the stage at which we had to face more than mere threats—the disappearance and actual murder of our loved ones, our families. And now they were talking about the systematic annihilation of the entire Jewish community, including our babies and children.

In response, a tiny cubbyhole was built into every Jewish home, a secret hiding place in which to hide. These hiding places took various shapes and could be found in different locations in the house, but they all had one thing in common: they were very small and had no windows or doors. They each had a small opening through which our gaunt bodies could crawl, before we were closed in on the inside. The cubbyholes usually measured about one meter by one meter, though some were even smaller, and they were built in such a way as to be completely hidden from view. Today, dozens of years later, I can testify that although these hiding places provided us some reassurance, they never actually saved any human lives.

Had we known beforehand what the occupation had in store for us, we would have prepared our hiding places earlier, if only to store our food in. But it's always easy to be clever in hindsight.

Like all the other Jews in town, my family started to sleep in our hiding place, in the hope of getting through the night with less anxiety. We entered a cage—the one escape cell that remained to us. Our skinny bodies would crawl into the miniscule room, which was closed on all sides, dark and tomb-like. There was not enough room to sit up and there was not enough air to breathe. After a night like this, we would be dizzy and headachy; after a while, we started to feel our health failing.

The Jewish community appeared to relax slightly. For the time being, no one had come to take away our lives. We still lived in our house; we had our beds and all the bedding for our basic needs. We dreamed of a peaceful sleep in beds where we could stretch out our legs; the younger children tried to see what it felt like to be on a bed. Mother and Father couldn't bear to force their children into the hiding place. It was bad enough not having enough food to feed them; they should at least be able to give them a decent night's sleep. My parents gave in to their emotions and allowed us to spend the night in our own beds.

The Jewish festival of *Shavuot* fell one day in May or June 1942. But in the early morning of the eve of the holiday, while it was still dark, we were woken up rudely by a loud string of multi-lingual curses: they flowed in German, Ukrainian, Russian and even Lithuanian, even though no Lithuanians lived in our region. We could feel the earth shaking under our feet, at the hysterical calls of "Yids! Kikes! Out, get out; death awaits you!" The murderers were shooting indiscriminately and within seconds, there was death and destruction everywhere. It felt as if all the murderers in the world surrounded us. My first thought was that I would not live to see the sunrise. There was no time to dress. On that fateful night I was sleeping next to my twelve-year-old sister Nina, who was about two years younger than I. Three-year-old Liuba slept between us. My gaze lingered for an instant on my beautiful sisters, with their blonde hair and big blue eyes, coal-black eyelashes and eyebrows, just like in the fairytale pictures of angels. The murderers had come to destroy this beauty! My sisters were in shock, their mouths wide open, unable to utter a sound, or make a move. They were terrified and fixed their eyes on me, as if they could see nothing but me. I grabbed little Liuba and brought her to me; she came willingly and clung to me for dear life. But Nina could not be moved; she remained glued to the spot like a statue. I tried unsuccessfully to push her forward and ended up pulling at her as I would an inanimate object. I don't know from where I got the strength to do it, I was only a child myself. I tried to make my way to the back door of the house and get into the storehouse but realized that the murderers surrounded the house. I thought I'd try to cross from the storehouse into the canteen on the opposite side of the street, but didn't really think we stood a chance of staying alive; the last spark of hope had been taken from me. But I wanted us to die as human beings, without facing our murderers, and avoid torture. Less than two meters separated me from the murderers; two more doors. The doors were open and temporarily hid me from view. It was dark in the house but the sun was starting to rise outside as I made my way, slowly and quietly with my two sisters, to the storehouse.

Just as I was ready to exit the storehouse, I saw that Father had arrived ahead of me. With him were my two brothers—eight-year-old Efi and five-year-old Leon, together with my four-year-old sister Raya. The murderers noticed Father and the children and started whooping in triumph. I heard loud curses, followed by a volley of gunfire. My heart sunk, certain that Father and the children were dead, but a part of me envied them. Maybe they had been fortunate enough to be shot on the spot and killed outright, feeling no pain.

In my confusion I banged into a ladder and looked up. Suddenly I realized that we could climb up that ladder to the attic! I was standing on a structure my parents had begun building that would eventually have been a house for me, the eldest. The unfinished building had two giant windows facing the yard where the murderers were standing, but above me there was an attic. For some reason I hesitated a few seconds and then I saw my mother behind me, holding my youngest sister Batya by the hand. My lovely blonde-haired mother with her blue-green eyes, always so neat and well turned out, now appeared confused. Wordlessly, I motioned to her to climb the ladder. But Nina, who seemed unable to take in what was happening or to move of her own accord, had me worried. How would we get her up that ladder? She did not respond to my silent gestures. Finally, I pushed and Mother pulled her all the way up the ladder. The other children followed and I was the last one to reach the attic when we heard running footsteps. We held our breaths until it was quiet once again. I peered through the holes overlooking the yard, which was empty; then I ran to the other side of the roof that overlooked the front of the house.

I had an excellent vantage point from which to observe everything around me; the streets and alleys near our house were spread out like a giant map. Chaos and utter confusion reigned, as people ran in every direction and filled the street. Almost immediately, I noticed Father being led by the murderers, with Raya in his arms and Efi and Leon walking on either side of him. The two boys were grasping Father's undershirt as they were led toward the Ukrainian municipal building, a building in our neighborhood that had once belonged to Jews. I followed the progress of my beloved relatives until they disappeared from view at a bend in the road. My father had been a courageous soldier, a valiant and daring man who was always able to get himself out of danger. But now, at this critical moment, he was incapable of protecting his adored children, the foundation of his very existence.

We stood in the attic watching, knowing that this was the end for us, too. But this did not alleviate the excruciating pain of watching, helplessly, as our loved ones were being led to their deaths.

I looked around the attic and noticed that the dirt on the floor was damp. Some of the roof tiles had been destroyed in the German bombing, allowing the rain to enter. I placed little Liuba, who was almost naked, on the muddy ground and she went straight to sleep, as if drugged. Mother and I exchanged looks before silently and carefully pulling the large, heavy ladder up into the attic. Down below us in the house, the windows and doors were still open. Mother came up and whispered to me, "If only we could find a way to smuggle you out to the canteen, Anna. You'll be safer there." She wanted to save me, but I knew better than to hang my hopes on the canteen ladies; those German 'nurses' had not been brought there in order to save Jews.

It was almost sunrise and I could now see more clearly what was happening on the street below. The streets and alleys were full of murdered Jews. Cries and moans of the wounded and ear-splitting screams of people being dragged out of their homes filled the air. German soldiers sauntered around, surrounded by murderers in Ukrainian police uniforms and large numbers of plain-clothed local youths with distinguishing armbands. I recognized some of them. The local volunteers were unarmed, but they tried to attach themselves to policemen and were sometimes allowed to borrow a police gun with which to 'practice'. We watched as entire families were dragged out of their homes. Even now, after so many years, I can still see the faces of those pathetic people, the small children clinging to their parents for salvation. Time has done nothing to blur my memories and banish those images.

Our house stood in the middle of everything that happened on that terrible day in which the Jews of our town were annihilated. From all around new victims were brought in and we saw them pass next to our house. It was increasingly obvious that the murderers had embarked upon their campaign of death against the Jews of Korzec.

Something was happening in the canteen and it didn't take long for the picture to become clear: about a dozen Jewish women, including girls, were being led out of the canteen kitchen. There were a few Jewish men with them. I recognized all the women as having worked alongside me in the canteen, though they had no permission to work with me in the kitchen. These young women were entrusted with cleaning the yard and especially the lavatories, and they also supplied wood for the ovens. But how did they get to the canteen at a time when no Jew was allowed leave his or her home at night? I thought that these Jewish workers had hidden themselves and their children among the buildings close to the canteen during the night; my own family had done the same many times, in order to breathe in some fresh air under the sky, despite the danger.

Then I saw the victims being thrown out of the canteen, under a shower of blows and curses. The children were shivering uncontrollably and weeping in terror, their voices gravelly and hoarse. One of the German women, Frieda, flogged the victims mercilessly with a horsewhip in an obvious attempt to curry favor with the German murderers. The canteen's entire workforce encircled the Jewish women and children and abused them shamelessly; a terrible crime was being committed openly, in broad daylight and no one said a word in protest. I kept my eyes glued to the scene and watched this and other groups of Jews being led towards a large open space in front of the Ukrainian municipality. It was here that all the Jews were taken to be registered, before they were murdered; the Germans were organized, even when it came to murder.

Here, again, I understood that the biggest and most dangerous predator on the face of the earth is mankind. As I stood and watched the way the non-Jewish townspeople behaved down on the street below, I began to understand that they had clearly been prepared in advance for what was about to happen. They wanted to get their hands on Jewish houses, land, and possessions, which drew them like a magnet. It seemed to me that they had been thoroughly primed as to what was permitted and what was forbidden. They walked behind the foreign policemen impatiently, hoping to be rid of them soon; they were especially afraid of the Germans.

A number of wagons began to draw up at the edge of the street, in the direction of the Ukrainian municipal buildings. They pulled up near our house and I could see that they carried the bodies of murdered Jews, thrown carelessly one on top of the other like pieces of surplus baggage. My eyes and my brain took in every single detail.

On top of a pile of corpses on the first wagon lay the body of my maternal grandmother. She was freshly murdered and I had no problem recognizing her. She was wearing one of her beautiful long dresses with lovely decorative buttons that had been sent by her sister in Boston. She must have been too frightened to get undressed that night and decided to stay in her dress.

Jewish men were tied to the backs of the wagons—the same wagons in which their relatives lay dead. I saw Jewish men tied by rusty chains to the wagons in such a way that they could barely move or breathe. Although I recognized many of my fellow Jews in that group, I was particularly drawn to the tragic sight of Shaike Zweig. To me, he seemed to symbolize the suffering of the heroic Jewish people, a kind of Samson figure.

Shaike Zweig's daughter was in my class in school, we had studied together and I visited their home often. All his life Shaike Zweig had done business with the ethnic Germans—*Volkdeutsche*—who lived in the region. Ironically, Shaike looked more German than the Germans he dealt with and also spoke fluent German. There must have been many Germans who dreamed of looking as Aryan as Shaike did. To this day I remember Shaike's store, stocked with milk products supplied by the Germans and Czechs from the neighboring villages. Shaike was never afraid of anyone in his life and was sure he had no enemies. He was a tall, broad-shouldered man, intelligent and well-educated, a good and brave soul, well able to make use of all his assets. I looked at him and thought, "If only he had had the chance to fight back!"

But we knew that we were too late. We had wasted our chance to escape or fight, and that knowledge was even more painful than the tortures we now faced. In the past, when rumors reached our community about anti-Semitic activity elsewhere, what did they say? "They are not all like that; you can't blame a whole nation because of the behavior of a few criminals." Yes, I remember that well. "All we need is patience and everything will blow over. After all, human beings are inherently good." My own parents were unable to imagine cruelty between one man and another. A Jew will never believe in anti-Semitic rumors, until they personally affect him. Even when this anti-Semitism takes the form of armed robbery, pogroms and murder, most Jews refuse to be afraid until their own families are involved. Even then, the Jew will try to rationalize things and avoid overreacting.

I had become conditioned to this Jewish way of thinking. Before World War II we had plenty of opportunity to learn about events in Germany, the way German Jews were being treated. Later, our town took in refugees, including survivors of German atrocities, who were free with their descriptions. The Jews in our town had plenty of time to run away. And how did the Jews react? By telling each other that the idea of destroying all the Jews is inconceivable. After all, what kind of person is capable of murdering little children?

Shaike was bound so tightly that he had to cling to the murdered Jews on the wagon. His shackles held him in such a way that his head and shoulders were bent over the corpses, while the rest of his giant body was dragged behind the wagon. He was covered with blood and could not raise his head or move an inch; I could not tell if the blood was his own or that of the corpses. He was still alive and forced to suffer this torture until he died.

I searched for my father but could not find him. If he was among the corpses on the wagons, there was no chance that I would be able to see him.

Mothers with babies in their arms and little children hanging to their skirts were led to their deaths under a hail of blows and cries of contempt and derision. Most of the Jews had not even had a chance to dress when they were woken up and thrown out of their beds. At such a critical time in their short lives, little children walked alone to their deaths because the murderers had deliberately separated them from their parents. With all my strength I grasped a wooden post that held up the roof, to prevent myself from falling over. I felt a primeval scream welling up inside me; the world spun dizzily around me. But I knew I had to stay quiet because any noise would jeopardize my three sisters. Silently, I hung onto that wooden post for dear life. I understood that as I watched the endless rows of women, children, and old people being led to their deaths there was nothing I could do to help my unfortunate fellow Jews. Everything was lost, but I could not take my eyes away; I had to look for my relatives, to see everything. In that line of death I saw my neighbors, friends, even relatives. And there I was, hiding with my mother and sisters, unable to do anything.

Is there anyone who can understand the feelings of a child, alone in a sea of hatred, separated from its parents at a time like this? What must he or she be thinking, feeling, on this last, long march towards certain death? And when they arrived, they would be forced to wait in line, naked, to be shot and then thrown into a huge pit full of blood and the bodies of other Jews.

The hours passed; it was already afternoon, I think. The procession continued on its way. Row by row they moved past our house, close enough that I could see them clearly and then they disappeared. But I did not take my eyes away; I was still looking for my father and the other children.

Suddenly I saw them! There they were, Efi and Raya. In the middle of a row my brother Efi marched along, holding the hand of his four-year-old sister Raya. She was having difficulty walking and Efi supported her. Occasionally he would turn to hug her, taking the place of his parents. It broke my heart to see so much love and compassion between those two children. They were barefoot and dressed in short, sleeveless turquoise summer pajamas. The march was hard on their bare feet, I could see that; the road was covered with particularly rough stones. Crying bitterly, the two children gazed up at our house as they walked past; they must have believed that none of us was still alive and were silently saying goodbye. My mother stood at my side watching with me as her children were led to their deaths. We both knew that we would never see them again and we could not turn our eyes from them. "Efi was born in December, he's still so young," my mother whispered. "He's trying to take care of Raya as a parent would, although he needs us himself." She stopped for a moment. "I should be there, with my children who need me, and not hiding here, watching." She was in agony, blaming herself relentlessly.

We were like two wounded lions in a cage, with no way out. Our suffering was worse than death. Mother said she no longer wanted to live; her place was with her children. But we still had three children with us, so we did our best to avoid being discovered. Mother kissed my foot and begged my forgiveness for her 'sin' of bringing a large family into the world and being unable to protect or care for it.

The two little ones, Liuba and Batya, had been awakened by the shots and screams. They were still lying on the wet dirt, but did not cry or ask for food or water. They knew it was useless.

How much longer could we keep small children with no food, water or clothes? But it was Nina who concerned me the most; she looked ready to burst into tears at any second. Mother tried to persuade me to let her go, to release her to her death and undertake the burden of caring for the other two. I tried to reassure her. "There is no need," I whispered. "They will have killed us by nightfall and this nightmare will be over." I, too, no longer wanted to live; I had lost my fear of death. It was easier to die than to suffer this nightmare existence; we envied the dead. Our time was running out; we had seen the long lines of Jews being led to their deaths. We had no choice but to stay with the children to the bitter end.

Still Mother wavered, agonizing over the possibility of taking my sisters and me to join the march of death. We both knew that as soon as one of us climbed down the ladder and left the house, the murderers would track us down and kill the children. I have no idea how the drama in the attic would have ended, but Mother suddenly collapsed and fainted. I was actually happy, and thought, "If only Mother were to never wake up, she wouldn't have to suffer like all the others." That's the thought I had about my lovely, dearly beloved mother of whom I was always so proud. I was so confused. It was a lovely, sunlit summer day, yet I felt as if I was in a dark tunnel with no way out. Once I had noticed Efi and Raya on that march, it was as if the skies had fallen in on me and everything had become black and cold.

Like my mother, I blamed myself for not joining them on their last journey. Instead, I, the eldest child, was standing aside, watching. What was I to do? I was confused, uncertain, and incapable, in an impossible situation.

My nails were still clinging to the piece of wood that kept me from falling. Suddenly I began clawing at my face with my nails, tearing off bits of my own skin. The pain inside me was so great that I needed something physical in order to stop myself from screaming. The blood that poured down my face mingled with my tears, until I felt I was crying tears of blood. Everything became black; a big black cloud shrouded everything. My strength ebbed away and I could no longer stand up. I had not had a glimpse of Father or Leon; I had not seen Mother's sister or her baby. I loved them all so much, but my body betrayed me. I simply could not watch the death march for one second longer. Slowly and quietly, I allowed myself to fall to the floor, dug my nails into the wet earth and averted my eyes from the horrors just outside my home.

Just then I heard the sound of boots inside the house; someone shouted in German, "Get out of here, I can manage alone. Just keep watch and make sure those filthy Jewish kikes don't get away." Then I heard a Ukrainian voice say, "Don't get him riled, let's get out of here." At first I thought someone outside had heard us, but there was silence. Was the danger over? Again I heard the sound of many pairs of feet walking around the house; it seemed an eternity before someone jumped suddenly on the steps of the porch and I heard the sound of jackboots trampling all over the house. Speaking in Ukrainian a man tried to chase a group of people from the house; then there were sounds of resistance. Someone cursed the intruders and told them rudely, "This is the first time in Ukrainian history that people like you became rich overnight! However much we give you, it's never enough!" It was as if the police were handing out their own possessions and not those of the Jews. Later, a group of men were discussing whether the house had been searched thoroughly enough. Finally, they decided to seal the house and someone was told to tape a notice on the front door. We didn't have a chance to relax and breathe a little before we heard people walking around the house again. I tried to listen even more closely. This time, the young voices I heard were telling crude jokes in Polish; at first I was sure they were planning to squat in our house.

Suddenly, a group of Polish youths appeared in the attic, right in front of us! There was something unreal about the encounter; the murderer comes face to face with his victim. Indeed, the

Polish boys had decided to search the attic, but they were just as surprised to find us as we were to be found by them.

Mother was still lying motionless in the wet earth but at the sight of the Poles, she mustered all her strength to come to. Her entire world had just collapsed and, as if that wasn't enough, 'they' had returned to kill her surviving children. With trembling hands she grabbed baby Batya from the ground and held her close to her chest. She looked nothing like the woman who was my mother, everything had changed; she was covered in mud and her long blonde hair was uncombed and hung to her knees. And I, with the deep, mud-covered, self-imposed scratches on my face, could have frightened away the devil. My hands and elbows were also full of mud and my blonde braids had lost their color. So sure were the Poles that no Jews remained in the house that they were quite taken aback at the sight of us; they fell to their knees, crossed themselves and mumbled a prayer. They then stood up and started to withdraw towards a corner of the roof, while we remained motionless. I was now able to get a better look at the group and saw that they were not teenagers but young men and women in their twenties. I recognized them all and they recognized us, although we had never had any kind of social interaction. I then noticed that three of them were even more familiar to me than the others; they were the three children of Paplawski the Pole.

In 1938, Paplawski had succeeded in renting a store and then he wrote antisemitic posters, which he glued to his store window. He called on his compatriots to "sever all business ties with Jews and send the Jews to Palestine." Following the German occupation, this same Paplawski had managed to appropriate machinery and tools from my father's store. In one single day, Paplawski stole everything that Father had collected painstakingly throughout his life.

At first, Paplawski's daughter appeared on the verge of passing out from the fright of seeing us, but the young Poles soon recovered and began discussing our fate with each other.

Our lives depended on them. We could hardly stand up after days of hunger and thirst but my mother and I did our best to steady ourselves as we heard our sentence. My little sisters stayed relatively quiet, except for an occasional sigh, which made those children sound like old women.

I listened as these Poles talked about their current economic situation as compared with earlier years, all thanks to the property they had stolen from the Jews. "Admittedly," they agreed, "we have achieved all this bounty in return for the annihilation of the Jews, but we Poles are not to blame for their misfortunes." Their consciences were clear, they told each other; it was not they who planned and carried out this mass slaughter; there was certainly no place for regret or remorse on their parts! "You must understand," they rationalized to us, "according to German law, you have no right to remain in this house, which no longer belongs to you. You must vacate the house immediately and go out to the road where the law enforcers are the only ones with the right to decide what to do with you."

We went down from the attic. Part of me was happy that our fate had evidently been sealed; our suffering would end, once and for all. What was the point of extending our torturous existence? Our strength was ebbing and the earth pulled us like a magnet. If only we could rest! But it was not to be.

Mother lay down with the girls on the porch and I sat on the steps. Not far from us, the quiet was interrupted by the shouts of a woman. We stood up to discover the source of the noise and saw the open gate of a courtyard that had belonged to the Wilner family. Earlier on that endless day, before daybreak, we had watched sadly as the Germans dragged the Wilner family out of their home.

Now we saw that two more members of the Wilner family, Zhenia and her brother Lyowa, were being dragged outside. I knew that during the occupation, the family of a Ukrainian fascist had moved into one of the apartments owned by the Wilner family, turned several of the rooms into storehouses for plundered Jewish property, and forced the Wilner girls to serve them. It seemed that Zhenia and Lyowa had managed to hide under the Ukrainian fascist's bed when the Germans had evicted the rest of their family that morning. But now the Ukrainian's wife had discovered them and was chasing them out of the house. The woman was dressed in a fancy outfit and adorned with expensive gold chains, bracelets, rings and precious stones. She actually sparkled in the sun, like a Christmas tree. She was holding a large garden broom with which she beat the weeping Zhenia and Lyowa on their heads. The woman knew no mercy, grabbing her victims and holding them tenaciously, allowing them no opportunity to escape her blows that were accompanied by furious shouting. Finally, local policemen took the two Jews away.

We were exhausted by now and indifferent to everything around us. All we wanted was to rest. No Jews remained anywhere near our street. The policemen started to press us to run in order to join other small groups of Jews, who were accompanied by armed policemen. We were like a flock of frightened sheep, surrounded by vicious watchdogs on all sides. We entered the main street and there we met a young woman by the name of Matia Buf. They had killed her two-year-old baby as well as her family; only she remained alive, but now they attached her to our group. We all knew that this was our last day on Earth; it was no secret that we were being taken to the murder pits of Kozak. We had seen so much death that day and were annoyed that we were not even allowed to die in dignity.

We were ordered to walk the eight kilometers to the Kozak pits. We had no choice but to obey even though our legs refused to carry us and we didn't have the strength to endure the murderous blows that were inflicted on us if we dared to stop. Dragging our legs as if they were inanimate objects, we prayed to die and thus end our misery. Why didn't they just shoot us on the spot and be done with it? Only later did we learn the answer. The murderers had wasted no time and patience on earlier groups of exhausted Jews, shooting them on the spot and saving them the walk to the pits. But then an order came to stop the murders in town, because collecting all the corpses that littered the streets had become a nuisance. This was the only reason that they did not shoot us, too.

Slowly we dragged ourselves to the Kozak Forest, which was adjacent to a village of the same name. That's when we saw the three enormous pits, full of the corpses of Jews of all ages. The murderers had just completed their day's atrocities and the corpses were still warm. Germans had been responsible for the murders of the Jews, enthusiastically assisted by policemen from Zhitomir, who used the Jews for target practice, together with policemen from Lithuania and local Ukrainian policemen. But I must point out that the German forces were the ones to carry out the mass murders. The others, policemen and Ukrainians were allowed to torment the Jews, to beat, and even kill them, but it was the Germans who were responsible for the mass murders.

At the site of the pits we saw extremely drunk German soldiers who told the policemen who had accompanied us that they "have worked harder than planned and now have to prepare for a party." As they murdered the Jews, they drank large quantities of alcohol and ate delicacies, right next to the pits that were filling up with Jewish corpses.

We waited at the pits. The local murderers were in a festive mood, so drunk they could barely drag their feet. Many policemen were busy rummaging through the piles of clothing that the victims had been forced to remove before being shot. There was a large selection and they had a hard time deciding what to take. I suspect that those policemen were happy to stay behind in order to look for hidden treasure or jewelry among the victims' clothing.

It transpired later that the people of Kozak had welcomed the unfortunate Jews making their way to the murder pits by falling on them screaming and shouting hysterically, to check their clothing and shoes for valuables. They ripped good jewelry off them and even checked their hands for wedding rings and other pieces.

We waited, our gaze fixed on the corpses of our neighbors. Tensely we followed every move of the German murderers. I don't know where I got the strength to listen to their conversations. They said that the Jews had been murdered in accordance with a special agreement. They complained that some of their helpers violated the agreement by continuing to send small batches of Jews, thus forcing them to work overtime, past the time they had set themselves for their day's work. They had no choice but to liquidate all the Jews who had succeeded in hiding themselves during the day. If that wasn't bad enough, they were now being asked to stay on even longer in order to murder such a small group as the one that included us! This time the murderers were furious because it was already 4 p.m., or so I believe I heard them say.

We waited tensely as the murderers talked among themselves. We sat next to the pits, stroking the ground that was wet with Jewish blood. As they poked through the piles of clothing, our tormentors talked about the parties they would be going to that evening. Although they said they wanted to leave already, they didn't seem to be in any hurry. They had time to jeer at us and mock us, to make snide jokes about our miserable appearance. My lacerated face provided them with plenty to laugh at and they sneered at the naked victims.

However, one thing gave us a little hope. The murderers were comforting those of their colleagues who were impatient to leave: "Alright, let's get out of here; we've done enough for one day. These Jews are finished anyway; why should we stick around any longer to do away with those lice? They can spend the night looking for their relatives in the pits. I say, they have nowhere to go, nothing's going to happen if they spend a few more days here and then we'll kill them." Shortly after, the monsters disappeared.

We were getting cold and started to walk, not knowing where we could go. Where, indeed? In the forest we encountered someone who had survived and witnessed the mass murder. He had succeeded in eluding the murderers by disappearing into the bushes. The man had no clothes and was afraid to approach the piles of clothing to search for his own. I have no words to describe his wretched appearance. But he was quick to describe what his eyes had seen that day and that he was the only one still alive after the hideous atrocities he had witnessed. His name was Yisrael Melamed.

As all this took place, we were sure that no one out in the big world knew about the Jewish nation being systematically annihilated. Our fear was that this terrible crime perpetrated by the German monsters would remain a secret until the end of time. And this fear was not unfounded. We saw how the Germans went to great lengths to hide their evil deeds and this pained us greatly. It was clear to us that the Germans wanted to erase the very existence of the Jewish nation from the face of the earth. And it is for this reason only that I, and others like me, made superhuman efforts to remain alive, if only for a short time. We had to be able to testify to what we had experienced. We were spurred on by the fear that no one would remain alive to tell the tale. We wanted the world to know what the Germans did to the Jewish people; we wanted someone to avenge our blood from those monsters whose evil has no comparison in human history.

In the meantime, we knew we were living on borrowed time. Having survived the Kozak murder pits, we were afraid to stay together and each went in a different direction. Sadly, I don't think there were any other survivors. Lyowa Wilner, the neighbor I had seen being hounded out of his home when we, too, had been caught, had been able to reach the partisans and was killed in one of their operations. His younger sister Zhenia had many non-Jewish friends before the occupation, most of whom severed all connections with her. I don't know how she managed to obtain a forged passport, perhaps through someone she knew, or even what kind of a passport it was. All I know is that Zhenia did not get very far from Korzec before she was caught and murdered. Matia Buf, also around twenty years old, remained with her mother who was still a young, strong woman. Their many non-Jewish friends broke contact with them after the occupation, but one heard that they were still alive and offered to hide them in her house. This woman happened to be our closest neighbor, a Polish woman by the name of Dajonowa, whose house shared a fence with ours and with whom we were friendly—until the occupation. But for some reason, she offered her protection to Matia and her mother, who handed over all their hidden valuables, some of which had been left with them by other families for safekeeping. But when the Germans came to collect the survivors of that dreadful day, Dajonowa chased Matia and her mother out of her house and the two were captured and tortured to death.

My mother, my sister Nina and the two little girls we carried tried to make our way back home. Ostensibly, there was nowhere to go back to because those young Poles had thrown us out. But, like house pets that tend to return to a familiar place, we too went in the direction of our familiar home. Our house was open and it was empty. The street looked like one big cemetery. An eerie quiet reigned and we saw hardly anyone on the streets. We did not know if any Jews were still alive, aside from those in our small group.

We barely made it up to the balcony; we passed by the hall and entered the kitchen. I could see that Mother was on the verge of collapse so I quickly removed Batya from her arms before she fell to the ground. Once again I thought, "If only Mother would die now, peacefully in her sleep, without having to suffer any more." I wished that we could all die in our sleep.

My entire body ached but, as the oldest daughter, I felt enormous responsibility toward the little girls who depended on me. That day they had seen dreadful things and had suffered quietly. They were afraid of being alone and their eyes followed me all the time. They did not cry, they did not utter a sound but their eyes spoke volumes and begged me to stay. I felt helpless; I knew we desperately needed food, clothing, shoes; the barest essentials to maintain our meagre existence. I searched the house, although I knew already that it was empty. At first, I found nothing and I was unable to properly search my parent's room because the glass panes in the big windows had been shattered and the feathers and down from the quilts filled the air. But I did find one prize: a black chiffon evening dress my mother had received in one of the parcels from America, a gift from my grandmother. Evidently there had been a fight over this dress because its bodice was torn and the thieves must have then discarded it. But the dress had a long, full skirt from which I was able to fashion a couple of headscarves for my mother and myself. I had no shoes and no dress. Still I managed to make myself a black kerchief, large enough to hide my face, which had swollen badly from the deep scratches I had inflicted on myself.

In the courtyard, I found some old potato peels left behind by the Germans when they evacuated their portable kitchen the day before the atrocities. I cooked the peels into a repulsive porridge, both in appearance and in taste; there was not even a grain of salt for some flavor. At least it was something to eat and I fed it to my sisters.

Mother was very sick throughout the next week, unconscious and with a high fever. She stayed on the floor because there was no one to help me pick her up and move her. Nina sat next to her and changed the wet rag on her forehead. From time to time she breathed heavily, I thought she was dying. It was so sad and touching to see my little sisters speaking with their mother, begging her not to leave them. The house was dark and we did not turn on any lights. I did not even bother to close the doors because anyone could have entered through the large windows. Experience had taught me that there was no point in hiding.

I was exhausted, but unable to fall asleep. I thought about the open pits I had seen in Kozak. I was depressed, confused and did not know where to turn. I couldn't see a way out of our predicament. Inside me raged a tempest, a desire to scream, a desire that tore me to pieces. In those days I had no peace and my thoughts were fixed on our terrible tragedy.

Time passed since we had returned from the pits and I had not found a way to improve our circumstances. I consulted with my twelve-year-old sister, Nina, about ways to get food for our hungry sisters. It was then that I remembered my parents' bag full of expensive jewelry and family heirlooms that they had hidden in their bed. Before the night of the mass murder, we would sometimes escape from the house at night to a nearby field, in search of some fresh air and to allow the younger children to relax a little. Mother always took this bag with her on these outings. It was a real treasure trove and could have provided us with everything we needed for many years, but my parents refused to touch it even when we were hungry. They were convinced that it was wrong, under any circumstances, to sell off the family jewels.

I was determined to search my parent's bedroom more thoroughly this time, despite all the feathers and down that filled the air. I went straight to their twin beds that stood next to each other, to form a double bed. Feathers covered them, but I resolutely overturned the pile of feathers, but found no bag. I stood by the bed, worried, unable to understand why a thief would rip open the brand new down quilts and the big pillows; they didn't even take the new cases. Mother had sewn all these herself for her daughters; they were to be part of our future dowry.

I reached the conclusion that a German murderer, on his quest for Jews, had come into the room and found the bag of jewelry. This encouraged him to search for more booty and he had used his sword to slice through the quilts and pillows. The feathers soon billowed out and filled the room and the local thieves had been put off from entering. If my theory was correct, I thought that there might still be a chance of finding some shoes under the bed. I stopped thinking and simply reached under the bed. I reached under one of the beds and found my five-year-old brother, Leon, lying there unconscious.

I cannot describe my feelings during those moments when I found my brother instead of the valuable jewels. Gradually, Leon returned to himself and told us what had happened after Father, Raya and Efi had left the house. He described how the Germans had fired in all directions in order to frighten their victims. There was pandemonium. One of the Germans fired a shot at Father's head from behind. Leon saw Father fall and roll down the mountain. But the Germans forced our children to continue marching towards the municipal building.

The Germans held a selection. They separated the men from the women, older people and parents from their children. Leon remained with Efi and Raya, since Father had disappeared down the hill. When the angel of death raged, the children were alone with no adults to comfort them.

Eight-year-old Efi, five-year-old Leon and my four-year-old sister, Raya, walked together in a row. Leon saw from a distance that the doors and windows of his home were open. He managed to slip away from the convoy and ran home, into his parents' bedroom, and hid under the bed. He was followed by a German, who had noticed his escape, and some Ukrainian policemen, but for some reason the German chased them away.

Leon lay under the bed and watched the boots of the German who stood next to it. The terrified boy lost consciousness until that critical moment when I found him; when I had thought he was no longer alive. I was so happy that instead of jewelry, I had received my brother.

As soon as he recovered, Leon took his place on the floor beside Mother. He sat and talked to her enthusiastically as if nothing had happened. Mother was still unconscious and did not respond.

CHAPTER 5

The Doors Close

About one thousand Jews were still alive after the big *Aktion* in Korzec. It appears that many had survived by seeking shelter in the homes of acquaintances in the villages; two hundred young women had been left alive to be employed in forced labor by the murderers. But not one Jewish family remained intact and the survivors were alone in the world, internalizing their pain and sorrow. Those of us who had made our way back from the very edge of death had done so purely by chance; but we were broken in soul and in spirit. We envied those who had died and fantasized about an easy death, devoid of torture and suffering.

After a few days, those of my family who were still alive were now back in our house; no one came to bother us. Most of the time we just sat on the floor and watched as our Mother slowly died. I took responsibility for the younger children, who were in desperate need of a parent figure, although I was no less needy. The tension we had lived under for so long had left our nerves jagged and every little noise from outside caused us to jump. The children were constantly alert, listening day and night for every sound inside and outside the house. We were like hunted animals.

Our biggest problem was finding food. Jews were still forbidden from going outside their homes and we had been warned of what would happen to us if we were caught anywhere near the village. I was afraid to leave the children alone to go out in search of food, not knowing if I would ever see them again. But I had no choice; I had to find some way to provide for them. The two youngest ones were listless and apathetic and I dreamed of finding some milk for them. I would have done anything for a cup of milk! The children had not seen any milk since the beginning of the German occupation.

After a few days had passed without so much as a crumb of food in the house, I made up my mind to go out through the back alleys toward the village. I felt duty bound to feed my surviving brothers and sisters. I didn't see the sun, nor did I feel the ground under my feet; I gave no thought to what would happen to me if someone were to see me; I just didn't care. But now that I had gathered my last strength and set out to find food, all the doors were closed in my face. When they thought I wasn't looking, they stared at me as if I had horns. I kept asking myself, "What makes me different from them? I even speak the same language, have the same accent!" I was fluent in all the languages spoken by the various ethnic groups in the region; I could have passed for one of them. But it made no difference; I was a Jew!

Also, I looked strange; a black kerchief covered my head and most of my face, except for my swollen, almost closed eyes. The villagers eyed me suspiciously, as if I had come to blame them. No wonder they didn't want me around, not even in their backyards. So, although the villagers needed cheap labor, no one wanted me, not even for the most menial, backbreaking jobs. All my life I had heard my parents talk about truth and justice, honesty and integrity; they had taught me and my brothers and sisters that mankind is inherently decent, merciful and compassionate. But in reality, it was just the reverse. My bitter thoughts stung like salt on a wound. My parents' blind faith had led them straight into the German hellhole.

The Jews all suffered from hunger and were forced to sneak into nearby villages, regardless of the danger, and the villagers took unfair advantage of our plight by putting us to work for a slave's wage. Jews could not ask for milk or bread in return for hard work and had to make do with any leftover scraps handed out by their employers. For all my hard work I was given a few potatoes. It was a horrendous situation, created just for the Jews.

But I quickly learned some street wisdom. Since the non-Jewish population preferred not to come face to face with our wretched situation, I was taught by others to stand upright, walk tall, fix a smile to my torn face. We Jews had to pretend that things were all right, to hide our tragic circumstances. Everything we did was above and beyond our power; just to earn some scraps of food.

One night, a few days after that horrendous day in which most of the Jews had been rounded up and murdered, I heard a tiny sound outside the house. I was sure this was the end for us; 'they' had come to take the rest of us and murder us, too. The children sensed the noise in their sleep, tossing and turning restlessly, before raising their heads and then sitting up, wide awake. There was no point trying to ignore the noise and going back to sleep: I mustered all my strength and quickly made for the front of the house. With one quick movement, I opened the two doors wide and walked to the porch, where I stood looking into the lovely darkness of the summer night. I did not see a soul, nor did I discern any movement. I wanted to double-check and make a more thorough search, but decided to run back into the house first, to reassure the children that nothing was wrong. I returned to the porch and suddenly who should appear in front of me, but my **father!**

I was scared to death by this unexpected apparition. I had been yearning for my father so much that I thought I must have been dreaming. The idea that I might be seeing an apparition was so overwhelming that I was quite speechless, unable even to scream. It had been several days since the *Aktion* and there was no basis for even a glimmer of hope that Father was still alive; with my own eyes I had watched him being taken out of our house with the children. Leon had described seeing Father being shot in the back of his head and the blood that flowed from the wound. He had seen Father fall to the ground and roll down the mountain that led to the river.

But it was no apparition. Even though he was badly wounded and barely recognizable, it was really him, my beloved father; but he was so weak he could barely stand on his feet.

I rushed to treat Father's many wounds as best I could and when I was finished, he told us his story. He and the children had been led by the murderers, under a constant shower of blows, towards the assembly point where the Jews had been congregated. But before Father could reach the assembly point 'they' had shot him from behind. He was standing at that moment on a steep slope and the unexpected shot caused him to lose his balance. He rolled all the way down the hill and landed in an orchard and straight into a tree. The tree had broken his fall and enabled him to stop and lie down, hidden from view.

Father stayed in hiding for a while, trying to recuperate from his injury. Then, sure that there was no one around, he mustered his little remaining strength in order to get away unseen. "I was sure no one from our family was alive," he told us. But he forced himself to overcome his fear, found a stick to help him walk and set out at night on the long crawl back home, hoping against hope to find some survivors. "I had to see if there were any Jews still alive," he said simply.

We all felt that Father had been resurrected from the dead. But our happiness at finding him was mixed with the pain of knowing that eight-year-old Efi and four-year-old Raya were lost forever.

Once Father was back with us, our situation improved somewhat. For one thing, he was able to slip out to the villages, where he managed to find work, while I stayed behind and took care of the children. Some of the burden had been lifted from my shoulders. But most welcome of all was the fact that, with Father's return. Mother began to slowly recover and return to herself.

But shortly after Father's return we were thrown out of our house for good. A group of Germans, accompanied by Ukrainian policemen, paid us a visit. They behaved as if we were breaking the law by squatting on someone else's property and forced us angrily out of the house immediately, telling us to find a place to stay in one of the empty houses in the ghetto. They then warned us that anyone caught outside the ghetto would be killed. So we left our house for the last time with empty hands, staring longingly behind us; we knew we'd never see our home again. Later, though, Father was able to return to our home and smuggle out some of our valuables and even a few family pictures. We moved into Grandmother's house, which was near the beginning of Berezdowa Street on the edge of the ghetto. Needless to say, there was nothing left of her furniture and possessions. The ghetto was very small; the Germans deliberately kept Jewish ghettoes as small as possible so as to be able to keep their eye on us all the time and to isolate us from the non-Jews. The only people we connected with were the other Jews in the ghetto.

Berezdowa Street, which ran next to my grandmother's home, was long and wide and cobbled. When German or Ukrainian policemen walked down that road in their hobnailed boots, they made an ominous drumming noise that caused our hearts to sink whenever we heard it. It was a sound that signaled approaching danger; it meant that our enemies were drawing close. To this day, I can still hear in my mind the terrifying click of those jackboots.

It is hard for me to describe the carnage on the ghetto streets; it was complete and utter chaos. The house, too, was in a terrible state. There was so much to do, that we hardly knew where to begin; we had to clean inside as well as outside.

We hadn't even finished, before there was a visit by several
Ukrainian policemen, who had come to commandeer us into
forced labor. They treated us like dirt and transported us in
cattle trucks. We were already used to the despicable way
they talked to us, full of insults and abuse. They took us
to work in a very large house outside the ghetto that had
once belonged to a Jew. The house contained no furniture or
other household goods, but the numerous, spacious rooms
all contained built-in wooden cupboards with shelves that
reached the ceiling. The house was clean and there were piles
of clothes on the floor in each of the rooms, clothes that had
been removed from the Jews before they were murdered.

Many of us became hysterical as soon as we saw those
piles of clothes, our throats choked with tears; some were
dumbstruck, paralyzed, unable to move. The angry policemen
spurred us on. Then they beat us. They began taunting us,
saying that soon, our own clothes would find their way to
these piles, that our days were numbered and that we, too,
were destined to die.

Our job was to sort the clothes according to type and size.
We separated the clothes into piles of dresses, pants, coats
and shoes; there was a separate pile for children's clothes.
Even though they didn't hide from us the fact that we were
also going to die, they did not refrain from demanding our
absolute obedience and precise work. When that didn't help,
they told us that they were only following the orders of the
German government to ship all clothes to Germany by a
certain date. We often heard the policemen say that all Jewish
possessions, including the clothes of murdered Jews, had to
be sent to Germany.

We all searched for some item of clothing that had belonged
to one of our relatives. We used all kinds of tricks in order
to be able to run our eyes over those piles of clothes. Still,
it was impossible to scan them all; there was just too many.
The piles also included winter clothes. Although it was still

summer and some of the murdered were wearing winter clothes, perhaps because they had not had enough time to get dressed appropriately when they were pulled out of their beds. We all knew that there was no rational explanation for our obsessive search through the piles to find something that had belonged to someone we had lost, unless we needed to pour salt on our open wounds; but we felt we had to do it. As we worked, reality and imagination became intermingled; as we sorted those clothes, we also saw our family members stand before us. Our eyes filled with tears as we stroked those garments; the clothes assumed the form of all those people who had worn them before being murdered.

And then it happened: all of a sudden, I came across the clothes my little brother and sister had been wearing! I cannot explain the coincidence that led me to my brother's neat little bundle of clothes, in the very pile I was working on, as if it was just waiting for me to find it. I lost my equilibrium. The women beside me realized immediately what had caused me to collapse and rushed to my side. It was thus that I was able to conceal my brother Efi's short-sleeved turquoise pajamas among my own clothes.

I was forced to continue working and not to attract attention. My hands worked mechanically, while my thoughts flew. Suddenly, I heard the faint jingle of something metal falling on the floor. I looked down and noticed a shiny coin near my foot. I didn't know what it was, but I was determined that it shouldn't fall into the hands of the Ukrainians. Carefully, I covered the coin with my foot. I looked around and, when the coast was clear, I slipped that coin into the hem of my dress.

Time passed slowly. One day it started to rain very heavily and there was even some hail, a very unusual occurrence on a summer's day. I stood beside one window in the house and my mother beside another and we both wept. There was nothing to say, we both knew that the murder pits near Kozak Forest were exposed and now would be flooded with rainwater.

Jews begged the German murderers for permission to seal
the open pits into which our loved ones had been thrown.
After a while, they were given the names of people to whom
they could pay large sums of money in return for the privilege
of closing the mass graves. Eventually the permits arrived.

Each permit enabled ten men only to go to the site. However,
wives and others also felt impelled to visit the mass grave
of their loved ones. On the other hand, some people were
suspicious of the Germans' motives. "Who is to say if we'll
ever get out alive from that place?" they asked. Eventually,
as a compromise, a number of Jews went to the forest one
night and split up into small groups. Thus, in the early hours
of the morning, small groups arrived from different directions
at the murder site. I was there, too, running after my parents.

Before dawn we reached the open pits in the forest, near the
village of Kozak. What I saw has been carved forever in my
memory. All three giant pits were completely covered by wild
forest animals. So numerous were the animals and so densely
crowded, that it was impossible to distinguish between them
and the corpses of the murdered Jews. We were dumbstruck
at the sight of those animals falling ravenously on the dead
bodies of our loves ones. But the predators did not compete
with one another or fight among themselves. Clearly, there
was enough food for them all and there was no need to fight.
Hovering overhead and standing next to the animals on the
ground were great numbers of large, swollen ravens.

I felt absolutely sick, but, like all the others, forced myself
to swallow my emotions and do what had to be done. Some
of the men took charge and commanded us to break branches
off the trees, to scare off the animals. Eventually, even the
women recovered from their revulsion and began to help to
the best of their ability. But the animals refused to budge. Our
next tactic was to cover the pits and the animals with earth;
only then did the predators start to retreat into the forest.
It was hard work, because we had no tools of any kind; we

were even forced to step on the corpses in order to access the center of each pit and cover it with dirt.

The men recited the Jewish mourning prayer, Kaddish, and the women repeated the words. We had completed our task and sat down on the covered pits. Not a word was uttered; everyone was wrapped up in his or her own inner grief. We had no more tears left; the silence could have continued forever. But then someone pulled us out of our thoughts, "When we are gone, there will be no Jews left to cover the pit into which our bodies were thrown. Will anyone be left to tell the story of the Jews in our town?" Someone else from the group said, "Eventually, the forest will cover our pit too," and my mother added, "Yes, and people will come to gather mushrooms above our graves and no one will know, or believe, the horrors that are hidden underneath." Then one of the men said, "Let's not torment ourselves with these pointless thoughts; we are suffering enough. It's time now to hurry back to the ghetto."

From the beginning, the occupation was accompanied by starvation and lack of sleep. I was confused and in despair; all I wanted was a hot soapy bath, a comfortable bed to sleep on with no worries or fear of imminent death, and the ability to straighten my legs as I slept. But in the ghetto, the Jews did not know a moment of tranquility, the earth burned beneath our feet. Constant tension had become a part of our lives. But that, clearly, wasn't enough; every day, unwanted guests appeared in the ghetto and spread rumors that the Germans were about to liquidate the ghetto. Father said, "If I can't feed and protect my own children, then I can't stay with my family. What kind of a man am I?"

Mother decided that we must try to reassure the children by taking them out of the ghetto at night. "There is no longer anything to lose," she would say. So when darkness fell, we looked for opportunities to slip out unnoticed. Mother and I would carry the younger children in our arms and go to places that were usually deserted, such as the cemetery, the garbage dump, or an empty field. If we were lucky, everything went smoothly and we were happy, even though we shivered all night from the cold. Then, before dawn broke, we'd go to the river and wash ourselves with the help of some chalkstone substitute for soap that we had found on the way. Somehow I couldn't believe that another nation would go to such lengths to maintain their human dignity in the face of so many fatal blows and such humiliation.

Sometimes we weren't lucky and were stopped outside the ghetto and separated from each other as 'they' cursed and swore at us. We thought 'they' were going to kill us and I tried to shield the little ones with my body. When 'they' led us to some obscure place we were sure it was our last day on Earth until, unexpectedly, we were released, but only after they beat us as a punishment and warning of things to come. Under constant suffering and fear, twelve-year-old Nina had a nervous breakdown. She was unable to cope with the knowledge that we lived on borrowed time and was constantly asking why she had to die so young. She cried all the time, even in her sleep. Until the end, she was naïve, dependent and very needy, no less than the youngest of the children.

According to our mother, a hiding place between the walls of the house would be useful in calming everyone's nerves, especially Nina's. There had been one in our own home, but here in the ghetto, we were not so protected. Admittedly, we had learned that it was futile to try to hide from 'them'. The Ukrainian police were recruited from among the local people and they knew everything there was to know about the Jews of Korzec. During the big *Aktion* on the eve of the *Shavuot* festival, most of the Jewish families hadn't even had the chance to enter their cubbyholes and few (if any) lives had been saved due to these precautions. But Mother was right—a cubbyhole would have benefited the children and quieted their nerves, even if only temporarily.

Then she had an idea. Her brother Menashe had been murdered, together with everyone in his large family. His empty house was located on the other side of the ghetto and Mother had a hunch that Menashe had built a cubbyhole somewhere in his home. We decided to take a look and walked over to the large, deserted house. It was completely empty; the thieves had been there first, of course. But after a thorough search we found a cubbyhole, which, by current standards, was a good one. Father flatly refused to use it, choosing instead to stay behind in our own ghetto house. But the rest of us squeezed into that small cubicle at Uncle Menashe's home. It was closed on all sides just like a dark, suffocating grave. We couldn't even see each other, but we heard each other's heavy breathing. Mother and I held the younger children on our laps, while Nina and Leon stood beside us. We were as crowded as sardines in a tin, and sweated profusely. It was a heavy price to pay for peace of mind and a chance to calm our frayed nerves.

We were inside our hiding place one night, when there was a noise from inside and outside the house. It was as if people were coming in and out of the house and we were terrified that we had placed ourselves in a trap; there had been cases in which 'they' had set fire to houses with Jews inside their cubbyholes. But we were afraid to emerge. Eventually, quiet reigned and I slipped outside to investigate. It was now quiet both inside and outside, as if nothing had happened. I signaled that it was safe to leave the hiding place and we all breathed a sigh of relief. We rested for a moment on the floor; the terrified children were on the verge of insanity and we needed to calm them down. We had to return to our house on the other side of the ghetto, to wash ourselves and fix some food for the children. But Mother said, "Before we leave Menashe's house, we must find out what happened here last night."

I accompanied her on a more thorough search. From the kitchen a door led into a storeroom, which led to a stable.

Mother noticed that a large supply of firewood had been taken. But our attention was attracted by something else: in a corner of the stable there was a huge pit, several meters deep, and inside were two enormous, hermetically sealed metal barrels. Various work tools were scattered nearby. Mother said immediately, "So this is the source of last night's noise! A group of men had been working here until they came across the pit and opened it. They must have searched all over the house for more hiding places; that was what we heard." Thieves preferred to work at night because they had a lot of competition, but mostly because they were afraid of the Germans who confiscated anything they managed to find. "Anna," my mother said, "please go and fetch Father now."

I did as I was told and brought my father to my uncle's house. After much hard work he succeeded in opening the barrels and removing their contents; we gasped at the treasure we saw inside them. There was a large amount of various kinds of things: elegant shoes, lovely blanket-sized woolen kerchiefs, coats and suits for every season, top-quality bed linens, etc. Father said, "We must get out of here immediately, because the thieves could return at any minute. Maybe the Germans frightened them off and that's why they stopped, but they are probably not far away and plan to return as soon as the coast is clear." So we left immediately.

Now we faced a new problem: where would we hide all this stuff? Since we had to act quickly and quietly. Father set himself the hard task of digging new pits in the bedroom in order to hide all the objects that had fallen so unexpectedly into our hands. His usual schedule consisted of slipping out to the outlying villages to work and obtain food for the children, but after finding the treasure, he had to prepare safe places in which to hide it.

One early morning, the ghetto was visited by a terrifying guest. Mitka Zavirukha, who was the commandant of the Ukrainian police, arrived in the ghetto accompanied by a police entourage. To the surviving Jews of Korzec's ghetto this was a very bad omen. In every house people waited tensely to hear what new misfortunes this murderer was planning to inflict upon them. But what could we do? How on earth could we defend ourselves? There was nowhere for us to run. The entire ghetto population went outside to hear what Mitka Zavirukha had to say; Mitka was very familiar with the Jewish community, as we were with him. In his youth he had been a notorious thief, the kind of criminal no one wanted anything to do with. How ironic that it was a Jew, Avraham Bardach, who had taken Mitka under his wing and tried to reform him. At a time when Mitka was at his lowest ebb, Bardach had taken him into his home, taught him a trade and treated him like an equal. Later, when Mitka was promoted quite suddenly to his present position, regardless of his criminal past, he turned viciously against the Russians and the Jews. According to rumor, he paid his henchmen well for carrying out his murders.

Mitka's whole objective was to get rich quick and to appropriate everything he could lay his hands on. To this end, he took full advantage of his rank to torment the Jews. He would summon wealthy Jews for interrogation in the cellars shared by the Ukrainian police and the Gestapo. Often, even after paying a handsome bribe, his Jewish victim would be murdered anyway, without ever again seeing the light of day. Mitka spoke fluent Yiddish and had a habit of asking in that language, "Doesn't the Ukrainian police commandant deserve to be rich?" He also used to say, "The Germans are strangers who came here from far off. They intend to kill all you Jews, but first they'll make sure to take control of all your property and wealth. So you have nothing to worry about, the Germans still haven't finished transferring all Jewish property to Germany." Mitka wore his police uniform and boots proudly, as symbols of his power and influence and the means by which he achieved all his desires.

And now, here was Mitka Zavirukha in the ghetto, looking at its Jewish inhabitants with cruel satisfaction. He stopped in front of my grandmother's house, the house in which we were now living. A policeman entered the house and walked out with Father. On that lovely warm summer's day, I was outside on the street with the other Jews, not far from the house. Seeing my father with the Ukrainian policeman, I felt only darkness and cold. I ran towards him and stayed close, but I was afraid to touch him. I knew my father well and recognized the expression of pride on his face. My heart was beating madly; I was terrified he would tell the murderer exactly what he thought of him. Things started to dance in front of my eyes. I saw Mitka nervously approach Father, standing so close that there was almost no space between them. It seemed as if Mitka didn't want anyone to overhear what he was saying to Father.

I managed to hear Mitka call my father by his Ukrainian nickname and say, "Volko [Wolf] I need you to work for me. I have sent my men to you and they tell me you are refusing to work for me. You have forced me to come here in person. Let me tell you, Volko, that you're playing with fire, you are risking your life."

My father screamed back his answer, "You killed my children and you can kill me too, but no power on Earth will force me to work for you. You are blind, Mitka, and you choose not to think about what will happen to you in the end. You will not escape your punishment!"

Then Mitka said, "Volko, forget your Communists, they don't exist any longer. The Russians are destined for the same fate as the Jews; the Germans will pursue them until they choke them to death, too." This was strange, because everyone in town knew that Father had never been a member of any party and was not a Communist.

"I am running this town now and nothing can change that! You are all my subjects and I order you to do the work I need of you!"

Mitka's policemen surrounded us as more Jews filled the street. People waited tensely to see what would happen. And then Father shouted, "You can murder every one of us, but the truth will follow you wherever you go. What kind of police chief are you? Have you forgotten the man who saved you when you were a juvenile delinquent and a thief? It was none other than the Jew, Avraham Bardach! You've come a long way since then, haven't you? Nowadays you are not only a petty criminal, you are also a cold-blooded murderer!"

This was the first time during this nightmare that was the German occupation that I heard my father actually say what he felt. From his own mouth, he was describing his pain and suffering and his loss of the will to live. I heard things I had not known about, even though we lived under the same roof. It was out of his love for me that my father had avoided talking to me, blaming himself for my suffering.

As my father spoke, Mitka's face turned white and he trembled; then he jumped backwards as if boiling water was being poured on him. His hands shaking, he pulled out his pistol and aimed it directly at my father's face. "You've crossed the line, Volko!" he shouted. "You're going to pay for this!"

Mitka turned quickly around, sizing up the situation on all sides. He realized that the Jews on the street must have heard every word of the insults my father had hurled at him. Even worse, his own men had heard, as they stood waiting for a command from their chief. I did not move from my father's side; I knew he was courageous and capable of doing something unexpected. There was nothing I could do. To this day, I believe that my father's words were no slip of the tongue. His harsh, public response to Mitka had been well thought out in advance. Mitka understood this and no retraction or apology could atone for the public humiliation inflicted on him. I knew that it was all over; Father had sealed his own fate. Out of pain I wanted to be the first to die and took my place in front of Father, in an attempt to cover him with my own gaunt body. But he pushed me aside angrily; he was deeply hurt by my attempt to protect him. I lost my self-control and started to scream.

Several minutes passed and we were still alive. I couldn't understand why Mitka hadn't shot Father, as he had seemed poised to do. Father, who stood right opposite Mitka, tore open his shirt and shouted, "Why don't you shoot me, you criminal? You won't escape justice!" Mitka seemed stunned as he tried to evaluate the situation. Then he said quietly, "Volko, is this what you want, a big funeral? You want to die a hero? Well, I won't give you that honor! I'll settle my accounts with you in the cellar, when it suits me."

Mitka slipped away quietly, as if nothing had happened. So long as there were still Jews in the ghetto, he never approached Father again. But years later, I found out that the criminal had settled his accounts with my father, as he had promised. I have felt guilty all my life for the torture that my father suffered. Had I known, I would have spared him those awful arguments.

Before the war I had had many non-Jewish friends and acquaintances, all of whom kept their distance after the German occupation. I particularly remember two older Ukrainian boys who studied at night school with me. They were older than me and came from wealthy, respectable families. They struggled with their studies, especially the German language, whereas I, on the other hand, did very well in all my subjects. We became friendly and I did what I could to help them and they seemed to seek me out everywhere. We had a nice relationship, although we knew that nothing would come of it, because of the invisible line that separated Jews from Ukrainians and the fact that there was no intermarriage between the two peoples. But they enjoyed teasing me, asking, "What kind of a Jew are you, anyway? You look just like us. There is no difference between us!" They thought it was hilarious and insisted that my ancestors must have been Ukrainian. But under the occupation, those same friends forgot all about me and the fact that I was starving and my life was in danger. How hard would it have been for them to offer me a few potatoes? But they never so much as came to visit; they simply forgot about me. I know that I would have behaved differently if my non-Jewish friends had needed my help.

I had a teacher called Rostikus, with whom my parents and I were on very good terms. He taught us botany and lived among the Jews. I treated him very respectfully and he treated me nicely in return. My parents used to say that he understood the challenges of a big family, as he (who was older than my father) also had a large family. He used to invite me to his house and I enjoyed going to visit him. He had fruit trees, vegetables, plants and even a beehive. I used to sit and watch the bees until the very last stage, when the beekeeper would extract the honey from the hive. Rostikus always found time for me and would demonstrate for me everything that I learned from him in class.

I had learned that Rostikus had become an important person during the occupation and was involved in all kinds of meetings and activities, as a representative of the town's Ukrainian population. Mother often told me that I should visit him, while I kept silent. Inside, I was irritated by her naïveté and the blind faith she still had in people. Did she really think that Rostikus would help us, if he hadn't done anything until now? I knew that no one would do anything for us.

Once we moved to the ghetto, we knew we did not have much time left and Mother insisted that I visit my former teacher. This time I agreed wearily. "What do you want me to tell him?" I asked. "He just needs to see you, Anna," my mother urged me. "Ask him for help, even advice. You have nothing to lose."

As I entered his yard I could see my teacher from a distance doing his best to avoid me. His wife was standing outside the house and with a sheepish look on her face she quickly went back in. I wasn't surprised; this kind of 'welcome' was commonplace nowadays, revealing the true faces of former friends, unmasking them. It was obvious that I was unwanted by the Rostikus family. At first, I was angry for having humiliated myself by coming at all, but then I decided not to give up so quickly. I have always been one for demanding clear answers rather than making do with guesses. Since I was already there, I wouldn't slip guiltily away but wait patiently. I wanted to be able to tell my mother that I had done everything I could and would have no regrets later. One of Rostikus' sons, who was a few years older than I, stepped out of the house, his eyes focused on the ground before him, as he slowly and unwillingly walked toward me. Still not looking at me, he asked, "What do you want?" I replied, "I'd like to speak to your father." The young man stood there uncomfortably before telling me he'd give his father the message. He returned and said, "Father is busy, he has no time to see you." I was not surprised and said calmly, "I have time; I'll wait until your father can see me." Embarrassed by my impudent answer, he hesitated for a moment before returning to his father with the message that I was still waiting to meet him.

Rostikus walked up to me, his gaze on the ground, refusing to meet my eyes. He asked no questions but chose instead to embark on a lecture: "I know you don't understand what's happening. Let me tell you that a man has to act in accordance with the dictates of the situation. It is no secret and I have nothing to hide. The Ukrainians are a weak nation, but they know how to use their brains. We were not capable of going to war against super powers like Poland or the Soviet Union. All these years we have been waiting for a strong country to do the work for us and we took advantage of the situation to stick a knife in the backs of the Russians. When the Russians were still ruling the Ukraine I was one of those people who worked with German spies. We Ukrainians are obliged to faithfully honor the treaty we signed with a superpower, so long as they stick to their side of the bargain. We have been given an historic opportunity that we must not give up. It is for this reason that I was one of those respectable Ukrainians who welcomed the Germans. Finally, we've released ourselves from the red plague (*Chuma*), forever! And now that you know everything, what have you to say?"

I was unimpressed by Rostikus' confession. His treachery and that of other locals was common knowledge. I noticed from the corner of my eye that Rostikus' daughter was standing behind one of the columns of the house, secretly watching me. Seeing that I had noticed her, she sat down on a nearby chair to listen to our conversation. Her father finished his soliloquy and waited for me to leave. I glanced enviously at the tranquil family life enjoyed by this man; I just couldn't understand it. The Rostikus family lived in a paradise, completely oblivious of the fact that behind the fence of their lovely garden, their neighbors and former friends and families were being murdered! I felt an overwhelming need to ask: "Doesn't it bother you that 'they' will soon come to kill me?"

Rostikus had known me for many years as a rather bashful, very polite child. I think my question might have shaken him a little because he looked at me sharply before responding, "Yes, I do have the chance to save you, but it's not at all simple. Do you want me to take action against the Church? The Church tells us not to have mercy on a single Jew! The Church sees the Jews as the root of all the evil that has spread throughout the world. Jews were the first to disseminate communism, a doctrine against God and the Church. All our church leaders warn us that the Jews are the only ones capable of bringing back communist Russia to the Ukraine."

My head spinning and my legs unsteady, I left the Rostikus' yard and returned to the ghetto and to death. When Korzec was liberated, the Russians imprisoned Rostikus for war crimes. I don't know what happened to him.

An old Polish acquaintance once came to visit us in the ghetto; I sensed his unease at seeing our misery at such close quarters. He noticed the little children watching him surreptitiously. Although naturally reserved, their lengthy struggle with malnutrition made them voice their hope that the visitor had brought something for them to eat. They were too young to understand that no one took pity on us and this man had not come to us for altruistic reasons. He had come on behalf of a Polish fascist friend of his, who was in need of a housemaid. He was, after all entitled to a Jewish slave worker, to whom he need pay no wages! Our acquaintance came to inform us that he wanted to recommend me for the job and that I should be pleased at the chance to move out of the ghetto and have food in my stomach and a roof over my head.

Parting from my family was unbearable. My mother was certain we would never see each other again and gave me a lot of advice: that I should take full advantage of being outside the ghetto; to consider distancing myself from Korzec and moving toward Poland. My blonde hair and fair skin gave me an 'Aryan' look and since I could speak the language and knew the culture, it would be easy enough for me to blend in with the locals. She begged me not to think of the family, that there was no point in doing so. She stressed the importance of someone from the ghetto surviving this, in order to testily later to the German atrocities. "You must stay alive and tell the world what the Germans did to the Jews," she said. "You must never allow the German murderers to whitewash their crimes." Mother knew how close I was to my little brothers and sisters and tried very hard to convince me that my mission in life was to survive. "Don't worry that others haven't succeeded," she told me. "You have nothing to lose, so just do your best. Move forward and get away from here so long as you have the chance." Mother was unable to withstand my emotional parting and fainted, tearfully, painfully, on the front doorstep. The neighbors, who were also outside and heard all the commotion, saw mother faint and rushed to her aid. I was shocked that my devoted father made no move to help, but stood aside watching others take care of his beloved wife. I knew that my parents had been, and still were, very much in love; it was common knowledge that they were an extremely happy couple, so his behavior now was surprising. He sighed and said, "If only she would die and no longer have to suffer." Deeply distressed. Mother was unable to control herself and told the children that I was leaving for good. They were too weak to cry, but shrieked loudly. Some of our neighbors led me out of the house and ordered me to leave the ghetto and never to return. Everyone asked me to remember them.

I was only a teenager, but the circumstances forced me to grow up very quickly. During the German occupation I had acquired a great deal of life experience and knew how to fend for myself. I had become a woman. Everyone told me that I had to survive, to be a living witness, to tell the story of the Jews of Korzec. So I left the ghetto at a time when my little brothers and sisters needed me more than ever before and my mother was dying.

I started working as a housemaid at the home of the Polish fascist. The work I was required to do was hard, physical labor and I was on my feet from early morning until late at night, in the kitchen as well as in the yard. It was a large house and some parts of it had been turned into a warehouse for confiscated and stolen Jewish property. The master of the house worked for the Germans and made it his business to 'visit' Jewish homes. Like all the other thieves, he took advantage of his travels to bring back parcels and suitcases full of objects; sometimes even furniture.

The hard work exhausted me, especially since the mistress of the house did not think that a Jewish girl from the ghetto needed food. I was tormented by hunger and suffered in silence, until I was on the verge of collapse, when I mustered all my courage to actually ask for food. My mistress shrugged, thought for a moment and then pointed at a sack of dried bread. "Don't forget to feed this to the chickens too," she said. I had no choice but to moisten the bread with water, and that's what I lived on. No wonder the family was satisfied with me.

I started to think about surviving. Unfortunately, I was fully aware that as soon as 'they' started to liquidate the ghetto, I would be among the first to be murdered, however much these fascists needed my work. They would never do anything to help me. I blamed myself for being so defeatist: here I was, slavishly serving my people's murderers until the very last minute. And the fact that I missed my family in the ghetto was the most painful part of all.

I thought of doing as my mother had begged me, leaving the Polish family, making my way on the 'outside'. Was it possible?

Whenever I went outside for anything, or had to work in the yard, I noticed that everyone had their eyes on me. I mentioned this to the mistress of the house and she made it clear that all the locals were instructed to keep tabs on strangers moving about the neighborhood and report anything suspicious to the local police. According to instructions issued by the local authority, it was forbidden to allow strangers into one's home without a license. In other words, everyone knew that I was a Jew and that my days were numbered.

At night I used to stand beside the kitchen window that overlooked a large, lush green garden. One night I noticed a dog kennel among the trees. But, instead of a dog, I saw the head of a little girl. Such sights were not unusual but still I was very moved. I strained my eyes and was amazed to see that the head belonged to one of the children of the best barber in town, who had lived with his many children on a side street near us. I had seen the family being led to their deaths and was amazed to think that this little girl had somehow managed to survive. No one in the ghetto was aware of her existence, and here she was, the top half her of body extending out of the dog kennel. She looked so wild and filthy and the sight of her sent a shudder through my body. I was the only person who could know who she was, because we had lived in the same neighborhood. Suddenly, a dog appeared beside her and licked her and she hugged him in return. I found this unbearable to watch, perhaps because of my own unhealed wounds. I wondered how this child had managed to survive for so many months. What did she eat? Where did she hide during the day? I hesitated over what I should do, but was afraid to approach and embrace her. Supposing someone else was watching from the window? I didn't even have food or warm clothing to give her. Taking her back to the ghetto would mean certain death, an ugly death with starvation, suffering and disease.

I tried to find this little girl after the war, but none of the people who had been with me in the ghetto had survived, so I was unable to get any information as to her fate.

In the end, I returned to the ghetto, to my family. Needless to say, my parents protested. But I could see that they were happy to see me again. At home the tension had reached the limits of human endurance. Mother described recent events in the ghetto. Three Jews, two boys and one girl, had somehow managed to escape death in Russia and arrived in the ghetto, taking over an empty apartment near my family. The apartment's previous owners had been relatives of the young people, but they had been murdered. The three hid forged documents, firearms and other items in the apartment, their plan being to get to the forests and join the partisans, or to find a place where they could organize their own partisan group. But they were unaware that our particular area of the Ukraine was not suited to that kind of anti-German activity. The ghetto Jews welcomed the newcomers, but knew nothing of their secret plans. Within a short time, the authorities caught the young would-be partisans some distance from the ghetto and imprisoned them in the police dungeon, where they were horribly tortured. The German authorities in Rowne (Rivne) then ordered the Korzec police to waste no time in transferring the 'offenders', under lock and chain, to Rowne, 60 kilometers away, in order to have them participate in a show trial. The Germans wanted to demonstrate that they could apprehend partisans wherever they chose. The poor youngsters were transported by truck under heavily armed police guard. But then something inexplicable took place: as the truck drove over a very wide bridge, the young men, who were already on the verge of death, managed to jump over the bridge and into the river where they were killed on the sharp rocks. Some of the ghetto Jews actually witnessed this with their own eyes.

In the ghetto the Jews were made to suffer after the three young people were caught; police forces were sent into the ghetto to conduct searches of all the houses and it was during a search of the house occupied by the three that they found the forged passports and weapons. My mother told me that our house, too, had been searched; indeed the police even sieved through the soot in the stove. Fortunately, one of the policemen said they were wasting their time in our house; he was personally acquainted with my father and knew for a fact that he would never abandon his young children to run off with a forged passport. The policeman had said, "Drop it! Use your brains; none of these little kids could possibly have a gun or a forged passport." And they left the house.

Mother finished telling me this tragic story and looked at me sadly. After a short pause, she said, "Believe it or not, Anna, we do have a passport for you! What luck that you weren't home; that the policemen didn't suspect us because the only ones in the house were your father and me and the little children, which is why they stopped the search at the last moment and a terrible disaster was avoided."

So now I knew that I had a forged passport. I realized that Mother could not have done this without Father; she never did anything without consulting him and it was he who assumed responsibility for the family. But they were in no hurry to show me the passport so as not to get me involved too soon.

Apparently, some Ukrainians made a business out of selling documents, such as passports, that had belonged to people who had died. However, these documents were dangerous to use and often the people who did make use of them were soon caught by the authorities. In a town such as ours, people knew all about each other and most Jews had no faith in Ukrainian dealers, but there seemed to be no other option. The passport my parents obtained for me had belonged to a young woman ten years older than me. Even worse, the document's entire stamp was imprinted on the picture. Thus, when Father replaced the original with my picture, it would remain unstamped. The Ukrainian counterfeiters were aware of this and evidently did it on purpose. My parents, therefore, had many reasons not to send me away unaccompanied and with a useless, obviously forged passport, even though it had been very expensive. But they still tried to convince me to leave nonetheless, without the basic necessities and without a proper passport.

My sister Nina was a very pretty girl, but as innocent as a baby. The rest of the family conspired to keep her hidden at home, well away from the slave labor we were forced into. When we were unable to replace her and there was no choice. Mother and I took Nina with us and made sure never to leave her alone. So Nina became increasingly dependent on me and I was happy enough to follow my parents' instructions and do as they told me.

One day, as my father stood on the doorstep, a young Polish man asked if there were any girls in the house who wanted to earn a few potatoes. Father said no and the Pole left, but he returned some time later. At that time, strangers were able to come and go from the ghetto whenever they pleased, even at night, and they were free to enter any Jewish homes they wanted. This man was very disgruntled, "After all," he said, "you have two daughters who could help me pull potatoes out of the ground. Why do you keep them at home?" He returned to our house three times in one day, begging us to come work for him! During one of these visits he sat down with his head in his hands and wept shamelessly. We stood by silently, waiting to hear his story. "I come from a big family and my parents never had enough money to set us up in life," he explained. "We all supported ourselves by working as hired laborers. In fact, my brothers and I were employed by Jewish landowners. But then came the occupation, and the Germans killed all the Jews and their land was abandoned. So I joined the other villagers and together we decided to appropriate these lands."

It was late July 1942 when this strong, healthy, well-fed man, who knew nothing about having to live under constant fear of death, was sitting in our home in the ghetto, whining and complaining and wallowing in self-pity! He was completely oblivious to everything that was happening to the Jews, the way we were being persecuted, abused and slowly starved to death. All that mattered to him was to find help in harvesting his crop. "We are able to save the lives of these two young ladies on our estate," he said and pointed to Nina and me. He promised Father repeatedly that he truly intended to save us. "Our fields are never visited by strangers," he assured us. "No one will ever know, or come to take your girls. You can trust me."

Mother looked at Father impatiently, but he took his time in answering. We waited. I waited behind Father's back for his decision. It's what we always did: Father was always the one to make the decisions. I was shocked therefore, that he rejected the man's offer. "Listen, my friend," my father said quietly, "everything you say is correct. It's no secret that people like you received everything the easy way and no longer have to work for others. But I have no doubt that you can find workers, if you pay them a decent wage. As for my children, they have suffered so much that you cannot begin to understand. I am responsible for them and I won't do anything to add to their suffering; I won't send them out of their home to be alone and unprotected somewhere else. I want my children to die quickly, to finish a life of torture once and for all." Barely able to stand up. Father walked into the bedroom and closed the door.

My father's opinion was always important to me; I saw him as the commander, the king, God even. Yet this particular incident has tormented me throughout my life and I blame myself for not being more courageous. Anyone who hasn't lived under German occupation will never be able to understand what I mean. The writer has not yet been born who can accurately describe the horrors of the Holocaust.

After the terrible day of the big *Aktion* at the Kozak pits, I overheard my father ask my mother, "Why are you weeping over our murdered children? They are at rest now; we can only envy them for no longer having to suffer. Instead of crying for those who were murdered, we must muster all our strength to do what we can for our surviving children. It is they who will have to suffer before they can reach eternal rest." I was aware that my father had lost his will to live and the only thing that kept him alive was his stubborn desire to care for the small children who needed him. My parents were desperate and tormented people. They suffered from insomnia, were constantly exhausted, and sensitive to the slightest noise. The buzz of a fly or the rustle of the wind in the middle of the night would have them leaping up from their bed in a second.

It was still dark one night, when my mother came to wake me up gently. Before she had a chance to say a word, though, my brothers and sisters jumped out of bed and ran to the window to see if 'they' had come to murder us. I looked down and was surprised to see two horses harnessed to a very big agricultural wagon, the kind used to transport sheaves of grain from the fields. Now the wagon was occupied by a large group of people I did not recognize and I was very curious. They appeared uncomfortable and worried.

A Ukrainian couple aged about forty-five years old walked into our kitchen, followed by their daughters who looked about eighteen years old; the last to enter was their only son, aged about twenty five. I watched them with interest, hoping that they had brought us some potatoes. The son seemed to have a dominant influence on the rest of the family. Apparently these people were old friends of Father and seemed quite comfortable in his presence. I learned that even after the occupation Father had been in contact with the young man and had even visited his home in one of the outlying villages. They apologized for their delay in arriving and explained that they had been unable to come two months earlier as promised. But it was late and everyone seemed in a hurry to cut short the meeting before the neighbors began waking up and asking questions. I had no idea what was happening.

My father was ready and helped load the wagon with various valuables, including three heavy overcoats for the girls, bolts of beautiful fabric, elegant wool and silk dresses, and men's and women's suits. These were followed by packages containing linen fabrics, fine leather for boots; everything was spanking new. Our visitors examined all these riches with great excitement, the girls danced and hugged each other happily, albeit a little tearfully. They were thrilled and completely oblivious of my parents' feelings. Mother held Leon's hand, unable to say a word. Suddenly I understood. Who better than I could appreciate how hard this was for her? She contained her grief and faced the woman who had agreed to save the Jewish child, our Leon, who had already had a taste of the Holocaust that visited our town. In a choked voice Mother said to the woman, "As a woman and a mother I beg you to take pity on this child who now has nothing in the world but your family. I place his life in your hands." The Ukrainian woman had no time for emotions and replied gruffly, "Very well. I cook every day and I'll make sure to feed him with the rest of my family. But we expect him to work hard; we have a large household." It was clear that the family's only aim in taking in Leon was material.

It was only now that I understood why my parents allowed their children to suffer the agonies of starvation and malnutrition, when they owned so many valuables that could have been exchanged for food. My parents had kept their plan to hand Leon over to that family for a long time; now that it was taking place, they wanted me to know as much as possible about the family and asked me to register the details in my mind, to remember them and to search for my brother after the war, if I survived. They told me that the young man, who had made a good impression on us, was a translator for the mayor of the town, an infamous Ukrainian fascist, who had appeared with the occupation from outside the region. This young man also mediated between the German occupiers and the local Ukrainians.

The Ukrainian family prepared to leave and we parted tearfully from our beloved Leon. The mother barely looked at us or at Leon; it was the family's son who stopped for a moment and swore to us that he would do everything in his power to save this Jewish child. The young man held out his arms to my father and said emotionally, "I promise you that so long as I live your son will live, too."

Forced to relinquish their son to strangers, my parents hoped and prayed that Leon would be strong enough to work hard and not be a burden on the people who protected him. It was this hope that gave them strength in the months to come.

Much later I discovered what had happened to Leon during the war. I was overjoyed to learn that he had survived, but more on that later.

One night there was a knock on the door and we heard our neighbor say, "Don't worry, it's only me. I have some important news and I can't sleep until I tell you." At that time we didn't turn on any lights; it was best for Jews to live in darkness. The neighbor was clearly shaken as he whispered to my parents that his niece had just slipped into his house. She had come from the nearby town of Rowne, having managed to escape death when all the other Jewish residents of the town were rounded up and murdered. The man said, "You can see now that it'll be our turn. All the signs are pointing to the fact that our days are numbered. No Jews remain in Poland, or in occupied Russia. We are the last. My father had many relatives in Rowne; now they are all gone." The poor man was distraught and joined my parents on the porch steps. There were no more tears left to shed; nothing more to say; our brains refused to function. Our neighbor was too agitated to sit in one place and left, but promised to tell us when we could talk to his guest.

Early the next morning my mother woke me up to say that we were invited to visit the girl from Rowne, who was planning to leave the ghetto. Next door, we were shocked to see the girl being embraced by a young Polish man. Embarrassed, Mother quickly closed the door. But the Pole laughed and said, "Come on in; we did invite you, after all. Please meet my wife!" The young man spoke only Polish.

The girl provided a vivid description of the hardships suffered by the Jews in Rowne under the occupation. "The German murderers had it all planned," she said sadly. "All Jewish men and boys were killed off gradually, in order for the women and children to remain defenseless in their most critical hours. The only thing left for the victims to do in the end was to burn down their own houses. It's what the Reisbergs, my own family, did too. Then, when the murderers came to drag us out of our homes, I managed to climb up into the attic."

With a massive fire raging, no one could have suspected that anyone was hiding in the Jewish neighborhood. The firefighters worked hard to prevent the fire from spreading throughout the city; when one of them went up to the attic to check, he was amazed to find a girl hiding in a distant corner, right under the roof. She had rolled herself into as small a ball as she could, caught between the water and smoke. After extinguishing the fire in that house, the firefighters let out the frightened young Jewish girl, in her nightgown and wet and dirty. For the young Polish firefighter this was his first experience of the terrible fear this Jewish girl was living under. He was nonplussed and not quite sure how to react. But suddenly he was overcome with love for this girl: he felt that he had been searching for her all his life. Indeed, in this unlikeliest of places, he found the love of his life. He was overjoyed, although he didn't even know her name. He knew he would have to fight hard to save this girl's life, but he was not afraid of challenges.

In those days it was no simple matter to save Jewish lives. The firelighter whispered to the girl that he would come back that night to take her to safety. He realized that the first thing he would have to do would be to distance himself from his friends and family, to avoid arousing their suspicion. He made up various stories in order to convince his colleagues to abandon this particular house and move on to other houses nearby. His beloved was waiting for him in the attic and he would do anything in his power for her.

The young firefighter went home and told his family that he would have to leave town for two weeks. He had no financial problems and, as a citizen of Rowne, he was well known throughout the region. He decided, therefore, to take the girl to the home of an old priest in a far-off village. He prepared a story to tell the priest: the girl he was in love with was pregnant and he was barred from telling anyone about the pregnancy because both sets of parents were opposed to their union. The sympathetic priest agreed to marry them right there and then! For the young couple it was a perfect opportunity to receive official documentation in the form of a marriage license. The young couple found refuge with the priest and the happy bridegroom took advantage of every minute to prepare the necessary documents for his Jewish wife, before the two set off toward occupied Russia. They reached Korzec at night, but had no transport to take them on to Kiev. In the middle of the road leading from Poland to Russia, they stood, surrounded by suitcases full of clothes, as well as gold and silver items, with which they were to start their new lives. They were standing right next to the pharmacy on the corner of Berezdowa, beside our neighbor's house. By this time, they needed a rest, so they went into the first house they came to in the ghetto, which turned out to have belonged to the relatives of the young bride from Rowne. The family had been murdered, but her uncle still lived there!

My mother had a lot of questions to ask and was happy for the opportunity to consult with the Polish firefighter about her plan to save my life by sending me in the direction of central Poland. We both thought this was a good idea because not only did I speak Polish, but I actually looked Polish and could easily disappear into the non-Jewish population. But the young man did not agree. According to him, many Jews had had the same idea but he had seen numerous cases of Jews being captured in the possession of counterfeit documents, no matter how well they thought they could blend in with the non-Jewish population. "Surely it's time you learned not to trust people?" he said. "Stop making the same mistakes. After all you've been through!"

The Catholic Church had a powerful influence on the Polish people and the Church had called on the people to help the Germans by turning in any Jews they knew of to the German murderers! In 1942 it was possible to get a kilo of salt or cigarettes—of which there was a dire shortage—in return for handing over a Jew to the authorities! Even small children were proud to search for Jews wherever they could, in order to sell them to the Germans and get paid in matches. Eventually, the young man said, "Forget Poland. No Jews are going to survive in Poland. It's too dangerous to stay here, which is why we are making our way to Russia. You'll have a much better chance there." He gave my mother a lot of useful advice with regard to me, telling her that strangers traveling alone can arouse suspicion and are liable to meet all kinds of danger. It is important, therefore, not to travel alone with a suitcase or money. "You Jews are as innocent as children," he said. "Even a thief has good reason to get rid of a Jewish witness to his crimes." He encouraged us to try to escape. "You have nothing to lose," he urged. "There are no Jews left in the German-occupied territory and your ghetto is now on the list for liquidation. What difference does it make where they catch up with you and kill you?" We had to hurry, he said, because now that that the Rowne ghetto had been liquidated, the Korzec ghetto was next in line. "Remember: Don't walk along the main road; don't waste any time on the way; and don't go into any of the houses. Try to stay away from people, stay alert, and be very careful. Finally: keep your sights on reaching Kiev and then mingle and integrate with the other residents.

The young couple quickly got dressed and set off on their way, afraid to spend too long in the ghetto. The door had barely closed behind them when my mother said, "You see that I am right. You must go, Anna, and prove to the German murderers that they cannot annihilate us all. You have to live and bear witness to the genocide of the Jewish people. They must not be allowed to destroy the evidence of their crimes. I wish I could live in order to avenge the death of my children."

She sighed. "If only I could see the locals when the Germans are defeated. It's going to happen, I can feel it, and I'm so sad that I won't be here to see it."

CHAPTER 6

Into the Cold, Alien World

The Ukrainian Preczysta holiday was approaching. We had learned since the beginning of the German occupation that national and religious holidays were to be feared. The Ukrainians would emerge from their churches brimming with the anti-Semitic hate instilled in them by the sermons of their clergy. Physical results soon followed; the thieves who came to take our property told us themselves that they had been instructed by their church leaders that anything belonging to the Jews was actually theirs. The 1941 Preczysta holiday reached a new record in anti-Jewish violence, when 550 Jewish men and children were abducted and disappeared without a trace; admittedly, this paled in comparison with the big *Aktion* on the eve of *Shavuot*. The uncertain fate of the 550 men and children remained an open wound in every Jewish home in the ghetto and people never gave up trying to ascertain the fate of their brethren.

Experience, therefore, had given us plenty of reason to fear the approaching Ukrainian holidays, bloody holidays, as we knew them. And true enough, just a few days before the 1942 Preczysta holiday, groups of local Ukrainians sauntered through the ghetto informing us that their holiday was to be our last night on Earth. There was nowhere to run and there was no point trying to hide because the locals knew all about us. We were caught in a trap, helpless. But as we waited for death, we felt unable to remain inside the four walls of our homes and went out to stand in the street, all day and all night. The days seemed to go on forever.

I remember my last night in the ghetto. We had spent the night huddled together in the street, as close to each other as possible, instinctively reaching out for human warmth, support and comfort. We could feel death approaching, almost sense its presence and were sure we would never see the morning light. People wished each other a speedy death, devoid of torment and suffering. Ukrainians started swarming around the outskirts of the ghetto sometime after midnight, all carrying sacks under their arms, a clear sign that they had been informed by the Ukrainian police that the Germans intended to liquidate the ghetto and the local population was invited to help themselves to any Jewish property still available.

There was no doubt that this was the end. We wondered how all these people had managed to travel to Korzec from their villages so early in the morning. It was a religious holiday but here they all were, waiting to pounce on every last piece of Jewish property instead of going to church! Could these people actually believe in anything? It had been only a few months since the 1942 *Shavuot* eve *Aktion* and here they were again, waiting with their sacks to pocket our last possessions and the clothing on our backs. They were waiting impatiently to see the end of those few who had survived the Kozak murder pits.

I envied every bird that soared in the sky above us, free and independent. I asked myself, "What was the point of surviving the massacre at Kozak Forest if it meant only a few more miserable months of starvation, suffering and terror? How many times can a human being prepare for death? What point was there in making superhuman efforts to prolong our tortured existence for a short reprieve?" We had neither the physical nor the mental strength to prepare for, and think all day long about, death; to wait at home for the murderers to line us up like sardines before murdering us. I thought a lot about how to cope with the pain and torture I would have to suffer before I could be free, finally, of this world. It was the endless waiting that was so unbearable and the yearning to be rid of this miserable existence, once and for all. I was sorry not to have died when the occupation began, or during the bombing, when many others had been killed near our house.

My last night in the ghetto seemed to last forever. I spent the night wandering restlessly from one group of adults to another, desperately needing to hear what was being said, my tired brain churning feverishly. Each time I moved to a new group of people, I'd experience a small glimmer of hope, of hearing someone say that this was not our end, something might still happen to change the situation. But it didn't happen. The conversations were impassioned, full of self-examination, scrutiny and regret. At last the Jews realized that they had been duped by the Germans, who had used vicious cunning in luring them into their deadly trap, leaving them unable to fight back.

Our feeling that night was a strange combination of misery, depression, suffering, unendurable pain and a powerful desire to stay alive, if only to witness with our own eyes the defeat and humiliation of the Germans. Everyone spoke of revenge and the anguish of having to face death, unable to leave behind some kind of monument to our existence.

All that night I was so immersed in my own self-pity that I didn't even notice that my parents were nowhere to be seen on the street. As dawn broke, the Jews started to return to their separate homes, reluctant to allow 'them' to notice any unusual movement in the ghetto. I was very tired and wanted only to sleep; even on the street I had wanted only to be left alone. But as I entered the house, my mother opened the door to the long hall that led to the kitchen and I had the feeling that she had been waiting for me. I noticed my father standing on the ladder that led to the attic, working on something. In the hazy light, I could see that a few planks had been lifted from the bedroom floor, to reveal a hole in the floor, which they used to hide our valuables. It suddenly occurred to me that my parents had been working all night.

Mother came and held me close to her; she then placed her hands on either side of my face and looked deep into my eyes and said, "Anna, your father has decided that it's time for you to leave the ghetto. You know yourself that it can no longer be delayed, this is probably your last chance to escape. There is not a moment to waste." Mother looked past me into the distance for a moment, before saying. "You know, of course, that anyone caught with forged documents is tortured to death. Nonetheless, your father is up in the attic, working to correct a forged identity card for you to use. You must be extremely careful; any mistake you make can result in your death. Use this document only when you have absolutely no alternative and you have nothing left to lose." Mother handed over the identity card with Father's revisions. I looked up at my parents, who stood waiting tensely for my response. I didn't know what to say. Even a child could have discerned the obviously forged stamp.

My 'new' identity card had belonged to a Ukrainian girl named Ulita Novkivska, who had lived in a nearby village and had died of tuberculosis in the summer of 1942. She had been ten years older than I! Putting his fears aside, my father had taken a chance and paid a high price for this document, suspecting that the shady dealers who were selling these forged documents were informers. Unfortunately, as the official seal had been stamped directly onto the owner's photograph, when Father removed the original picture in order to replace it with mine, the seal went with it. And if this wasn't enough, traces of the original picture remained on the document. Father glued my photograph into the document and created a primitive seal out of a two-centimeter-long pencil stub he had found in a garbage pail after much searching. The 'official ID document', therefore, was no more than an old, wrinkled and crumbling piece of paper, with a photograph, covered by a crudely forged seal, stuck in it. And this was the identity card with which I was to embark on a new life!

Mother told me to come into the yard, where Father had prepared some well water. "After this long night you are going to have to wash yourself in cold water." There was great agitation in the ghetto because of the forthcoming *Aktion*. My neighbors couldn't understand why I was getting washed at such an extraordinary hour, but since the entire ghetto population was behaving insanely, they probably assumed that I had gone crazy, too.

Mother did not leave my side for a moment. She had made me a dress that would give me the look of a village girl. My identity card and gold coin had been cleverly sewn into the dress; this was the same coin I had come across by chance when I was sorting clothes belonging to the victims of the June 1942 massacre at Kozak. Mother had also prepared a bundle for me, which she had shaped into a ball and tied with a piece of rope so as to appear unobtrusive, valueless and above suspicion. The bundle contained some lovely items, such as a woolen shawl the size of a blanket, with large colored squares of material; a few lengths of dress fabric; two large white bed sheets edged in light blue stripes; an elegant lady's suit and several frocks and shoes. I was now the owner of some very smart new clothes. Mother also gave me bank notes, evidently currency that had remained in circulation from the time when Korzec was still under Russian rule. She said, "You'll have something to start with, to sell for food, until you find work."

It was not the first time my parents had provided me with the necessities for setting out on my own, but how different it was from the others, when they had been able to prepare a proper suitcase full of everything I needed. Indeed, times had changed; the last time I had been encouraged to leave the ghetto Mother had advised me to dress elegantly and taught me how to reach central Poland. Now she was only able to provide me with this modest package, which contained no food; and I was not on my way to Poland, but to Russia.

I also had a collection of family pictures left behind after the robbery on the day of the June 1942 mass murder. I examined the pictures in order to pick a few to take with me. But Mother gently removed them from my hand. "Enough, Anna; we've finished with our memories. You now need to get used to living alone, with no family pictures even. You have no choice." I suspect that my mother didn't want me to have any pictures that could arouse suspicion that I was Jewish. Mother looked over my head and said, "Anna, we have wasted far too much time because I believed I could convince your father to leave, too. But I couldn't. You know him; he cannot live without his children. He decided to stay with us right to the bitter end. But a large family like ours needs to have a survivor. So it's up to you to try; maybe you'll be the one to succeed."

Noticing all the commotion, the children were watching in astonishment, but not in fear. They had seen me leave home several times, then return, so this time didn't seem any different. It was my sister Nina who first understood what it was all about; she hugged me and begged me not to abandon her. She wanted to run away with me, to escape the certain death that awaited her in the ghetto. It broke my heart; my conscience wouldn't let me abandon the children. "I'm not going anywhere," I said. "I'm staying with you until my last moment on Earth."

My mother's face changed in an instant; she seemed absolutely crushed, feeling that all her efforts had been in vain, that she had failed. She went to Nina and released me from her grasp. She held the frightened Nina tightly to her chest, to pacify her. Then, in a choked, trembling voice. Mother said, "You must understand my dear child that your sister is not going on an outing. Once she leaves the ghetto, she will be completely alone in an extremely hostile environment.

I know my daughter well; even if she defeats all her obstacles, her life will be worse than death." Mother looked at me as if asking for mercy and forgiveness, "If I had known what kind of life my children would face, I would have killed myself before they were born. But I couldn't have known what these murderers would do to us. I wanted a big family, so you would have brothers and sisters to help and support one another. I was wrong; please forgive me. Try to understand and not blame me; my intentions have been nothing but good."

I was firmly against my parents' plan to send me away, but Mother would not relent. Finally, she took me aside and said, "We don't have time for arguments. This is your very last chance to get away; look at those birds of prey circling the ghetto!" she sighed. "Your brothers and sisters are not your children, Anna. Responsibility for them is mine and mine alone. You have to accept the fact that you can no longer help us; you must help only yourself."

She sighed again and said, "Look at Nina; see how she radiates fear. If you take her with you, you won't even reach the main road because she'll attract the attention of the first policeman you meet. But if you go by yourself, I will go to my death with the knowledge that you could still be alive somewhere, and that will be a huge comfort." Gently my mother removed the black chiffon scarf I was wearing. The wounds on my face had started to heal and I looked normal. "Now go into the bedroom," Mother said. "Your father is waiting for you."

Mother had tried on numerous occasions to explain to me that Father was avoiding me because he regretted not having listened to me when I said we should all leave Korzec when we still had a chance to do so. I, in turn, had become accustomed to my father going out of his way not to meet or talk to me, although we lived in the same house. But I knew in my heart that his love for me was infinite and Mother was a faithful go-between in maintaining contact between us. She kept me informed of Father's activities and feelings and vice versa.

I went into the dark bedroom, where Father was waiting for me, damp with tears and sweat. After months of no contact, we now fell weeping on each other's shoulders. He hugged my gaunt figure as if I was his baby and wouldn't let go. I had yearned so long for this moving reconciliation; only now did he give me an opportunity to approach him, as he had before the occupation when we were so happy. I wanted to stay there forever; I needed my father, and I loved him deeply.

Father couldn't bear to tear himself from me, but it was getting late. As tears poured down my face, Father said in a strange, hoarse voice, "Don't ever forget who you are. You must remember all that you saw and heard during the occupation. Now go; Mother wants to say goodbye and accompany you, to make sure that you really do leave Korzec."

I never told Father what I really wanted to because it wasn't the right time, and I didn't want to rub salt in his wounds. But I knew how lucky I was to be born to such wonderful parents and it broke my heart to have to leave such precious relatives, whom I loved more than my own life. But my father was right, all the signs pointed to the fact that this was the ghetto's last day. Rumors were rife that police from Zhitomir had already arrived, in order to help the Germans liquidate the ghetto and all the Jews in it. And here, on a morning like this, Mother insisted on leaving her babies at home to accompany me, despite the terrible danger a Jew faced by being outside the ghetto. The Ukrainians in the area surrounding the ghetto were so hostile and violent that the Germans didn't even need to employ guards to watch over us.

Mother and I walked along the alleys so as to avoid meeting other people, and she continued offering me whispered advice as we walked. "It is no easy matter, being alone," she said sadly. After a few kilometers we left the area of the town and continued towards the main road leading to Warsaw and Kiev, an area that was very dangerous for Jews.

But it was very early morning, and we were fortunate not to encounter a soul. I was amazed at the lack of traffic on the road. Looking back, I can't believe how reckless we were, stopping right in the middle of the road to say our farewells. How can I possibly describe my feelings at that moment? How can anyone describe the final parting between a mother and a daughter? I had always believed that we shared a single soul; and now we were being forced to part forever. I knew I would never see her again, never be able to embrace her again, never be able to speak to her. There are no words to describe the agony we were feeling. We could only stand, hugging each other in silence; we held each other so closely that we almost became fused into one entity, a motionless statue of grief, love and torment. All this took place in the center of the usually bustling main street, a spot that was treacherous for Jews. Mother did not move, and I did not want to leave her. Once again, I was full of doubts; I knew I would be unable to live without my family. But I could not disobey my parents; I could not deny them their last wish— not to see me die. It had taken much persuasion, but I, too, had reached the conclusion that it was best for us to die separately.

I could no longer watch my mother's suffering. She was a woman who never thought of herself, only of her loved ones, and I was now witnessing her utterly selfless devotion to the very end. I knew she would not move away until she was sure that I would continue alone towards my future. I felt as if my throat was on fire; I opened my mouth but could say nothing, and then I felt myself about to collapse. No, not here! I shouted to myself. I gathered my strength and ran forward, trying to put as much distance between myself and my mother. I knew I could not allow myself to fall.

I turned to look back; Mother had not moved. A scream welled up inside me, threatening to erupt, and I feared losing control. My mother stood there, full of grace, noble, tall, slim and blonde. Her sunken green eyes had taken on a uniquely piercing gaze. Her long, black shawl fell from her head to her shoulders. Her long, thick blonde hair, usually pinned up on the top of her head, was now loose over her back. It was an awe-inspiring sight, my mother's anguish. This last vision of my mother will remain eternally carved in my memory.

I wished the earth would swallow me, so that Mother could no longer see me. It was so dangerous for her to remain there in the middle of the road; I had to force myself to put some distance between us so she would go home. Then I noticed a deep ditch to my right that ran the length of the road and rolled myself down and into it. In the ditch I found myself next to a tree, which I hugged with all my might; imagining that it was my mother. I sunk my teeth into that tree trunk, to quieten the storm that was raging within me.

I don't know how long I lay in that ditch, but I remember suddenly hearing voices from afar, sounds of laughter and people shouting and talking. A group of girls was coming in my direction and, as they were within a few meters from me, I emerged from the ditch and joined them surreptitiously. The girls were all barefoot, as was I. I lived in an area in which the local population was not poor and people generally did not lack proper clothing or shoes, but the village girls would sometimes remove their shoes and carry them, in order to enjoy the comfort and pleasure of feeling the ground under their bare feet. I joined this big happy group of girls and acted among them as I would with old friends.

It was the summer of 1942, the day of the Ukrainian Preczysta holiday and the girls were disappointed that the sacks they were carrying were still empty of the Jewish loot they had been promised. They were annoyed at having been duped. "They spread the word throughout the villages," I heard them say, "that they planned to kill all the Jews in the ghetto during the holiday." To me, this meant that my family was still alive; I allowed myself to feel a spark of hope even though I knew that it was no more than a temporary reprieve.

I listened intently to these girls' chatter, horrified at the matter of fact way they complained about the postponement of the ghetto's liquidation; it was as if they were talking about the weather. How bizarre and evil this world was, I thought; here I was, walking among girls who had been awake all night, waiting impatiently for my death so that they could inherit the clothes on my back. And now, not knowing that I was Jewish, they welcomed me into their group as if I was one of them.

They were indeed very friendly to me, each vying for my attention, trying to tell me all about their successes. How chillingly ironic it was that these nice young girls could have been among those who plundered our own house during the *Aktion* that night at the Kozak pits. But I needed these girls as cover. I dared not allow myself to be separated from them. There was a lot of traffic by now but the girls refused to walk on the side of the road and insisted on remaining in the middle. At first, I saw no signs of villages, but then after a while I noticed that gradually paths began leading off either side of the road and the girls disappeared in different directions. They didn't even say goodbye to each other, simply turned to leave and it was then that I realized that they didn't even know one another, and it was for this reason that they had accepted me into their group.

And then I was alone; by now there were a lot of German army vehicles moving on the main road. I knew I had to get off that road and look for side roads leading to Novograd Volynskiy. I went into a grove of trees and must have gone in too far because I soon lost my way. In the middle of a field, I suddenly came upon a large house, which appeared to have been moved there from elsewhere, as many of its parts still remained disconnected. It lacked a stable and a shed and it looked totally out of place in the field; it was clear to me that this house had been stolen from a Jew.

The house stood next to a well-cultivated plot of land that appeared much higher than the field surrounding it.

Overgrown red onions, the size of large grapefruit grew on this piece of land; in fact, they were so big that I thought at first that they were red cabbages. On an impulse, I sat down and stroked an onion curiously. A man of about forty five walked suddenly out of the house, followed by his family. They were obviously very angry at me and demanded an explanation for my trespassing. I realized that I didn't have a story for my new identity and was unprepared for possible interrogation. In order to stall for time, I looked at them and calmly asked a few silly questions. But I saw that the man was furiously awaiting my answer and became quite frightened; I blurted out that I lived in Zhitomir and had just visited my grandmother in Poland. I was now on my way home.

In order to justify my sudden appearance on their property, I explained that I had tried to hitchhike home and although I usually stick to the main road, I had made an exception this time to get a closer look at this lovely area. Of course, they started asking questions about Zhitomir and Poland, demanding all kinds of details. Although I had never actually visited those places, I somehow managed to pass the test. The family seemed to enjoy my made-up stories and warmed to me. They told me how happy they were to be rid of the hated communist government, and praised the new fascist rule. Also, they were convinced that the Germans would soon occupy Moscow. I said nothing. Suspiciously impatient, they asked me a few leading questions regarding my own impressions of the mighty German army and waited for my answers. I had to say something positive, so I responded, "You are right, of course. The massive German military presence on the highway is very impressive."

The family took a liking to me and asked again about the Polish natives and what my own family thought about the new political situation. When I said that everywhere people were hoping for better economic conditions, the man of the house was very satisfied and laughed smugly as he described his own economic successes. The family then started competing with each other with stories about themselves and how they had managed to grow those enormous onions. Then they told me something horrendous: that they had brought earth that was saturated with Jewish blood and were using it as fertilizer in their onion field! I froze on the spot; but they continued to boast about their sweet-tasting onions, which they shipped to Germany for high prices. The man even offered to let me taste one of the special onions, to prove that it was as sweet as a fruit.

I then discovered, purely by chance, that this family knew what had happened to the 550 Jewish men who had disappeared during the Ukrainian Preczysta holiday the year before. Apparently, the men and boys had been murdered in the field on which I stood, in Szytna Forest. One of them was one of my mother's brothers, my beloved uncle, Menashe Weiner.

True, we had been visited by greater tragedies since the disappearance of the 550 men, but knowing the facts made me feel as if sparks of electricity were coursing through my body. My face might have registered some of the horror I felt, because the Ukrainians came closer to me, scrutinizing me suspiciously and listening attentively to my every response and reaction. I knew that during the occupation the inhabitants of this area were very suspicious of strangers, and many of them dealt in robbery and murder, as well as betraying people to the authorities. I knew I should get away from these people as soon as possible, but also that I shouldn't appear afraid or that I was running away from them. I said my goodbyes politely and set off on my way.

I walked along the footpaths without looking where I was going. It was a lovely summer's day, but for me it had become dark and frightening. I was terrified of the approaching night and didn't want to be alone, without a roof over my head, on the perilous main road. I yearned for my family, but knew that this time I had left for good and would never see my family again in this world. I reminded myself of the mission that my parents had thrust on me: to stay alive, to prove to the murderers that they could not annihilate the Jewish people. I was longing to witness the German defeat with my own eyes, and it was for this that I was willing to continue my tortured existence.

I walked along a path, without knowing where I was going. After a while, I reached a village and was able to ask for instructions on how to get to the city of Novograd Volynskiy via side roads and not the main road. At night, I reached a bridge, then a road leading to the city. Before I could breathe a sigh of relief, I noticed that the bridge was totally destroyed. I looked around and saw no one. Where had all the traffic disappeared to? Where were the military vehicles? There must be another bridge, probably nearby, but where? Should I go right or left? There were no road signs anywhere and darkness was already beginning to fall. I continued to walk along the riverbank, looking for a place to rest. It was a big river, but I had no way of knowing if it was so wide and deep only in this part of it. On the other side, I caught a glimpse of a forest but couldn't tell how big it was. The bank on which I stood was much higher than the water, like a steep wall, and I could not reach the water from it. I had the impression that this remote place was not often visited. The grass under my feet was very wet; I didn't know if that was because of the heavy dew, or because it was so close to the water, or even perhaps because it had rained during the day. In any case, the wetness didn't bother me; I had more serious matters to contend with.

I lay down on my stomach, still unable to quiet the storm within me; my hands clawed the earth next to my body. Since the dirt was wet, I soon found myself covered in mud and slime. I don't know how long I struggled with my internal anguish before I heard a male voice shouting from a distance. I thought at first that someone had lost his way and was calling out to someone else, but then I noticed that the voice was coming closer to me. With great effort, I gathered my strength and raised my exhausted body. Dawn was breaking. I was barely able to remain standing; I felt dizzy and cold but my brain still functioned. I was worried that others might see me in this condition.

I noticed eventually that the voice was coming from a boat in the river, making its way in my direction. An old man sat in the boat and instructed me on how to get down to the water, then he helped me onto his boat without asking any questions. In fact, he didn't even try to talk to me. He led me to a wooden house in the forest; an iron stove burned in the middle of the room, which I found strange, because it was only September (I think). I was soaking wet, my teeth were chattering and I had every reason in the world to be afraid. The old man stood in front of me, chain-smoking his homemade cigarettes, silently staring at me through penetrating, suspicious eyes. I kept thinking that my life was in danger, but I calmed down after a while. Through the window I could see that the dawn had risen; outside it was green and lovely. I realized that I was this man's prisoner and should not make the mistake of hurrying away until I had received a sign of agreement from him. I learned that it pays to be patient.

The old man had a cunning look about him and obviously didn't trust me. He seemed to be trying to get at some truth about me and scrutinized me as one would a map. He must have become tired of second-guessing me and started speaking in Russian. He told me that he had come across many people who were on their own and seeking shelter in this region; but they all met a bitter end. "What brought you here?" he asked. "Why are you wandering around by yourself on these deserted side roads?" I had no answer for him because of my confused emotional state and, worse, because I hadn't yet prepared a suitable cover story for my new identity.

I felt like a plant that had been uprooted and was now having to grow and develop all on my own, with no time to spare. My upbringing had been based on honesty and integrity, and now I found myself having to create an imaginary persona for myself that was nothing short of a lie. Flustered, I began with my grandmother. "I was living with my grandmother, who, before her death, ordered me to go and live with my uncle in Zhitomir." The old man continued to watch me slyly, as if I had not said a word; I noticed a thin smile on his face, before his gaze moved to a far-off spot just above my head. He continued to ponder deeply until he appeared to have made up his mind and had come to a decision. He stood up and I was sure I had fallen into a trap. My eyes followed him tentatively and I wondered what kind of death he had planned for me. Every second seemed an eternity. Then he appeared with a piece of bread and some water and I knew that the danger had passed. The old man's behavior had changed and had become friendly. He told me that he had been watching me since the day before and had seen me near the bridge. He introduced himself as a hunter of Jews seeking shelter in this deserted area; I knew immediately that this old murderer turned in Jews to the authorities in return for bounty. He told me he had stayed awake all night, so there would be no chance of my being able to slip away from him. He was very experienced in this, he told me, and had developed his own system. Naturally, I had plenty of questions, but thought it wiser to keep silent. I checked if he would let me leave and said, "I think I've wasted too much time already, I must find a ride soon if I am to reach Zhitomir at a reasonable hour." Slowly I walked toward the door, telling him that his place was lovely and I was sorry I had to leave but that I would visit him as soon as I could.

I walked down a path that led to the main road of Zhitomir and didn't see Novograd Volynskiy at all; I had somehow managed to go past it. To this day, I don't know where I was all that night. Was it really a large forest, as I had thought? If it was, why were so many policemen patrolling the area? What were they trying to find? There were certainly no Jews left alive there.

I was already more than 40 kilometers away from my town, yet there was still the danger of someone recognizing me. So, in order to get myself further away from Korzec, I opted for the main road, although I was aware of the danger this entailed. Several people from nearby villages were engaged in road repairs nearby and had scattered large quantities of gravel all over the road, which made things very uncomfortable for my bare feet. Admittedly, this was the not first time I had walked barefoot on gravel—I had walked through snow during the early stages of the occupation. But then I had known that my family was waiting and worrying about me at home and I had had someone to cry to, to complain to. Here, I was completely alone; now, my whole world had fallen apart.

The workers told me I was about 20 kilometers from Zhitomir. I noticed that a temporary water pipe had been erected for the workers a little way off the road and I was very pleased as I drank my fill of water from that pipe and washed my face, hands and feet. My legs were swollen and bleeding from the cuts I had incurred walking barefoot on the roads and uneven terrain. I didn't know what to do. By now I was so close to the city, but unable to put on my shoes. How could I go about barefoot in the streets of Zhitomir? I decided to linger as long as I could, to walk from place to place so as not to attract attention. But I realized I needed an organized, ready plan. Meanwhile, I had to do something about the way I looked; I forced myself to take care of my long, heavy hair.

I stood some distance from the road, with my back to it. A strange man came up to tell me that he had a truck not far away and that he provided the workers with gravel. "I have been watching you for a while," he said; he looked as if he wanted to know more about me. Although I had put so much effort into saying as little as possible, I suddenly burst out,

"I have family in Zhitomir, I lost all my money on the road. Usually I am fond of walking, but I decided to rest a little this time because my legs are quite bruised." The driver told me he lived in Zhitomir himself and would be happy to drive me there after work.

So I had time to wander around all day, though there was nothing much to see, until finally the driver finished working. He said I could hop up on top of the truck even though there was no one with him in the cabin. I sat there, looking out on all sides, while the driver continued chatting with his friends, who were mostly the men he'd worked with on the road. The truck moved off eventually; the driver was forced to drive very slowly and carefully because the road was so uneven, and the wheels kept sinking into the holes and pits.

Suddenly, who did I see striding quickly behind the truck, but a neighbor of my grandmother's, Avraham Huk! I hadn't seen where he had come from; it was as if he had just materialized out of nowhere. I had not seen him since the beginning of the occupation, and was overwhelmed at the sight of a familiar face. Later, I learned from survivors that during the great *Aktion* of June 1942, this young man had been among those who had wanted to get away but it had been too late. And here he was, striding down the street. He seemed to be in a hurry to arrive in time to a party. Avraham Huk was about thirty, tall and handsome. His clothes appeared new and he was carrying a large straw basket. His trousers reach to below his knees and he wore them with long socks and straw sandals; and he wore a strange straw hat on his head that seemed vaguely out of place. He was dressed like a Ukrainian from the forests of Belorussia. I laughed inside, because I had known him as a born actor and this outfit was perfectly in character. Avraham Huk was signaling with his hand, indicating to me to keep quiet and not let on that I knew him. But so great was my pain at leaving my mother and so happy at seeing a familiar face that I wanted more than anything to approach a kindred spirit, another undercover Jew who suffered as I did, someone who had known me since I was a baby. I just didn't think of the outcome and started knocking frantically on the driver's window; I even bent over and asked him to stop and let me off. But for some reason the driver ignored me. I was miserable and afraid of losing contact with the only person who could understand me. But then I saw Avraham turning off onto the first broad pathway he came to. He obviously had a plan and knew exactly where he was going. I followed him enviously with my eyes.

After the war, I searched for Avraham Huk, but no one had seen him. Until one day, forty-six years later, an acquaintance called and asked if I would be willing to meet a relative of his. Of course I agreed, and rushed to a meeting in Tel Aviv. It was there that I learned that although Avraham had survived the war, he had volunteered for the Red Army immediately after liberation and was killed on the Russian front.

My heart was heavy as I waited for the truck to reach Zhitomir. It was the first time I had ever traveled alone to an unfamiliar place and I was consumed with fear. On the one hand, I needed to be among people; on the other hand, I was terrified of the hostility and hatred I would encounter. And I didn't want to arrive in the city at night, in the dark.

I reached the remote, foreign city towards evening, on top of a truck. All I knew about the city was that men of the Zhitomir police had been the chief helpers of the Germans in carrying out the murders of the Jews of our town. Also, I later learned that the Zhitomir police had been those who had accompanied my father to his death.

The memories were fresh. I had even come face-to-face with the Russian murderers from Zhitomir because I had seen them in our backyard; young men who spoke only Russian. The mighty German conquerors had blinded even the Russians, who did not believe that their country was capable of liberating itself from the occupier, so that they became traitors.

What, then, could I expect from this town, so many of whose inhabitants had collaborated with the evil occupier and murdered Jews in order to steal their property! I tasted the bitterness of complete and utter isolation. I had left for good, and there was no going back.

I felt great apprehension at the sight of the first neighborhoods as we entered the city. Soon we would reach the city center, which would be full of Germans. I knew that the streets would be full of policemen and, no doubt, various 'volunteers' would be roaming the streets flushing out and exposing Jews, in order to prove their own loyalty to the government, or in return for exemption from military service. I was still trying to decide what I should do and where I should go, when the driver pulled up suddenly and said, "This is as far as I can take you. I have to go somewhere else now." I jumped down quickly and the driver disappeared without a backward glance.

In the middle of the road, I stood hoping to meet someone who could tell me how big Zhitomir was, where was its center, whether I could access the main road to Kiev without having to go through the city center. I knew I had to stick to the side roads in order to avoid the dangers of the main thoroughfares. But none of the people I met on the street were of any help; they all claimed that they, too, were strangers in the city, before hurrying off to safety, before the nightly curfew. How unfortunate, I thought, that the only people I meet are provincials. Isn't it strange that all these people were walking around Zhitomir without knowing anything about the place? And where were the locals; where had they all disappeared to?

It was getting dark and I was very tired and depressed. I walked up to some houses near the road and asked for a bed for a night, which I would pay for, of course. But everywhere I went I was told that they were under strict municipal orders to report all suspicious strangers. So I remained on the street, but felt I would faint or lose consciousness if I didn't get some rest very soon. At first I could find nowhere to lie down, but I forced myself to crawl on the ground until I was able to lie next to a tall wooden fence. My body shook with the cold, my teeth chattered uncontrollably. I yearned for some kind of cover, but was afraid to take out the large kerchief in my bundle because it was so beautiful that it might attract the attention of thieves. The slightest glimpse at the contents of my bundle would immediately reveal my identity.

I awoke early in the morning. My mind was at first foggy, my first thoughts going to my family. I sat up and tried to see if my sisters were beside me, but I quickly remembered where I was; and I knew that it was extremely dangerous to be seen like this, sleeping outside. Ironically enough, the curfew had allowed me to get through the night unobserved. Then again, who was to know if someone had been watching me from a window? I had better get away from here before the streets came to life, I thought. I tried to prop my back up against the gate, to create the impression that I was simply sitting down to rest.

I started remembering the stories that circulated in the ghetto of those youngsters who went off to other cities in the hope of saving their lives and starting anew. Sadly, most of them eventually returned to the ghetto. "Jews have no chance of staying alive these days," they said. I was just beginning to realize how difficult it was going to be for me, too.

My best bet was to take the road to Kiev. It's always easier to lie down on the side of a main road, than in a city street. I made my way toward the city center, where I finally got information about the police and the municipality, before going to see them in person. I stood watching people going in and out and thought that if I were to go in, I wouldn't be allowed to leave in one piece and decided to avoid government offices at all costs. Germans and local policemen walked past and I decided to leave that frightening place before arousing any suspicion. I was glad that I wasn't carrying a suitcase.

My mother had done a very wise thing; the bundle she had prepared was heavy, but much less conspicuous than a suitcase.

I walked along the main street of Zhitomir, searching for a glass window in which to look at my own reflection. I hadn't really looked at myself in a mirror ever since the beginning of the occupation, mostly because there were no mirrors in the ghetto, but also because we were too preoccupied with survival to worry about how we looked. But now that my circumstances had changed and my life depended on my being able to avoid making mistakes, I saw myself in a mirror, and was quite shocked. Was this really me? I had aged! The only thing that looked familiar was my long blonde hair, but I decided that the hairstyle of a young innocent girl no longer suited me and had to be changed. So I braided it and fixed it in a bun on my nape.

Convinced by now that there was nothing for me in Zhitomir, I made my way to the main Kiev road. I was completely unprepared for what I saw. Although I was expecting there to be a lot of traffic and German military movement along the road, I was overwhelmed by their sheer density and number. Where had they all come from? I started to look for footpaths leading off the road and found somewhere to sit down beside a fence that separated the two traffic lanes. For a long time I sat motionless, until I noticed that it was beginning to get dark. It was too dangerous to stay here; there was no choice but to turn back to Zhitomir in order to find shelter, at least for the night. I started walking, not even looking where I was going, until I eventually found myself in the same place I had slept the night before. Again, I spent the night beside the fence.

After two nights of sleeping on the street, I decided to try to find some temporary accommodation in the area. Local folk began showing an interest in me. There was no shortage in housing, but everyone demanded official documents as mandated by German law. I considered moving to a different neighborhood, where people wouldn't know that I was a newcomer who lived in the street, but just then a storm began,

with heavy rain and strong winds. I could find no shelter from
the downpour and was soon drenched to the skin. I trembled
with cold, my teeth chattered and I cried bitterly, sure that this
was the end of me. It was one of those low points during which
my life was so miserable that I saw no reason to continue the
struggle. I wished I was dead and went to sit in the middle of
the road, hoping that the storm would cause a car not to see
me and run me over instead; or that some sadistic German
murderers and their henchmen would come and put an end
to my suffering. But that isn't what happened.

I was still the same Jewish girl who had secretly escaped
from the ghetto, yet something had changed in me. There was
nothing about me that could betray the fact that I was Jewish
and people were no longer hostile to me. In fact, everyone
I came across was very pleasant and made me feel welcome—
although, of course, they all asked for a document with a
special permit allowing me to stay in the city. But that was
not because they suspected me of being Jewish; if they had,
they would have handed me over to the Germans without a
single qualm. But, unfortunately, I did not have a permit, and
so I remained on the street.

I was exhausted; I had forgotten when I'd last had
something to eat, except for the piece of bread at the old
man's near the river. However, it wasn't food I was thinking
of. All that concerned me was having a roof over my head.
I was overcome by the desire for shelter, however temporary,
even for one night; I didn't care what happened after that.
On the other hand, it was clear to me that no one in this city
would allow me into their home without an official permit.
Deep in thought, I walked down the street, wondering what to
do when I passed by a large detached house with its windows
open. The front door, too, was wide open. My curiosity was
piqued and I walked toward it.

A woman, who looked older than my mother, was sitting in
the center of a large room, gazing outside. I slipped into the

house and told the woman that I had come from Poland and wanted to reach Kiev, but I was exhausted from the journey and had decided to take a break in Zhitomir. I could see that the woman liked me immediately and didn't try to hide her delight at our sudden encounter. To my surprise, the woman saw in me someone who could help her. Thus, I discovered that many of the houses vacated by the city's Jewish population had remained empty. She told me that she had lived in a village, where her family owned a nice farmstead. When they had heard that Jewish houses were being handed out in Zhitomir, they decided to claim one. Her husband traveled to Zhitomir and picked out a furnished apartment, which they thought would assure their future and that of their children. From what I could see, the house was fully furnished and ready for people to move in. But the woman's children were still too young to move away from home and wanted to stay on the family farm; so the house remained empty. Every once in a while, however, a member of her family would come to Zhitomir to put in an appearance as the new owners of the house, so as not to lose their ownership rights. It was this reason, too, that they opened the windows and doors at every opportunity.

The woman tried to convince me to move in with her on a permanent basis, to stay in Zhitomir and familiarize myself with the city. "There's no reason to rush to Kiev," she said. "It's much easier in wartime to get along in a small place like Zhitomir where everyone knows everyone else." And what about the permit I needed? "All you need to do is go to the municipality in the town center and ask the clerks for the permit; actually, you only need to say a few words, that you are permitted to live in this city." She gave me a piercing look and said, "Don't worry, that's the way everyone gets a license." She even offered to accompany me to the municipality.

How could I respond to such generosity? I decided to take advantage of the chance I'd been offered and asked to be told all about her and her family, including their name and address. I thought it would be good for me to possess the details of a family who lived in the city and who wanted me to live with them. However, I still thought I would never be able to go to the police or the municipality for a permit to live in the city, since they would certainly ask to see my forged identity card. I was truly torn over what to do and decided to play for time. I mustered my courage and went to the municipal building and watched enviously as people entered and left unhindered.

I decided to climb the steps tentatively, and then I had no choice but to step inside. The reception room was large and crowded. I sat on a bench trying not to attract attention and carefully watched what was going on. I must have sat there too long because a policeman walked over. I jumped, then attempted a smile and said, "Thank you, everything is quite alright." In my heart I knew that I could not run away; I simply had to take my chances and go to one of the clerks, the way everyone else was. I went to a young woman who was busy typing, having specifically chosen her because she was clearly swamped with work. "What do I need in order to receive a permit to live in Zhitomir?" I asked her quietly. All I could think of was what would happen to me if they asked to see my forged document. I felt faint at the very idea of submitting that identity card to them. Suddenly one of the clerks went over to the secretary and whispered something in her ear, although she had not yet seen the forged identity card. I froze to the spot. The secretary gave me a penetrating look; she said nothing and my imagination took off. I was ready to give half my life to know what she was thinking at that moment. The two clerks continued to talk for what seemed like an eternity. Finally, the secretary told me that I had to return in the morning, when the mayor was in. At that moment he was in a meeting.

Drenched in sweat and deep in thought, I left the municipal building. As it happened, I found myself in the neighborhood where the driver had let me off a few days earlier. I decided to go back to the woman who had offered me lodgings; I now had an excuse—I would describe to her what had happened at the municipality and tell her that I had to return the following day for my permit. In the meantime I could ask her to let me stay in her house for one night.

I had started searching for her house, when I suddenly noticed from a distance a large group of nicely dressed girls. They were high-spirited and laughing loudly, as if they had just been let out of school. Walking over to the girls I said that I came from Poland, was on my way to Kiev and needed a place for the night in Zhitomir. "Do any of you know where I can sleep for one night? It doesn't matter how much it costs." To my great surprise they all wanted to take me in, but one of them, who seemed to have the most self-confidence, announced that I would go with her. I thought, "This looks very nice indeed, but what'll happen when her father asks to see my permit."

The girl was very lively, with a deep need for someone to listen to her. Perhaps all young people behave like this, I thought; I couldn't really judge because I had no idea how youngsters my age behaved. But we got on well; she was so busy talking that she didn't bother me with too many questions about myself. We became instant friends; her name was Niusia Grigorevich and she insisted that, in me, she had finally found a soul mate! But my bitter experience had taught me that her family, too, would ask for the permit and I didn't really believe that my luck would be better tonight than on the previous ones.

We were almost in the center of town, when we arrived at a side street lined with detached houses. Each house was surrounded by a garden, and the area looked lovely and well-tended. Halfway down the street, we entered a closed yard, and walked up some steps. But before entering the house, Niusia was already shouting, "Come see who I brought home!

But don't forget, she's mine." I thought at first that I wasn't hearing correctly, it had been so long since anyone had been so kind to me; and I still feared her father's reaction. For a long time I had wondered what causes people to love or hate each other for no special reason. But instead of the father, I was surprised to be greeted by a group of well-dressed young girls in a pleasant, clean home. The excited girls all spoke at once, wanting to know everything about me and to tell me all about themselves.

The girls' mother, Anastasia Ivanovna, looked young, strong and full of energy, as well as wise and shrewd. Vera, the oldest daughter, resembled her mother and was holding her six-year-old daughter. Vera told me that the Russians had jailed her engineer husband in 1937 and she had not seen or heard from him for five years since. She and her daughter lived with his parents in the Romanian town of Ananiev and she was convinced that the Russians had killed him. I think this was the reason that the whole family hated the Soviet regime, although they had lived in Russia for generations. Instead, they were pleased with the fact that the German occupation had improved their standard of living. Apparently, the family had moved into this house quite recently.

I saw Vera, who was visiting her mother and sisters in Zhitomir, for a brief time only. Who would have guessed that in a year's time unexpected circumstances would force me to search for her in Romania?

Ira was the oldest unmarried daughter in that family and was followed by Nadia, then Liuba. The fifth and youngest daughter was Niusia, and it was she who had brought me to their home; and she didn't leave me alone for a moment. As we all sat around a table I became sure that there was no man in the house; they made no mention of a father.

Suddenly, the girls happily announced the arrival of guests. "It's the Koch family, our relatives. Uncle Evgeni, Aunt Dusia and their son, Anatoli." The girls' mother served me millet porridge in a pretty bowl; I noticed all kinds of lovely dinner services in the house. It was a long time since I had eaten; but I couldn't force myself to touch the food. When I looked at my plate, I thought of my starving family and wished that I could give this porridge to my sisters. Concerned, the family was urging me to eat and out of politeness, I tried to taste the food but it stuck in my throat; I just sat there drawing circles in my bowl with a fork. They continued to watch me closely until Aunt Dusia said, "Why do you expect everyone to be able to eat this kind of food? You can see for yourselves that this girl is as delicate as crystal, she's not big and strong like you."

That night, I slept on the large sofa in the kitchen. It felt heavenly and I finally managed to get a good night's sleep with a roof over my head. Unaware of the family's schedule, I awoke early in the morning, got dressed and organized the bed, intending to wait until the family came into the kitchen, when I would thank them and say goodbye. But things, as usual, do not always go according to plan.

Anastasia came out of a room and was surprised to see me dressed and ready to leave. She wanted to talk to me, but seemed unable to begin; I thought she was trying to ask me for a favor. She hesitated before telling me that her daughters wanted me to come and live with them and had asked their mother to persuade me to stay. It was my decision and I didn't know what to say. I was flattered, of course, but since my plan was to continue to Kiev, I needed to look into some things, before giving them an answer. The girls were waiting impatiently to hear that I would delay my trip to Kiev. I had no explanation for these people's behavior; but I had no illusions and didn't want to raise my hopes. I left the house and made my way out of Zhitomir, to the highway leading to Kiev. Noticing a low metal and cement division in the road, I sat down to think things through and reach a decision. Heavy traffic passed on either side of me and the noise was ear-splitting, but I was determined to ignore all distractions and think. Although I had few options, the decision was not easy. If I went to Kiev, I would still have to present my forged identity document. It was clear that no one would take me in, under any circumstances, without that permit everyone was talking about. There seemed no point to running off to Kiev; why play for time, when all I could gain was another week or two, before having to show my forged document? It made no sense. It was now or never; better to get it over with and die now. I would never again meet such a warm, welcoming family as the Grigorevichs, in Kiev or anywhere else. This was not an offer that I should take lightly.

I was deep in thought, when suddenly someone asked me, "Why are you sitting here? It's extremely dangerous and, anyway, it's forbidden." I jumped and looked up to see a young man who was obviously worried about me.

I said nothing and the young man must have felt he owed me an explanation, "I own a store nearby. After work, I like to meet my friends not far from where you are sitting. We noticed you and thought you might be considering suicide, so we decided to see why you were here." I thanked him and said I hadn't known I had chosen a dangerous spot and went on my way.

I decided to return to my new friends. Even though I didn't know the name of the street I found the house immediately. It took me a few minutes to muster the courage to go inside and explain to Anastasia that I would be staying in Zhitomir for the time being, although I might still go to Kiev in the future. As for paying for my lodgings, there would be no problem. "I hope your daughters don't mind me staying here," I said, and they all looked at me happily. "Of course we don't mind!" they cried. "We understand you had a hard day and need to rest, but we need your papers in order to register you with the city council." I was careful not to hesitate and answered immediately, "Of course, of course! But let's do it all tomorrow." I even tried to smile.

Although it was wonderful to sleep in a proper bed, I couldn't enjoy it as much as I had the night before, because I was sure that this would be the last night of my life. In the morning, I gave my papers to Anastasia and left the house; I couldn't bear to just sit there waiting for the police to pick me up. Outside, I tried to distract myself by familiarizing myself with the neighborhood. I needed to escape from myself and walked around all day until I had no more strength left. I went back to the house worried that the family would be waiting for me, thinking I'd run away and was some kind of fugitive.

I walked into the house to see Anastasia standing in the middle of the living room surrounded by her daughters, each trying to get a peek at my identity papers. As soon as they noticed me, they froze awkwardly in their place. They looked at me suspiciously, as though I had horns. Anastasia told me that the girls had been to the municipality, where the mayor himself had examined my case. Since he could not dispense a residence license on the basis of the document presented, he ordered me to come in person to his office that afternoon. Casually, I said, "Of course. I'll do that." Inside I trembled.

I needed to be alone, so I borrowed a book and sat in the yard for a while, angry and embarrassed at my own weakness. I kept telling myself I had nothing to fear, that I was not a spoiled child; that it was time for me to grow up and accept death, if there was no choice. I deserved no more than my little sisters. If I were really brave, I wouldn't have left them.

At the municipality, I stood beside the desk of the German mayor, who was too busy to notice me; a policeman paced around the room. I was impatient, desperate for the interview to be over. Eventually, the mayor raised his head and I hurried to hand him my forged document. I told him that I had come to Zhitomir to visit friends and I wanted to stay with them for a while. Also, I needed a ration card, which is why I was asking for his help. He looked at me curiously, then shifted his gaze to the document, made a face, and scratched his nose and the back of his ears with his pen. He appeared undecided. Perhaps he didn't remember seeing my document in the morning, or maybe he did remember. I watched his face; he seemed to be talking to himself. Then he shrugged, shook his head and began writing quickly. He handed me a piece of paper, which he told me to take to the police passport department, where the clerks would know what to do. I had been granted permission to stay in the city for one month.

I went outside and took a deep breath. In my hand were one month's worth of food coupons. That meant another month of life. I could show Anastasia what she had asked for; a municipal residency permit.

Deep in thought, I didn't pay attention to where I was going and found myself in an unfamiliar part of town. Angry, I told myself to stop thinking of the future and the past and to focus only on the present. No matter how short my life would be, there were things I had to take care of. I needed a job; I needed papers in my new name; and I needed a German employer.

Finding work was a problem, because the German occupiers exploited the local population and paid them minute wages. As soon as the Germans occupied a city or region they took over businesses, factories and all local resources; then they would appoint Germans managers. All the merchandise produced from local raw materials was promptly shipped to Germany or straight to the front lines.

I needed some advice and thought of consulting the Grigorevich family, but I was surprised to discover that none of the girls worked. They had all been born and brought up in the city but knew nothing about the local job market.

I thought that the best way to find a job would be by visiting public places where people met for company and conversation. I decided to mingle, although this has never been my nature. I am naturally shy and, to be honest, all my life people have found it hard to become friends with me. But there was no choice now; I desperately needed a job, both for the money and in order to obtain a work permit.

After an unsuccessful day, I returned to the house in a gloomy mood, though, as usual, I tried to hide my feelings from my hosts. In the living room, children were playing under the table. The sight of those well-fed children carelessly having fun, when my own brothers and sisters knew nothing but suffering, was unbearable. It was the first time since leaving the ghetto that I was in the company of children, and I had to get away. I left the house and started walking. Because of the curfew there was no one on the street, so I had to knock on people's doors to ask for directions. I went up to several homes, but no one could help and I was getting worried. I hated to bother people so late in the evening, but I couldn't spend another night outside during a curfew. In the end, a ten-year-old in one of the houses explained that everyone was new in the area and had arrived from the villages to occupy the empty houses. But the child had a good friend on the street who was one of the original residents. And it was thus that I was able to get directions to Gonchama Street where the Grigorevich family lived.

I was deeply affected by that small episode, which showed me how few of the street's former residents remained. Most of the new residents had moved into the homes of murdered Jews, houses that were still full of their former residents' possessions. These people had become wealthy and successful, on the bodies of murdered Jews.

CHAPTER 7

Living in Zhitomir
Under a False Identity

Every evening the Koch family came to visit their relatives, the Grigorevich family; at first I had no idea that this happened because of me. The two adults and their son did their best to get close to me, to win me over. After a while I learned that the two families had not been on very friendly terms, but became closer when I appeared on the scene. It seemed that I provided a center of attraction. They all wanted to know everything about me, and it didn't take them long to start asking me how and why I had come to Zhitomir. It felt as if I was being followed and was all rather complicated. All my life I had been conditioned to be honest and to tell the truth. What could I say when every word I uttered could be used against me? There they all sat, waiting impatiently for my replies and I remained silent. Anastasia demanded to be told what it was that I was searching for in this area. I began to wonder if they weren't trying to trip me up by persistently pressing me for answers as to what I was hoping to find in Zhitomir. But I was beginning to learn a few things about giving people the replies they wanted to hear. I told them that I had come to Zhitomir to live with my uncle, but so far circumstances had prevented me from actually meeting him, although people had seen him in Kiev.

After all, I was no more than a naïve young girl, who had been forced, unprepared, into independence. As it happened, my story only served to pique their interest and they asked for details about my imaginary uncle. I now had to invent a name and age for someone who didn't exist, where he worked and what he did, in short, everything about him. There I was, surrounded by a large family whose members were pressuring me from all directions. All those pairs of eyes were following my every move and making me extremely embarrassed. I did not mean to, but in the end I said too much, including some things that were totally illogical, but by the time I realized that I had been rather too enthusiastic in my description of my imaginary uncle, it was too late and my audience was watching me, speechless. It would have been wiser of me to depict 'him' as a nondescript kind of person, with an ordinary name.

I was embarrassed later to discover that some of the neighbors had already told the Grigorevich family about me; that they'd seen me walking around the neighborhood for days, as if I was looking for someone. It was quite disconcerting to discover that the family actually knew more about me than I'd supposed. I didn't try to excuse or defend myself; instead I made it a habit to be as silent and inconspicuous as possible. I wanted people not to notice me, as if I didn't exist.

One morning, I was in a corner brushing my hair, when the Grigorevich girls walked out of their bedroom towards me and started crowing over my long, blonde hair; they asked if they could comb it and try fixing it in a new style. As quite a modest and shy girl I didn't really want to change the hairstyle I had adopted recently, but I couldn't refuse them. So I sat there motionless like a wooden doll while they played with my hair. They found a white hair and wondered how someone as young as me could have white hair like an old woman? They each insisted that they could create the nicest hairstyle until in the end they constructed a tower of hair on top of my head, and ordered me not to touch it. When I looked in the mirror, I was amazed to see how my whole appearance had changed: from a young schoolgirl I had been transformed into an elegant woman; even my own mother would have been unable to recognize me now! Niusia was especially proud of me and often announced that she would pluck out the eyes of anyone who dared hurt me. Her mother, Anastasia, confided that Niusia had a crush on me and was very protective of me, as well as jealous of the others. I knew this was true and was a little worried, because it seemed excessive. Apparently, I was Niusia's first close friend and the first to 'belong' only to her. We were about the same age but, more importantly, I was always ready to listen to her for as long as she wanted. It was convenient, because it allowed me to stay silent and focus on her.

The family obviously loved me, but I knew this was only because they didn't know who I really was. It wasn't Anna the Jewish girl they loved, but my alter ego, Ulita. Anastasia remembered that I had to go to the town center to sign on for food coupons, and then to pick up my food rations for a week. Niusia was happy at the chance to go with me. It was early and there weren't many people on the street. From a distance, I noticed a group of youngsters near the German canteen. They were all dressed nicely and chatted with each other as if they were old friends; now and then they would burst out laughing. Niusia and I arrived at the entrance to the local police station opposite the canteen and stood facing the young people.

I held my breath suddenly; I could have sworn that among those youngsters were a Jewish boy and girl I had known in Korzec. Now they seemed to be a couple, but in Korzec I had never seen them together; they had lived in different neighborhoods and, as far as I knew, were not in contact. Were my eyes deceiving me? Was it possible that ghetto Jews had been resurrected from the dead to reappear among a group of non-Jewish youngsters in the middle of Zhitomir? Where did they find so many friends? And above all, were they the same Jews I had remembered from Korzec? Or was I fantasizing?

It was September 1942, when there was no trace of Jewish life in Zhitomir. No wonder, then, that my heart was pounding furiously. I stood glued to the spot, staring at those youngsters and they stared back at us. Indeed, that girl looked just like the one I had known in the ghetto, the girl who had run away from Rowne during the occupation and come to live with relatives in Korzec. Her name was Kranzenberg and she was a real beauty with long blonde hair. I remembered seeing her on the eve of *Shavuot*, during the big *Aktion* the Germans carried out in Korzec.

I didn't move until they had dispersed and gone off in different directions. I often looked out for the young couple in the town center, but I never saw them again.

As I got to know the Koch family, I discovered that Mr. Koch was the director of a bakery in Zhitomir that baked bread for the German army. I immediately thought that here was a chance to get a job with the Germans; I was willing to do anything, swab floors and sweep streets, in order to earn a living. I was sure that Mr. Koch could get me a job requiring unskilled labor and that this would provide me with the work documents I needed. I tried very hard to convince him that I was reliable and hardworking and genuinely interested in learning all about bread baking. But Evgeni Koch said that he was sorry to disappoint me, but would not recommend me for work I was not suited for. I was terribly disappointed.

Two days later the Kochs once again paid their relatives a visit. This time, things were different. Evgeni rushed up to me and said he had good news. He told me that he had visited an acquaintance who had moved from Berlin to Zhitomir and needed a housemaid. I was barely able to contain my excitement, I wanted to jump and skip for joy. We went together to visit the woman and I was amazed that someone actually wanted to do me a favor.

My new German employer was my mother's age and she liked me from the moment she laid eyes on me and she needed me as much as I needed the work. She wanted to know how much German I spoke and I didn't know what to say. At first I kept silent, because my mother had warned me not to speak German. However, I could not afford to lose this job so I said, "I know a little German and I'm sure I'll learn more when I work for a German family."

The house was neglected so I went to work immediately. It was obvious that here, too, Jews had once lived. Every day I scrubbed the wooden floors while the German woman went to her important job in the mayor's office. My employer was very frugal with her household expenses and gave me so little food as to just keep me above the starvation line. If she could have saved on the air I breathed, she surely would have done so. But she provided me with a document, signed and stamped by the mayor, certifying that I worked for her. This was very important, because I needed new papers to go with my new Ukrainian identity of Ulita Novkivska. Although it did not constitute an identity card, a temporary work permit was an important milestone in establishing my new identity.

The German woman treated me with respect; she liked me and praised my housekeeping skills and my upbringing. She used every opportunity to sing my praises to Mr. Koch for finding her such a successful maid, and Evgeni in turn told everyone how happy he was with me. In my heart I was grateful to Mr. Koch for the job he found me and for his kindness.

The German woman liked my cooking. I found this strange because although she hated Jews, she certainly seemed to like Jewish food; since everything I cooked I had learned from my Jewish mother, in our Jewish home. Often I thought that if my employer knew I was Jewish, she would kill me. Still, I hoped to stay at this job for as long as possible, at least until the end of the occupation. I had good reason to fear the Germans and the local collaborators, and tried to stay inside the house, even when it wasn't necessary; I felt safer there.

In time I learned why that German woman had come to Zhitomir. She had arrived in occupied Russia before the full-scale murder of the Jews had commenced, with the purpose of amassing Jewish wealth. This was nothing new to me; I had seen too many such cases in the Korzec ghetto, when large numbers of Germans flocked to occupied Russia to get rich quick by laying their hands on Jewish property, money, gold, diamonds and furs.

After a month, I still hadn't been to the police station although I had received orders from the German mayor to return to the station for an identity card. One day I came home and Anastasia asked me angrily why I hadn't yet brought a police permit to stay in Zhitomir. My ration card had already expired and I needed a police permit in order to receive a new one. I realized that I could no longer postpone the much-dreaded visit.

At the police station I explained that I had not returned because I was now working during the day for Germans who had promised they'd take care of all these administrative affairs on my behalf. Fortunately, I was able to produce the work paper that proved I worked for the Germans, and I made the most of it. After a few more lies, I managed to obtain a temporary permit to live in Zhitomir; this was a major achievement. However, they locked my forged document in their safe and ordered me to report back in three days. It was obvious they suspected me; they could see that the document was irregular. But then I also had another document, signed and stamped by the mayor and authorization that I was working. Finally, I told them I was living with friends who could vouch for me. So I came back three days later and was instructed to return regularly twice a week; each time I had to deliver a report on my life in Zhitomir. Every time I entered that police station on those twice-weekly sessions I was sure my end had come; I needed nerves of steel to face the psychological pressure they inflicted on me.

And then one day the German woman told me she intended to return to Berlin. She was very polite and gracious about it and even offered to give me all her clothes. I wasn't sure I had heard her correctly, and asked her to repeat herself; I certainly hadn't anticipated such kindness, and tried to refuse at first by telling her I didn't want to take advantage of her generosity. I discovered later that she needed to make room in her luggage for all the Jewish wealth she had appropriated! In the end, therefore, I received all her clothes and even some money.

Aware that I should maintain good relations with my hosts, the Grigorevich family, I gave them the clothes and money I had been given. For myself I only took a skirt and blouse and handed the rest to Anastasia to share among her daughters. I felt it important that they should all enjoy my gifts. They said I was very noble-hearted, and I could see that my offerings cheered them up.

But I was worried about having to look for another job. During her last days in Zhitomir, the German woman occasionally shared confidences with me and I told her that it's not important during wartime where one works, the main thing is to be able to earn one's keep honestly. She agreed and added, "If you insist on working as a maid I can introduce you to my friend who is also from Berlin. I hope you'll enjoy working for her." Naturally I agreed immediately and sighed with relief.

We walked together to the town center and went into the German canteen, whose director was a plump German woman, who occupied a small apartment on the floor above. My chubby new employer was a cheerful woman with a loud laugh. Her expensive dresses and jewelry—numerous diamond rings on her fingers and many bracelets—gave her a distinguished appearance. She had a daughter who lived with her, a girl of about twenty.

My new employer was shrewd and inquisitive and wanted to know all about my family. I told her that my mother was sick and incapable and that my sisters were grown up with families of their own and could not care for me. Eventually, she provided me with a document stating that I worked in the German canteen. This precious document was more important than food; I felt that my entire survival rested on that piece of paper.

I worked hard and did everything I was told. Every morning I'd be given the day's work plan and started by cleaning my employer's apartment. Every day I did some laundry and ironing, almost always I did sewing and mending and sometimes I sewed new clothes. When I had some spare time, I went to the canteen kitchen for food. I never took anything myself, not even a drop of water, and always made do with what the cook gave me and she was a very difficult woman. The cook spoke Russian and German, I thought that she was German, but couldn't be sure. Fortunately, I was fed a full, three-course meal at lunchtime: a hearty soup, a main course and even dessert. Still, although this was the only meal I was given all day, I only ate the soup and asked permission to take the remainder home. Every day I took the food back to the Grigorevich family; it was my own idea to do so and I'm not sure they understood my motives, but I had been brought up to share food with my family and that is exactly what I did now with the Grigorevich family. I have always made sacrifices for others; it is the way I am.

The day came when my employer's daughter announced her engagement to a young officer in the German army. Immediately, preparations were underway for a party and everyone was very happy. Just before the party, my employer told me that I would be required to wait on tables with the rest of the canteen workers. I was very worried and afraid of being recognized by a German guest who might have seen me doing forced labor in the canteen in Korzec.

The engagement party took place in the canteen's large salon and the guests, who came from far away, had to produce special permits to be allowed in, since it was attended by high-ranking military personnel. I kept myself as unobtrusive as possible, constantly looking around in fear whenever anyone looked in my direction; I was terrified of being recognized. Suddenly, a high-ranking officer walked up and asked me to dance. Fear pounded in my temples; this was the last thing I needed. If he knew who I was, there was no doubt in my mind as to what all these fine 'gentlemen' would do! I told the officer that I couldn't dance and, anyway, it wasn't something I liked. But the officer was persistent and said he would be happy to teach me how to dance.

I said, "Why would you, an attractive man and a high-ranking officer in the German army choose me, a housemaid, to dance with, when you could have your pick of all the lovely German girls in this hall?" He replied that he didn't care where a girl worked; the important thing for him was her inherent personality. What an absurd situation! Here was I, a Jewish victim of German cruelty, forced to take part in this party; and now I was being told by a German officer that I had 'value'!

I said to him, "I am sorry, but I'm really very busy. As a servant I am not allowed to talk to the guests; I can be fired for having this conversation. If you really care what happens to me, please let me be." But my words only intensified his interest and he followed me wherever I went. He then stood in a corner, so as to be near the table I was working on and took advantage of every opportunity to talk to me.

Eventually he told me, "I have a large household in Novograd Volynskiy in the Ukraine and I'd like you to run it for me." He went on to inform me that he was the manager of a large factory that produced wood products that were promptly shipped to Germany. The German officer was an old friend of my employer and he promised me excellent work conditions and begged me to work for him. He tried repeatedly to convince me that I would never find better employment than with him.

My brain was in a whirl; my instincts told me I'd be looking for trouble if I went to manage a household for a man. But above all, I realized that he lived only 30 kilometers from the place I'd escaped from to save my life. It was no secret that many locals from Korzec worked in that factory in nearby Novograd Volynskiy, and any one of them could recognize me and testify that I was Jewish. It was out of the question—far too risky.

But that stubborn officer treated me very respectfully and I had to be careful to find some plausible excuses to explain why I couldn't work for him. "I am sure you are a wonderful employer and many girls would love to work for you," I said. "But I simply can't come with you, because I have to stay with my family in Zhitomir. My mother is very sick and I have to help her; my sisters also need me. Please understand that I am not at liberty to leave them." The man then said he wanted to meet my family! At that point my German employer came to give me permission to collect leftover food to take home. The officer watched me and when he saw that I was getting ready to leave, he offered to drive me. Although it was forbidden for locals to be found on the streets at night without a special permit from the German authorities, I was far from happy to be escorted by a German. But I had no choice and climbed into the jeep next to the officer, holding the package of leftovers in my lap.

I had to think quickly because I didn't want the man to know where I lived. I knew the girls were waiting impatiently for me and the food I always brought. I also knew that they would love to host a handsome young German officer in their home. That family was permanently on the lookout for guests just like this one and those girls would be delighted to meet him.

The officer drove through a neighborhood of large private houses that I had never seen before. I asked him to stop the jeep and when he tried to escort me home I told him I'd invite him in some other time; meanwhile, I slipped off into a strange yard to get away from him. Fortunately, there were no dogs in that particular yard! I heard the jeep drive away and breathed a sigh of relief. I started to run not knowing where I was; it was dark and very quiet; I couldn't even hear a dog bark. After wandering around the streets of Zhitomir, I finally got home just before dawn. I then had to tell the girls, who were dying to know, all about the German engagement party; they were also delighted with the fancy leftovers I had brought them.

The following day I returned to my job at the canteen, hoping not to run into that German officer. To my surprise, my employer ordered me to pack suitcases for herself and her daughter as they were leaving for an urgent trip to Berlin. She told me to stay in her apartment and to assist the cook in the canteen. I was careful to follow the cook's instructions implicitly, to avoid providing her with anything to complain about. And I continued to receive my daily lunch.

During the day I worked in the kitchen, where I noticed some wheeling and dealing going on. Apparently, people on the outside were running some shady deals with the cook because I often saw them leave with large quantities of provisions, including sugar, meat and butter. I tried to turn a blind eye, to neither see nor hear, so as to avoid being a witness, but I was quite curious as to whether my employer knew what was taking place behind her back. I knew that the cook was a good friend of my employer and they seemed to share secrets but was she really aware of these particular shady deals?

One day, I was working in the kitchen as usual, when the cook accused me of spying on her. I told her quietly that I was not that kind of person. She then came up to me and said angrily, "You think you're so clever, don't you? You think if you go telling tales to our employer, she'll believe you. But let me tell you that I have only to say the word, and you'll be out of a job!" I said nothing; a Jewish girl who has to report to the police station twice a week is in no position to argue.

But I couldn't understand what I had done wrong and why she was picking on me.

I soon found out. Full of high spirits my German employer returned from Berlin and spent a lot of time in secret conversation with the cook. One day, as I was leaving the second-floor apartment on my way to the kitchen, I overheard the cook telling my employer that she wanted to hire her granddaughter to work in my place. I was in shock and froze in my tracks. When the German woman said she was satisfied with my work and there was no reason to replace me, the cook responded with some fabricated accusation that I had been using her cosmetics and face powder in order to catch a German husband. The German woman was intelligent enough to burst out laughing at this barefaced lie. She knew I had no need for her makeup, because I am one of those lucky people to be born with perfect coloring. Nature gave me a complexion most women would envy. Even now, in my old age, I can honestly say that I've never needed or used any cosmetics.

But some time later, my German employer told me that she was planning a grand wedding for her daughter in Berlin. I understood the message: she would be leaving Zhitomir soon, which meant that she no longer needed my services. I'd be out of a job yet again and urgently needed to find a new one.

The Koch family did everything they could to befriend me. At first, I did not attach too much importance to their overtures, but when I started to work, Mr. Koch would accompany me every day to my job. Evgeni Koch must have noticed that I was uncomfortable with this special treatment and explained that the German occupiers of Zhitomir were press ganging local youths on the streets and sending them to Germany to work; he only wanted to make sure I would not encounter a similar fate. I was grateful for his concern but still felt awkward at appearing to take advantage of an older man who worked hard and held a responsible position.

I didn't know how to thank him, especially when he told me, with a flourish, that it was a great pleasure to serve me, as if I were his own daughter. I wondered what was it all about, but held my tongue, not wishing to offend this devoted gentleman.

The winter arrived and with it, heavy rains. The streets were often slippery, yet Evgeni continued to arrive at the door every morning to accompany me to work. Sometimes he told me to hold onto his arm, but I was shy and didn't know how to react. Finally, I worked up enough courage to ask him the obvious, "Why do you go out of your way for me?"

Evgeni Koch answered me honestly, "I have two sons to worry about," he explained, "and I am hoping that you will choose one of them; and then you will be like a real daughter to me."

I found this strange and thought, "What is this man chattering about? It is common knowledge that one of his sons is away in the Russian army, at the front. No one knows where he is, but they are still looking for a bride for him?" As for the younger son, Anatoli, I had heard that he had had a lovely fiancée, from whom he had separated when I arrived on the scene. This is all I need, I thought, and tried very hard not to give them any reason to believe that Anatoli had left his girlfriend because of me; although everyone knew that this was the absolute truth.

The problem was that I was afraid to say flat out that I wasn't interested in Anatoli. I had to please everyone, all the time, because I couldn't afford to have enemies. That was the mantra that guided my actions, and there was some justification for that approach because anyone who had anything at all against me could accuse me of being Jewish. All the police had to do was take another look at my fake identity document, and all would be lost.

Anatoli Koch brought me expensive gifts when I wasn't home and left them on the dining table because he didn't dare give them to me in person. He bought me a phonograph and a lot of records and even an expensive camera. The Grigorevich girls were thrilled but I got very angry and told everyone in the family not to accept any more gifts on my behalf. I even threatened to look for somewhere else to stay.

From the day she met me, Dusia Koch had taken me under her wing. Every afternoon she would arrive with a cooked lunch, which I never touched, leaving it for the other girls to eat. The last thing I wanted was to be beholden to the Kochs or to give them the impression that they could give me things in order to bribe me into marrying their son. I wanted to keep my distance from them, but it wasn't that simple. The Kochs blamed the Grigorevich family for taking advantage of my naïveté and taking everything away from me. I was caught in the crossfire of mutual recriminations, while struggling to stay on good terms with everyone and keeping my mouth shut.

I had to find a new job and, once again, the Koch family came to my rescue by telling me there was work to be had at the butter factory; I applied and got the job. What a relief! The factory I was now employed by manufactured butter and various kinds of cheeses. My job was to stand by the scales and weigh one-kilo slabs of butter, which were then packed into pretty packages in special paper. On the first day of my new job, I passed through a checkpoint into the factory yard, which was crowded with young female workers chatting loudly with each other. At a distance I noticed a train full of merchandise coming to a stop next to the warehouses. In those warehouses Russian prisoners of war worked at unloading cargo, heavily guarded by German soldiers. Suddenly there was some commotion among the Russians who were standing close together and two prisoners started running straight towards me. One was tall and dark and the other was stocky and blonde. As they ran they shouted and wept and were pursued by armed German soldiers. To my great surprise, the two prisoners fell upon me with hugs and kisses, shouting "Sister Olga!"

Even the Germans were stunned and stood staring at me as if I was a creature from another planet. I was speechless as I wondered, why on earth they picked me of all people? I wasn't exactly the only person in the yard. Quickly the prisoners told me that they worked all day in the warehouses, unloading merchandise such as sugar and flour from the trains. After work the prisoners were taken back to their prisoner of war camp.

I pitied those Russian prisoners; I knew all about what happened to Russians in German prisons. The two men whispered that they desperately needed tobacco and that they had had nothing to smoke since being taken prisoner and that this exacerbated their suffering. They told me they would risk any punishment if they could have a single cigarette and pleaded with me to bring them paper and tobacco in exchange for large quantities of sugar and flour. I started to shake with fear. Here they were, offering stolen merchandise from the German military to a Jewish girl with a forged identity card in the police safe, who has to report twice a week at the police station to account for her actions! I was not going to risk my life for any Russian prisoners of war, so I told them I was a stranger in the city, living with a local family and had no way of obtaining tobacco. The two men sighed in disappointment, wept like children and told me that I was their last hope. I felt so sorry for them that I ended up agreeing to their dangerous request, regardless of the threat to my personal safety. I was angry with myself—I was running away from death, yet here I was letting myself into a dangerous trap.

The prisoners taught me how to smuggle foodstuffs out of the yard and make the exchange without being seen. At the end of the workday, I'd meet the prisoners who would give me sugar and flour, which I would promptly place on the stone fence facing the street. It was far enough from the main gate, so I could then pass through the checkpoint empty-handed. Then, I'd simply take the food packages from the other side of the high fence. The following day. I'd bring tobacco and cigarette papers, which were wrapped in several bags. These bags were then recycled as packaging for new merchandise.

The Grigorevich family was thrilled with the large quantities of sugar and flour I brought them, especially since they received them for free, without putting themselves in any danger. The family also instructed me to smuggle them some butter every day. To accomplish this, they brought me a pair of galoshes to wear over my shoes in order to protect them from rain and puddles. I would fit blocks of butter into the galoshes as insoles and smuggle home more than half a kilogram of butter every day. Despite all this, I never received anything to eat because the girls did not give me anything. Their callous exploitation hurt me but there was nothing I could do about it. When I worked a night shift, I often left the house without so much as a piece of bread in my empty stomach. The other workers sometimes took pity on me and gave me a potato. I ate only enough so as not to starve to death; at the same time, I made other people happy.

On my days off I used to visit our neighbor, Elena Nikolayevna, to help her with her housework in return for some food. Even though there was no food for me at the Grigorevich home, I was happy to able to sleep under a real roof and wash myself with water and soap. What more does a Jewish girl need to make her feel like a human being!

One day I arrived at work to find all the girls sitting in the courtyard, staring nervously in all directions. The yard was flooded with Germans talking quietly among themselves, in spite of all the commotion around them. It transpired that the company's warehouses had been full of goods ready for shipping to Germany; all the merchandise had been loaded onto large trucks brought in by drivers and loaders masquerading as German soldiers. The trucks finished loading and promptly vanished. Soon afterwards, more trucks arrived, this time driven by real German soldiers, who demanded to receive the goods destined for the German market, which is when it was discovered that the first trucks had belonged to Russian partisans, who had driven off with the entire shipment. Pandemonium reigned. German detectives and SS soldiers soon arrived to investigate exactly what had happened.

The Russian prisoners who worked in the plant were immediately transported to some unidentified location. The local female workers were forbidden from leaving the site for the duration of the investigation, so we remained sitting in the factory courtyard. The other girls lived locally; they knew each other and chatted among themselves. I was the only stranger and was afraid to open my mouth. I was quite encouraged by the partisans' success and was glad to know that there were still people who fought the Germans in every way possible.

I sat there trying to collect my thoughts and prepare an alibi for when it was my turn to be interrogated. I felt like the stranger I was, afraid of being singled out from among all the other girls and wondering if anyone had seen me smuggling food out of the factory in return for tobacco and cigarette papers, which I provided to the Russian POWs. Suddenly we were free to go home, but warned not to leave the city without permission because the investigation had not ended.

I left the factory premises, still very tense, and walked around aimlessly. I was talking to myself and didn't respond when someone suddenly grabbed my arm. It was Anatoli Koch.

Anatoli obviously had quite a crush on me. From our first meeting in the Grigorevich home he seemed compelled to know everything about me; also, it later turned out that he had been secretly following me. I suppose this was normal for a young man with an unconquerable infatuation, but I was running for my life and didn't know what it was like to be young and carefree like other people my age. Anatoli told me he had been following me home from work every day. I had no idea! He said he always walked on the other side of the road, and even passed quite near me. I supposed I hadn't noticed him because I was so immersed in my own troubled thoughts.

Anatoli scrutinized me and said he was convinced more than ever that I had something to hide. Maybe I was struggling to recover from a tragedy or misfortune. He even told me that this time he had actually walked behind me and eavesdropped on my conversation with myself. I was worried; how much had he heard? What exactly did he know about me? This was a very dangerous development. I tried very hard to act normally and change his impression of me; I needed to dispel any suspicions he had. But I couldn't seem to find the right words or stories to explain myself, to tell him how I had come to be more mature and serious than other girls my age.

We stood talking, when I remembered with dismay that it was today that I had to make my weekly visit to the police, and it was already late. All offices had closed for the day and I was sure the staff at the document department had already gone home. My heart sank; I knew that if I didn't report on time, the police could pay a visit to the Grigorevich home. So I told Anatoli that I had an important matter to take care of at the police station and that he was bothering me. Anatoli laughed and said, "But you're standing right in front of the station! If you really had to take care of something here, why didn't you go in hours ago?" Without saying a word, I rushed into the station.

At first it looked empty, as I had thought, but then I saw that the department manager was still inside. As usual, the man pulled out my forged document and started asking me questions. I was sure my luck had run out, until suddenly the manager told me I was free to go, until the next time. I was drenched in sweat as I left the building. To my dismay, Anatoli was still there, waiting near the gate. What bad timing!

All I wanted was to be alone but Anatoli insisted on walking me home. Suddenly, he stepped in front of me and wouldn't let me pass, saying he had something important to tell me.

I didn't want to argue with him, but I was so tired and anxious that I couldn't even listen properly. Anatoli blocked my path again when we arrived at the house. He sat on the edge of the fence and said, "You don't live here, Ulita. This isn't your address. You belong in my parents' house, not here."

It was no surprise that Anatoli's parents were waiting impatiently for me to move in with them but I begged him to let me be and just go home but he was unmovable. In the end, I said that I had had enough of this and would be looking for somewhere else to stay first thing the following day. He gave up and allowed me to pass.

Exhausted, I lay down on the sofa, still in my clothes. Anastasia and her daughters were already in bed, except for Ira Grigorevich, who was busy writing letters. All the Grigorevich girls saw me as their confidante and messenger. Each was certain that I was there to serve only her interests. Ira was especially needy and insisted I get up early every morning when everyone else was still asleep. She made a habit of sending me out to deliver her letters and I was always required to add some verbal message as well. But on this particular morning she was unable to shake me awake; I was unconscious—ice cold and not breathing. She was so frightened that she started screaming and awakened all the women in the household. The previous day the Germans had imposed a very strict curfew because someone had killed a German on the street. In reprisal, the German authorities had rounded up 50 innocent men off the streets and hung them. There were no Jews left in Zhitomir so the Germans hung Russians. It was a terrible, terrifying night, but the girls insisted on summoning a doctor for me.

Dr. Visnevski arrived with his two daughters and, together, they helped me regain consciousness. I was groggy and not quite aware that other people were caring for me. In the morning they told me that I had had a heart attack and had to say in bed. I wished they had simply allowed me to die a natural, painless death. I wanted only to die, without torture and suffering; it seemed even that was beyond my reach!

As soon as I could rise from the sofa, the girls sent me to Dr. Visnevski, as he had instructed. He examined me, gave me medication, and told me I must undergo a physical examination because I had a heart condition. I appreciated the doctor's dedicated concern but was disconcerted to learn that I had to remain under his care for medical follow-up. There was nothing for it but to swallow my pride and tell the truth: that I was a lowly housemaid, working for the Germans for a paltry wage; I had no money to pay him. I thanked him for all his help and tried to tell him that I would manage on my own, but he seemed oblivious to my confession. Instead he said I had nothing to worry about; he would continue to treat me for free until I was fully recovered.

Dr. Visnevski sat with me in his clinic and he told me things I had not realized. To my surprise, I discovered that his family had taken a liking to me from our first meeting. Indeed, they had decided to take me under their wing and make me a family friend, rather than just a patient. My God, I thought, how was I supposed to handle this? The doctor and his family showed a warm interest in me and often invited me to visit their home. I always paid for the love I received.

Anastasia later informed me that she had known the doctor and his family for many years. I asked her what kind of person this physician was, who treated me like an angel. She looked at me suspiciously, and gave me an enigmatic smile. At last she replied, "What can I say; it's common knowledge that the Visnevski family is very close-knit and keeps to themselves."

"How can that be?" I answered. "Look at all he did for me!" Anastasia then told me that she, too, was surprised at the special treatment the Visnevski family had accorded me. At that moment, Mr. Koch walked in and added his own insight, "Everyone knows all about Dr. Visnevski's obsessive antisemitism. Even now, when no Jews remain in the region, that family doesn't miss a chance to rant against the Jews." Anastasia interjected, "Who cares? Everyone knows the Visnevski family also hates the Russian regime; remember how they celebrated Russia's downfall? That little doctor is so full of hate, he'll always find something new to detest."

My weekly visits to the police station continued; and each time I was re-interrogated. In addition to the department head, my interrogators consisted of two men and an older woman. She was the worst of all. One day I came home early and found her talking to Anastasia. My blood froze in my veins, but I acted normally and did not show that I recognized the policewoman. I assumed the terrible woman had not told them she was from the police because I don't think the Grigorevich family was aware that I was making twice-weekly visits to the station. Had they known, they would surely have thrown me to the wolves.

The questions were the same every time I went to the police station. They tried to trip me up by asking me a second question before I finished answering the first one; or someone would hurl a question at me that I had already answered. I don't know how I managed to stand firm against all that pressure. They had murdered all the Jews long ago, but they still searched high and low for any survivors, so that the entire Jewish nation would be annihilated. I had no illusions whatsoever that all those people who professed to love me would have had me killed without a qualm if they discovered I was a Jew.

On one occasion I made a point of arriving late at the police station, after regular work hours. Luckily, the manager was alone. He appeared worried as he stood by the window facing the inner courtyard, gazing into the darkness below. I was still recuperating from my illness and had no work. It was crucial to hide this information from him so I told him I was late because I had been working. I apologized for my tardiness and whipped out a bottle of alcohol, which I promptly gave this head of the police passport department. I told him it was a present, to compensate for the inconvenience I had caused him. He gave me a sly smile and hurried to lock the bottle in a closet. He then came up close and scrutinized my face as if it would reveal to him everything he wanted to know about me. I thought he was debating how to react and what to do. I was afraid, but remained rooted to the spot, staring him straight in the eye. An eternity passed until he opened his mouth to tell me to come back the following morning, when his staff would be in the office. I had no idea when I left whether my little gift had been a help or hindrance. I then waited tensely for the next visit, but then nothing had changed; I was asked the same questions and they continued to use the same technique.

But they still didn't issue me a new set of identity papers and I wasn't able to get a job. Would I ever manage to get out of this trap? It was obvious they were playing mind games with me and all I could do was stay strong and not give in to their pressures.

I walked out of the police station slowly, certain that time was running out for me. I had tried everything I could just to stay alive, but was clearly not having any success. Suddenly, I felt someone grasp my elbow, but I was so engrossed in my thoughts that I didn't respond. Next, I felt an arm around my neck. I looked up, and whom did I see but the doctor's daughter, Ira Visnevski! I smiled and did my best to hide my inner turmoil.

Ira Visnevski held a senior position in the city's German mayor's office and had just stepped outside for a few minutes to enjoy the lovely weather. She was happy to see me, and hugged me as she would a dear friend. She asked what I was doing there and I told her that I had been to the police station because I needed to change my identity card. Ira told me that everyone in her family was talking about me and invited me to visit their home. Moreover, her father was concerned because I had stopped attending his clinic; also, she reminded me gently, I was still under medical supervision.

Ira told me that she had already completed three years of medical school and hoped to be a doctor like her father, but in the meantime, she had a good job that she was very happy in. Ira knew everyone and I knew she could help me find work, and could even be instrumental in obtaining the papers I so desperately needed. But I didn't dare pour my heart out to her; I knew she would soon figure out the reason behind my forged identity paper and would turn me in to the Germans without a qualm.

The weather was perfect for a stroll down the main street of Zhitomir. Many high-ranking German officials walked toward or past us, many of whom raised their hats to Ira. Everyone recognized her and greeted her with respect. Yet Ira, who was a Russian, living in her Russian hometown, was uncomfortable talking to me in Russian and asked me to speak German. I tended to avoid speaking German and only did so when there was no choice, such as when I was at work and had to communicate with my employers. But Ira was clever and knew I must be fluent in German since I had German employers. Not wanting her to suspect anything, I had no choice but to converse in German and Ira immediately told me that my German was excellent. "I simply won't have an intelligent girl like you working in menial jobs," Ira exclaimed. "You have to get yourself a respectable position, Ulita."

"Yes," I said. "I have plans to study, but it's wartime. It doesn't really matter where I work, any job, if it is honest, is better than being idle. There is nothing disgraceful about domestic work." However, I did drop a tactful hint that, given a choice. I'd prefer to work in a factory.

"I know the kind of work that best suits you," Ira announced, "and I promise I'll take good care of you, don't worry. You can count on me."

CHAPTER 8

Trapped

Ira Visnevski was as good as her word and barely a day after bumping into her I was invited to the management office of the factory that produced and repaired rubber tires. I was amazed when they offered me work as a Russian-German translator! However, although I was desperate for work, I felt under-qualified for this particular job and tried tactfully to ask for something less demanding. The factory's German managers were surprised and explained patiently that they had enough shop-floor workers and the only vacancy they had at that moment was for a translator! There was nothing for it but to start work immediately. Luckily, they didn't ask me for any identification. Indeed, the German managers appeared not to want to know anything at all about my private life. They treated me with respect, as though I was already part of their team and they already knew everything they needed to know about me. This, obviously, was thanks to Ira Visnevski, and I owed her a debt of gratitude; she, in turn, was very proud of me, her protégée. Nonetheless, I had no doubt that if Ira ever suspected I was Jewish, she would hand me over to the German murderers without a qualm.

My time during the day was divided between the office and the factory, both of which were located in the same building. I tried to do my job well, but was constantly concerned about my official documents. Whenever I could, I printed out various documents for myself on official company paper;

I made a point of appearing in photographs with my German employers. I even had one taken beside the factory's sign.

The work provided me with a certain amount of security and confidence so I decided to adopt a different attitude to my regular meetings at the police station. No longer waiting for the designated date, I visited the passport department earlier. As before, I described my work, but now I boasted about my success. I asked—on behalf of my German boss—what the Russian police required with regards to my identity card. In my zeal, I allowed words to pour out of my mouth inadvertently and was amazed to hear myself say that my German boss was annoyed at the delay in my paperwork and that he would be complaining in person to the passport department! I waited on pins and needles for their reaction. To my surprise, I was issued a bona fide identity card on the spot!

At long last, I owned a legitimate identity card. But I couldn't let myself forget that the forged document remained in the police safe and could still be used against me. I toyed with the idea of leaving Zhitomir for good. If I went to Kiev with my new papers, no one would ever know about the contents of the Zhitomir police safe. But this was not so simple and I had a lot to lose. I never forgot my first days in town, before I found a place to live and people who cared enough to call a doctor when I was sick. I now had medical problems and in Zhitomir my medical treatment was free. Finally, I had an excellent job, and was able to support myself. Further thought convinced me that it was unwise to give it all up.

However, I continued to be troubled by the knowledge that on my forged papers in the police safe, I had the Ukrainian name Ulita Novkivska, whereas my legal document had been issued in the name of Lida Nowakowska, a Polish name. And on my legal document my age was ten years older than my real age, and there was nothing I could do about it. There was no way of knowing whether I would do better in a city or in a village, although I thought that a big city like Kiev would be ideal because people there didn't know each other. But then I realized that the Germans had arrived in Kiev, too.

I waited impatiently for my first paycheck and wondered what my landlady would say when she received only half of my salary, since I had always given her everything I earned. I told myself that I had to be strong and take care of my own interests; also I had to start saving if I planned to travel.

Unfortunately, things didn't happen according to plan. On the very day I received my salary, Ira Grigorevich became very sick. I realized that my money was needed to pay for Ira to have an abortion. I wasn't in a position to ask too many questions but this was not the time to desert the Grigorevich family.

One day I returned from work depressed to find the mistress of the house, Anastasia, waiting for me impatiently. She described a bitter argument she had had with her daughter, Nadia, whom she suspected of not holding a job and going out every night. Anastasia asked me to follow Nadia and not let her out of my sight, until I discovered where the girl was spending her time. I tried unsuccessfully to wriggle out of this mission, which placed me in an awkward position, since my objective was to be as unobtrusive as possible and on good terms with everyone. I wasn't about to become the family's informer.

There was nothing for it but to follow Nadia, who very rudely did her best to shake me off. She treated me like a child who was incapable of understanding her and claimed that her 'entertainment' was inappropriate for me. After a while I became disgusted with having to spy on someone older than myself who didn't want me around and I told Nadia that I had been ordered by her mother to do so. When I said miserably that I was unable to keep everyone in the family happy Nadia relaxed and became very friendly toward me. We chatted amiably to each other until we arrived at the upper class neighborhood with its posh villas.

At the entrance to a large house we were greeted by the housekeeper, a very large, fat woman. She obviously knew Nadia from previous visits and said angrily in German, "What took you so long? The master has been waiting a long time and is furious with you." To my great surprise, Nadia started to apologize and make excuses as if her life depended on this crippled German man. Introducing me as her sister, Nadia asked tentatively if I could spend the night. The housekeeper treated Nadia with obvious contempt and told her to hurry to the bedroom and not annoy the master any further.

I was stunned. Suddenly I noticed the German director of the meat factory, standing in pajamas at the bedroom door, curious to see who had come with Nadia. He recognized me from his visits to Nadia and looked at me in surprise.

The housekeeper then showed me into a guest bedroom. I was very tired and happy to be left alone at last. I was fast asleep when Nadia came in, dressed in a lovely, expensive nightgown that did not belong to her, and shook me awake. "Get up, get up!" she said. "You can tell mother that we spent the night with old friends, but not a word about that German. Don't forget to say that we were together all the time." She gave me half a bar of chocolate and told me to eat it on the way home.

Nadia knew I could keep a secret. She was later forced to get away when Zhitomir was liberated by the Soviets, because her activity during the German occupation had been common knowledge. She wrote me letters describing her life with her husband in the city of Batumi, where she was doing well. Although she didn't like the city, her husband had a good job as an oil engineer. Still, Nadia often complained about her husband, claiming that he didn't appreciate her; when he was in the army, she had raised their son all on her own. After all, Nadia wrote to me proudly, all people have the ability to control their own destiny; your happiness depends on your ability to grasp the wheel of life and follow your own fortune.

In 1943 the Zhitomir population was convinced that the occupation would last forever; to me this was a very frightening conviction. I had become extremely alert, both day and night. The couch on which I slept was positioned next to the window, facing the street. Many were the sleepless nights I spent beside that window, waiting for the break of dawn.

Once, when I was unable to sleep, I kept looking obsessively toward the window; outside it was dark and quiet, but suddenly I thought I heard noises in the street. I held my breath to listen; at first there was silence, but then I heard the sound of hobnailed boots, cautiously surrounding the house. I was taken back to the German occupation of my hometown, when the sound of those boots was a sure sign of impending danger. I was never able to overcome the fear the sound of those boots instilled in me. And now I was hearing them again. Were they coming for me?

Suddenly, I heard whispered male voices, trying hard not to waken the household. I was sure the house was surrounded on all sides and was terrified. There was no way to escape because the house had only one door. I was sure my end had come; they were here to get me, the stranger, the suspicious one. My forged document was still in the police safe. What terrible luck, I thought; I had been to hell and back to get a new identity card and now they've found the forgery and are here to get me!

I pretended to be asleep, but could hear everyone else start to wake up. In the adjacent room, the Grigorevich girls were getting dressed. Anastasia appeared beside me with one of the girls to shake me awake. They said nothing, but motioned me to follow them. Then Anastasia opened a door, ushered me inside and closed the door quickly behind me.

I was shocked at what I saw. That tiny room, a cubbyhole, eerily similar to the ones Jews had built in houses in Korzec, contained the entire Grigorevich family. I had no idea this house contained one of those cubbyholes; I had never opened the mysterious door to see where it led. But this room was mute testimony to the tragedy that had obviously taken place in this house and proved that the Jews of Zhitomir had also used hiding places to try and escape death. I noticed that the cubbyhole had once been part of a double wall that served as a shelter. There were other such hiding places in the house, all connected by the oven behind the wall. I assumed that this had once provided refuge to a large Jewish family. Part of the structure had been demolished; probably by the German murderers, who destroyed it when they pulled their victims out.

I sat in the partially destroyed cubbyhole with the Grigorevich sisters, not knowing what was happening outside. To them, the occupation was paradise. They had German lovers. So whom did they fear? The house was obviously surrounded by Germans or local police. Anastasia, it seemed, had remained in the kitchen to open the door. It later transpired that a group of men burst in and strode through the house in their heavy boots. I heard male voices and knew that I was the one with the most to lose; a Jew has to avoid interrogation at all costs. But what could I do?

In the end, I was lucky again and everything ended well. I was greatly relieved when danger passed and we were able to leave the cubbyhole. I didn't dare ask questions, but I looked pointedly and inquisitively at the girls, with a gaze that demanded an explanation. Was I also involved in this? Somehow, the girls seemed to be party to a secret and looked at one another with a strange expression, as if they were undecided what to tell me. It seemed to me that they were embarrassed to tell me the truth. Finally, Anastasia allowed her girls to confide in me, because I was already privy to many family secrets. This is what Anastasia told me:

With the German occupation, Ira had become friendly with a Russian policeman who worked for the Nazis. She needed his help in getting her hands on abandoned Jewish property. In fact, with his help, she managed to get everything she wanted. But the policeman had an ulterior motive; he wanted to marry Ira! She agreed and promised to be a devoted and loyal wife. They were happy together, but did not rush into marriage. But things changed. The Jews were all murdered and there was no more property to be had. There was nothing left to steal and the local policeman no longer served a useful purpose. Ira then left him. With my own eyes I had seen the results of that relationship.

Ira was a lively soul and wanted only to enjoy life to the fullest. She had many men 'friends', German as well as Russian. Consumed with jealousy, the Russian policeman started stalking her; he recruited some friends and colleagues and decided to take revenge on Ira and her beloved sisters. I discovered eventually that the girls had known beforehand that the men would be coming that night to haul them off to a forced work camp. They went into hiding and took me with them.

One fine Sunday morning, Ira Grigorevich awoke in an excellent mood. Telling me that I was looking pale, she persuaded me to join her on a long walk. I agreed reluctantly and was angry with myself for always giving in to the domineering Ira. I kept my eyes on the ground as we walked and thought about my family. I kept asking to turn back, saying that we had walked enough for one day. Ira agreed, but said we'd take a different route, one that passed through neighborhoods I had never seen.

At one point, we met some railroad workers, which led me to understand that we were in the neighborhood where the railroad workers lived. There was no reason for me to suspect anything, ha stopped suddenly by one of the houses, opened the gate, and laughed, "Come on in; let's say hello to some friends of mine." I wanted to walk home alone, but she insisted I stay and we entered a nice, well-tended garden, ha climbed into the house through one of the open windows and

I could soon hear her laughing. When she finally remembered that I was outside she opened the door to let me in and meet her friends.

I thought I must have been dreaming, as Ira went to wake up two men who were still in bed. These were German officers I had met occasionally in the Grigorevich home. The young blonde one was called Hermann and was Ira's boyfriend; the other, dark-haired one was Nadia's boyfriend. Hermann's bed was near the window and Ira slipped into it beside him. The second officer awoke at the sound of Ira's laugh and hurried off, explaining that he had important work to do. I discovered that the two Germans were responsible for the railroad and were quartered nearby; naturally they were thrilled at not having to fight on the battlefront. Instead they enjoyed a peaceful life in occupied Zhitomir and had a wonderful time with the local girls.

We all went into the garden and I planned to make a getaway as soon as possible. But to my surprise, I noticed a man in the uniform of a Hungarian army general speaking with some soldiers. It was the first time I had seen a Hungarian uniform, and I wondered what these men were looking for in occupied Russia. I was overcome by revulsion and longed to be able to run away from these people who had wreaked tragedy on my family.

All my excuses were futile; I could not free myself of them and, although I hated them with a passion, I found myself agreeing to re-enter the house for some chocolate. They sat me down and blocked my way, so I couldn't escape. The Hungarian general ordered his men to bring food and drink. I had eaten nothing all day, but now could not touch a thing. I felt my bile rising, I was suffocating. All I could think of was how to get out of there.

All at once, everyone burst into a spontaneous singsong. They laughed a lot and were in very high spirits. I noticed Ira and the Hungarian general exchanging confidences in a corner.

Curious to know what they were saying I eavesdropped on their conversation and was horrified to discover that they were finalizing the terms of a monstrous business deal.

I couldn't believe that even Ira was capable of selling me to the Hungarian general, as if I was some kind of chattel! It was inconceivable; after all I had done for that family!

The general didn't quibble over the exorbitant price she was asking; he was quite happy to pay her with a whole warehouse full of groceries and even with the rest of his cash. But Ira asked for a down payment: a truck full of delicacies, to be sent to her home immediately, plus a large sum of money for her mother. And this wasn't all; according to their 'agreement,' Ira would visit the Hungarian army quartermaster stores later to pick up the rest of her fee on site.

I was clearly in a trap. Although I was in shock, I told Ira in a choked voice, "I am not playing this game of yours, Ira. You tricked me into coming to this house; now I insist that you get me out and immediately!"

Ira retorted, "How childish you are, Ulita. Anyone would think you were still in nursery school and know nothing about real life. Time you grew up, little girl."

Then she became serious and added, "Where else could you earn such a fantastic sum of money? I know how hard you work, Ulita, and that you even risk your life to earn more money for our family, because you love us."

Ira was aware that I gave her family everything I earned, even food from my mouth. There was every reason, therefore, for her to believe that I'd sell my body, too, if it meant supplying her family with enough food for a year!

I felt myself suffocating on my tears. Indeed, Ira understood and remembered all I had done for her family and this was how she chose to repay me! My brain struggled feverishly to find a way out. Where could I go; whom could I turn to? I went across to Hermann, the German officer, who was standing in the middle of the room, smoking a cigarette and begged him to help me get away from the house. Instead of answering me, he smiled and blew thick smoke rings towards the ceiling. I lost control, gripped him by the lapels of his army greatcoat and pulled his head down; I don't know where my strength came from. In a voice full of venom I said to him, "You, you proud German officer, where is your honor? Aren't you ashamed of what is happening in your own house? What kind of man are you, to refuse to protect a weak, defenseless girl? Have you forgotten that I am your guest!" I took a deep breath and went on, "My German employers will never forgive you for this!"

Hermann knew where I worked and I watched him sink into thought, his eyes looking out somewhere above my head. I waited tensely, not knowing what he was thinking. Finally, his face darkened with anger and he threw down his cigarette. Without looking at me, Hermann said he had a plan to free me from the group of drunken Hungarians. He said that he'd rejoin the party and engage Ira and the Hungarians in conversation, allowing me to slip out to the bathroom. "A door in my kitchen leads out into a field," he told me. "Get out of here as quickly as you can, before the Hungarian general notices that you've gone." I did as he said and ran like a lunatic. As I reached the field I heard gunshots and was sure the Hungarian general had shot Ira.

It was early spring in 1943 and the ploughed field had absorbed a lot of water, making it very muddy. Once in that mud field, I could no longer move; I fell on my face and couldn't lift an arm or a leg. I turned into a ball of mud and there was no one around to hear my screams. My legs were as heavy as lead, the mud tripled my weight and I swung around like a drunk. I had had nothing to eat or drink all day and I was shivering with cold.

Mustering all my strength, I pulled myself across that field, inch by inch. It was after midnight when I eventually reached the Grigorevich household. Ira and the German officer were approaching from the opposite direction, holding on to each other and laughing. They were surprised to see me and said I looked like a statue made of mud. I was obliged to remove all my clothes and wash in ice-cold water.

The tire factory in which I worked was usually busy and noisy; occasionally it was visited by military and police personnel who came from far away. Whenever any of those noisy, jovial German visitors came in, I couldn't control my fear and tried to stay out of their way. One day, however, someone started a rumor that I was a Pole, a native of Warsaw, and had come to German-occupied Russia to look for relatives. Where this rumor started I don't know, but one morning when I came to work two men ran toward me, glowing with happiness and introduced themselves as Janek and Frank. Apparently they, too, had been born in Warsaw, just like me! They, too, were rather lonely in Zhitomir. They were sure we'd be able to share memories of pre-war Warsaw, when Poland was free and independent.

The men tried to convince me that, as former natives of the same city, we needed each other and should spend all our free time together; they invited me to join them in all their after work activity as well as at church on Sundays. It was quite difficult to produce endless excuses to avoid them as we worked in the same factory and saw each other every day. I decided to play safe and refrain from fabricating stories about my past. Although I knew the Polish language and quite a lot about the country's history, it wasn't enough to masquerade as someone who had been born in Warsaw. So I just kept quiet, and excused my inability to join them by being inundated with work. The result, of course, was that they became very annoyed. In fact, they began to suspect me and resorted to spying on me.

Things became complicated and dangerous when Anatoli Koch, who also spied on me, joined forces with the two Poles. Maybe Anatoli's real motive was infatuation and jealousy.

Nonetheless, the three started to meet every day to discuss me and came to the dangerous conclusion that the only kind of person who would behave the way I did, cutting myself off from almost all social interaction, had to be Jewish. Fortunately, they were not in consensus over this and decided to wait and see. But Anatoli was impatient and rushed to pour out his suspicions to my landlady, Anastasia. He even threatened to go to the police.

The Grigorevich family was soaked in anti-Semitism but couldn't believe that someone as strong-minded and confident as I could be Jewish. And those girls needed me, since I had become very useful to them; actually, the entire household needed me. Anastasia was sure that Anatoli was trying to manipulate her into throwing me out so that the Kochs could take me in, and told him angrily that she was not so stupid as to believe that I was Jewish.

I was concerned by all this, but knew that it was too late to run away. I couldn't change anything and all I could do was to act nonchalantly, as if I hadn't a care in the world; luckily, it seemed to work.

Still, people saw me as an unfriendly loner and therefore an object of suspicion. So I decided to befriend a young co-worker, a Polish girl of about sixteen who was a devout Christian. I hoped this friendship would help lessen my standoffish reputation. I visited her often in her village not far from Zhitomir and made several new friends there. On one visit I even received a gift from my friend's mother. It was a beautiful old holy book, bound in brown leather with a frame of golden copper. It was a magnificent piece of folk art and, at first, I refused to accept something so obviously valuable. The mother suspected that I couldn't read Polish and asked me to read aloud from the book. I was surprised at the way everyone there was impressed with my Polish and was moved by the friendly atmosphere. I decided to learn a few verses from the book by heart, which made my new friends very happy. They

Anna's mother,
Idit Rubinstein (neé Weiner)

Anna's father,
Wolf Rubinstein

Anna, 1944

Anna, 1944

Anna, a nurse at the military hospital, 1944

Anna, 1944

Anna and her son, Vladimir, 1951

Anna's brother,
Leon, 1948

Anna's husband,
Aharon Podgajecki

Anna Podgajecki

then asked me to accompany them to their church, which was quite close to their house. At first, I intended to join them, but then discovered that they planned to introduce me to their priest. My conscience troubled me for being unable to be open with these lovely people who had taken me under their wing from the start. Sadly, I decided to distance myself from my new friends and gave them no explanation.

During my time as a translator I was able to relax slightly and appreciate my good fortune. I had a place to live, I earned my keep, I was a meticulous and scrupulous worker and my employers were satisfied with me. All I needed now was peace of mind and security; but I dreamed of remaining in these circumstances until the end of the German occupation.

One beautiful late winter morning in 1943, I sat in the office practicing my typing skills, as I did whenever I had any spare time. My boss was at his desk and we were chatting casually, when a charming, well-dressed and attractive young Russian woman came in asking for work as a translator. I was afraid she had plans to usurp me in my job, and threw an envious glance at her documents and certificates, which included references from various important people. She was a native of Zhitomir and lived in the town center quite near the factory. I sighed; of course someone like that would have a better chance of succeeding, and it was no wonder that she was soon hired! I thought, "How could I, an escapee from the ghetto, compete with this girl who has everything?" I waited tensely to hear that I was to be fired, but to my welcome surprise, the director said there was plenty of work for both of us.

During our lunch break, the girl tried to befriend me and hugged me at every opportunity. She even asked to meet me after work. Zoia Spiegel was a well-organized young woman, who had studied medicine for three years before the war. As a child she had learned to play the piano and invited me to her home in order to perform for me. She lived in a large, furnished apartment that she shared with her maternal grandmother; I got the distinct impression that it was dirty and neglected.

Zoia's father had been a physician in one of the city's hospitals and was a native of Zhitomir. A Jew from a distinguished family, he had fallen in love with a simple Russian girl and married her despite his family and friends' disapproval. When war broke out, his wife decided there was no need to run away from the Germans who were swiftly advancing on Zhitomir. Of course, the fate of the Jews in German-occupied Russia had already been determined. Dr. Spiegel viewed the calamity that befell the Jewish people with great pain and understood that he, too, was part of it. It was as if he had finally woken up from a deep sleep, but by then it was too late to reverse the situation.

Zoia took me to the assembly area outside to describe the tragedy of Zhitomir's Jewish community and her parents' role in it. Her father, a caring Jewish husband, had done wonders for her Russian mother, but now she treated him callously. She took a lover, who stole all of Dr. Spiegel's wealth. Then, when the *Aktion* began in Zhitomir, she chased her husband out of their house and into the hands of the Germans, even though everyone knew that the Jews were going to be murdered. Zoia's relationship with her father had been especially close and she felt her world collapsing. She ran after her beloved father, but her mother followed her and saved her from sharing the fate of the Jews. Zoia showed me the exact spot near the fence where she swore to her father that she would not keep silent, but would avenge his death.

So here we both were, two Jewish girls working in a German factory, after all the other Jews in the Ukraine had been annihilated. Still I could not open up to Zoia. My life was in danger and I dared not discuss my own Jewish background. Instead, I tried to create the impression that everything was in order with my life. Ironically, Zoia knew nothing about my past, which is why she envied me and wanted to be like me.

Once I knew her problems, I wanted to help her. I wanted this to be a lasting friendship, but experience had taught me that my life was often interrupted by unexpected events and occurrences. Every day, when we said goodbye, there was no knowing if we'd meet again the following day.

When the Koch family slaughtered a pig and everyone said they were planning a banquet in my honor, I was acutely uncomfortable; I didn't want to be in the limelight and I certainly didn't like being seen as a potential bride for their son. But they assured me that the reasons for their celebration were quite different. First, there was my miraculous recovery; second, I had secured a very good job under the Germans; and third, I was fortunate to be loved by all whose lives I touched! I didn't know what to say, so said nothing. In my position, one cannot afford to argue or annoy.

On banquet day I returned to find no one at home; everyone was at the Koch house, helping set the tables. I really didn't want to attend a banquet in my honor. Anatoli had already reminded me twice that everyone was waiting to begin the meal. I knew they wouldn't start without me and I couldn't afford to turn them into my enemies. As I stood there grappling with my dilemma, the door to the kitchen opened and Ira Grigorevich walked in. She laughed her loud, happy laugh and hooted, "Here's someone who came especially to meet you, but don't forget that I'm a jealous type." She was followed in by a man of about twenty-eight, elegantly dressed in a crisp black suit, coat and shoes; the kind of clothes usually worn by well-to-do Jews. Who was this man? Could he have been sent by the local secret police?

The man, who appeared relaxed in this strange house, removed his coat and walked toward me. My fears intensified. He was handsome and elegant and a lot older than I was. He must have noticed my discomfort, because instead of asking awkward questions, he told me about himself. His name was Valeri Bulavin and he was a surgeon. He had been drafted into the Red Army when war broke out and later taken prisoner. Eventually, he was brought to the prison in Zhitomir where he performed operations in the local clinic. He had plenty of patients to treat and conditions were primitive. The Germans provided him with clothes and the occasional day off, as a bonus for his good work.

Dr. Bulavin said he had spent this free day with some friends and had met Ira. I kept a close eye on this man, still a bit wary of him because he seemed too interested in me, and I watched my words carefully. Suddenly, I noticed that Dr. Bulavin's smile was full of pain; it was a smile that conveyed more than any words could. I didn't notice that Ira had disappeared—gone to the Kochs, to join her German lover.

The kitchen door opened and Anatoli Koch ran toward the bedroom where the German officers' coats had been placed. I heard a shot ring out and started shaking, thinking Anatoli had killed himself with a revolver from one of the Germans' coats. I tried to run into the bedroom but Dr. Bulavin held my elbow tightly and ordered me not to move. Instead, he told me to look at him and try to smile, as if we were having an intimate conversation. The Kochs' German guests heard the shot and understood immediately what had happened. They were well aware that it was against orders for them to leave their personal weapons unguarded and they were seriously worried, knowing they faced prosecution if anyone had been hurt. Fortunately, even this incident ended happily. Anatoli was so afraid of death that his hand shook and only his ear was hurt, not his head. After a sigh of relief, we were all able to relax and enjoy the meal.

Dr. Bulavin and I were the last to arrive at the table, where we were seated next to each other. The German officers opposite us raised their small liquor glasses in a toast. They were in excellent spirits and tried to make small talk with the doctor, about whom they knew nothing. Bulavin ignored the Germans, claiming that he did not understand the language.

I found this hard to believe, but, as usual, said nothing. Bulavin did not look at me, but whispered discreetly in my ear that he was at the party only for me. I eventually plucked up the courage to ask him what we had in common. Suddenly, Mrs. Koch came over and forced me politely to go into the next room to try on her beautiful clothes.

I was modelling clothes for the others, when Dr. Bulavin whispered that he had to go but needed to talk to me before leaving. He insisted I accompany him outside and I decided to comply with his unusual request in order to discover what he had come to tell me. He placed his arm around my shoulder and whispered into my ear that we had no chance to escape these people. He looked at the floor and I could sense his inner struggle, as he tried to decide about something. Finally, he whispered, "There is no choice; we have not succeeded. Your life is in danger. Save yourself. Get away from here before it's too late." Then he rushed off without saying goodbye.

I was rooted to the spot, deeply troubled by this encounter with the mysterious guest. That night I tossed and turned restlessly in my bed. Bulavin's words echoed in my consciousness because I had heard the same words in a dream only two weeks before. In my dream, my mother banged on the chair next to the couch on which I slept, and shouted, "My daughter! Run to save yourself, because your life is in danger." I had tried to ignore this message, telling myself it was only a dream, but now a real person had come to give me the very same message! I knew Bulavin was right and that I should leave Zhitomir, but I was also acutely aware that my forged identity card continued to languish in the police safe. Still, I decided to wait for an opportune moment. I didn't want to anger the Grigorevich and Koch families. My escape from Zhitomir had to be planned in absolute secrecy; I even thought of searching for an underground or partisan unit in the nearby villages.

The next morning I awoke feeling unwell; the newspapers and radio gave the name of the escaped Russian prisoner as Valeri Bulavin. Apparently, the doctor was in contact with people from the local underground who helped him join a partisan company that was desperately in need of an experienced surgeon. The Germans were furious and regretted having allowed the prisoner a day off, during which he had slipped away. They promised a large sum of money to anyone who would hand the doctor in.

I envied those people who could fight the Germans. I, too, dreamed of joining the partisans, but I hadn't been able to make contact with them. I was in contact with people who disseminated news about their doings and talked openly with me about it but I had never heard of any local underground organization. It occurred to me that the Ukrainians and other locals were so enthusiastically pro-German that any chance of underground activity in our area was out of the question. Moreover, the Germans were very sensitive to any sign of rebelliousness and beat it out with an iron fist. Whenever the partisans killed one German in Zhitomir, for example, the Germans killed fifty innocent local men in reprisal and as a warning. In this way, they succeeded in intimidating the local population. But I had heard during 1943 that there were many partisans in the vicinity of Zhitomir—only not in the city itself.

CHAPTER 9

On the Road Again: A Prison in Romania

In the early summer of 1943 I was still working in the tire factory as a translator. I enjoyed my job and now I also had a friend, Zoia, whom I loved dearly. It was ironic that she, of all people, envied me. But although we were really good friends and I loved her, I could not allow myself to tell her that I, too, was Jewish and had run away from the ghetto.

When I came home one day in a good mood, even though I was tired and hungry, Ira Grigorevich suggested I grab my documents and go to town with her. In those days, no one went outside without his or her identity papers.

I don't know why I agreed to join Ira; I still hadn't forgotten or forgiven her for the previous time, when she tried to sell me to a Hungarian general. I could never refuse her anything.

We stopped beside the movie theatre and I was sure Ira had brought me there to see a movie. I was never happy about taking part in recreational activities that involved mingling with the German military personnel and their local henchmen, but I had never learned to argue with Ira and, besides, I was afraid to raise her suspicions. An army jeep pulled up next to us, driven by Boris, a neighbor of ours, and one of Ira's lovers. The two carried on like a happy couple while I stood by, open-mouthed. They giggled and ordered me into the jeep.

I was sure we'd be going home, but this time, too, I was wrong. Boris drove very quickly, then stopped and let me off in some desolate, unfamiliar place. "Wait here and don't

move," Ira called to me and off they went. I was as innocent
as a shy schoolgirl and I believed that all they wanted was to
have a chat in private. They disappeared without a trace and
I was left alone; night started to fall and I had no idea how to
reach the road to Zhitomir. I started to walk towards a nearby
orchard; in front of me were endless fields and railroad tracks.

With the passing hours, my anger grew; all I ever wanted
was to survive the German occupation, but I had had enough.
I despised my people-pleasing role as the see-no-evil, hear-no-
evil fool who was constantly taken advantage of. Ira probably
intended for me to lie to her mother and say I had been with
her all night. My eyes filled with tears when I remembered
the last time with Ira and the Hungarian general. I decided to
take the first train that stopped. I had my papers with me and
that was all I needed. Hadn't I been warned to get away from
Zhitomir? Surely it was high time I did so. Good riddance to
that selfish, manipulative Ira and her parasitic family.

But no train arrived and it was already after midnight. I was
freezing and tired and sat curled up to conserve warmth, trying
hard not to fall asleep. People started to arrive, which meant
the train would be leaving soon. It suddenly occurred to me
that I had no money with me. How would I pay for a ticket?
What if the Germans were to take me in for questioning?
I was examining my options furiously when Ira reappeared,
drunk and barely able to stand up. She went over to a water
tap, washed her face and hands, extended a weak hand and
muttered incoherently, "Let's get out of here."

A heavy rain began to fall, it was cold and there was a
strong wind, so I followed Ira; I had nothing to lose. It was
too dark to see anything. We stood in the open air, exposed to
the elements, as close as possible to the train tracks and a train
finally pulled up next to us. The inclement weather evidently
helped Ira to sober up a little and she ordered me to follow her
and climb up into an open coal car where we actually sat on
a pile of coal. I strained my eyes to look around me and was

surprised at the number of people who quickly scrabbled onto the open coal cars. Ira promptly fell asleep, while I wondered where we were going. Here we were, on the way to who knows where, and all my clothes were in the Grigorevich home! I was furious enough to explode. Drenched to the skin, my teeth chattering, I had nothing with which to cover myself.

After living in Zhitomir for almost a year, I had a good job and a salary large enough that I did not have to sell the valuables my mother had sent me off with. I had put them aside for a rainy day. And now, here I was, penniless on a rainy day, with only a thin summer dress to my name. The rain didn't ease for a minute and I was extremely hungry and thirsty. And I still didn't know where we were going.

Eventually, I calmed down and became apathetic, resigning myself to my fate, over which I seemed to have no control. I curled up in a fetal position in an attempt to get warm. Suddenly, I heard a horrible shriek; a woman was screaming wildly that a man had fallen under the wheels of the train. How awful! I wouldn't have believed I still had enough emotion in me to care what happened to others, but I must have still had some sympathy left in me. Even Ira noticed and tried to comfort me. People said there were villages in this region, close to the train tracks and the train deliberately picked up speed in order to prevent local people from climbing onto the moving cars.

When I asked where we were, Ira said we were three kilometers from a town called Vinnitsa. The train passed by the town without stopping. Who would believe that three years into the future I would be living in that very town? Ira knew exactly where we were and called out the name of every town as we flew past. She felt quite at home in these surroundings; I now noticed that she was wearing warm clothes under her overcoat and that she couldn't care less if I was freezing to death in my thin summer dress. Now the train was approaching a major station at Zhmerinka and I got the distinct impression that Ira traveled this route frequently. I couldn't help but envy this daring woman, with her devil-may-care attitude and excessive self-confidence. She had no doubt she could do anything she wanted, take on any task, do the impossible and intimidate anyone else into helping her. If only I could have been like her; I might have been able to save my little brothers and sisters and my poor parents.

In the morning the train stopped in a field and Ira said, "Let's get out of here quick, we have to warm up and dry your clothes." I was sure she was joking, but she grabbed my shoulders and ordered me to enter the only closed train car. On the way she stopped to see where we could wash up. Ira laughed her head off, saying I was a real sight, covered in soot as I was. My summer dress looked like a crumpled, filthy rag and I was embarrassed to be seen; I was also reluctant to enter the only closed car in the train, to join people who had paid their fare. But the car was clean and warm, with a red-hot heater in its center and a number of small tables and benches all around. German military personnel were talking with uniformed train workers and border guards were moving from table to table. We had obviously arrived at the German–Romanian border. Ira ordered me to sit next to the window and warned me not to open my mouth. I was happy at the chance to warm myself and waited tensely to see what would happen next. The border police arrived eventually and asked to see special passports containing a visa issued by the Romanian embassy in Kiev. In addition to these, we needed tickets and other documents in accordance with Romanian law. It was amazing to see Ira calmly deliver all the necessary papers. How unpredictable she was. She even told them I was her little sister. I was unable to see what documents she had, but evidently they were accepted without complaint.

I watched Ira, still unable to understand what was happening. Why was she taking me on this trip to Romania? All the time I was living with the Grigorevich family I thought

I knew more about Ira than her family did, but I was wrong. She was a complete enigma to me.

We reached the town of Troitsk. The passport authorities led us to the customs building. Again, everything went smoothly. How had she managed to engineer all this, I wondered. Then I remembered her boyfriend Hermann, the German officer; he was a director of trains in occupied Russia. He must have supplied her with all the necessary tickets and documents.

I contemplated my new circumstances: Had Ira taken me away from Zhitomir in order to settle in Romania, where I would have to start from the beginning, in a new country, with an unfamiliar language and with nothing except the dress I was wearing?

Ira brought me to the center of Troitsk. We found somewhere to sit down to rest and she told me she had to leave for a meeting, to arrange something important; she stood up and left. Once again, she left me on my own. Obviously, she was no stranger to this place; here, too, there was someone waiting for her. Again, I waited a long time with no idea where she was. I realized that I was in need of shelter, a roof over my head and work. I don't know how long I sat there, tired and weak from hunger, before Ira rejoined me.

She was drunk again, but she noticed that I was suffering and this time she brought me some bread and apricots. The apricot season had just begun and this was the first time in my life I had ever seen this fruit.

Finally, Ira actually discussed her plans with me, albeit in a roundabout way, but I was too tired to pick up her hints. Apparently, she had good reason to spend time in the city. She tried to reassure me that I had nothing to worry about; she had plans for me, too, that included work and a place to live. "We can be settled in within a day," she said confidently.

After a while she admitted that she was in some trouble. Little by little, Ira revealed her secret; she was in urgent need of a lot of money; her life and happiness depended on it. While living in her mother's home, I had seen and heard things about Ira that I didn't understand at the time, but I said nothing. I did the same now. After hearing her out, I decided to give Ira the gold coin that was sewn into my dress. I was hoping she would say that the coin could help solve her problems, or at least that she was grateful. I knew that Ira was aware of the coin's value. But she said nothing; her sly smile said it all. Clearly, she thought I had a secret stash of such gold coins!

Next, Ira jumped up suddenly and announced that we had to hurry to get to the village of Mayovka. In that charming village we were welcomed by a large, wealthy Russian family, whose daughter, Maya, was a good friend of Ira's from their student days at the university in Odessa. Ira asked her friends if I could stay with them until her return. "I'll pay them," she whispered to me. "Everything will be alright." She warned me several times not to leave the house because she needed me; but she refused to tell me where she was going or what her plans were.

In the morning I set out with the family to work in the large field they owned. But I was very worried; the clock was ticking and I had to act quickly because I was sure Ira had returned to Zhitomir. She had told me in Zhitomir that she had a plan to kidnap a two-year-old girl from her lover Boris, in order to force him to marry her. Ira had insisted that I help her take care of the child, but I refused to have anything to do with this crazy plan. I warned her not to play with fire. Now I was afraid she might return with the child. So I used every chance I had to find a job in Mayovka, so as to leave this family and find lodgings of my own.

One Sunday morning I awoke early; my hosts were still asleep and I thought about a local farmer who had promised to give me work the following day. I was encouraged by the thought that I could earn my keep and some extra money that would enable me to travel back to Troitsk and to look for work in the wealthier neighborhoods. I was at the door, ready to leave, when I realized that it wasn't polite to go without saying a proper goodbye.

I was about to leave after saying goodbye when I noticed a horse-drawn wagon near the house. Two men approached me and asked in Russian for my documents. My passport wasn't stamped with a visa for Romania and I didn't know who these men were, or what they wanted from me, but they ordered me into the wagon and drove me straight to the Troisk prison. For two days I was held without food.

My interrogators decided to do a thorough job and discovered that although my identity card from Zhitomir was legal, the document added almost ten years to my real age and they wanted to know why I looked so much younger. They asked how I had managed to cross the border without a visa and why I had chosen a place where I had no friends or family. Although they obviously suspected something untoward, they did not come close to revealing the truth about my identity. Luckily, I had plenty of documents to testify that I worked for Germans; and there were also all the photographs I had saved. I swore that the uniformed Germans in the photographs were my friends. All this conflicting evidence must have confused my interrogators, because the prison commandant decided to send me to the local police station.

I was taken under heavy guard, like some dangerous criminal; even my personal documents were treated like criminal records. The police station was located in two adjacent houses. I was locked up in a filthy room with no furniture, just a window facing a long, narrow yard. The police department promptly forgot about my existence, while I was in desperate need of food and access to the outside lavatories. All I could do was sit on the floor, tormented by hunger.

At the time I had good reason to believe that all the Jews in the territories occupied by Germany had been murdered. As far as I knew, I was the only Jew left alive, and now I, too, had fallen into the murderers' hands. In order to escape my

terrible loneliness I resorted to memories; until suddenly
I heard male voices, speaking Yiddish! I thought at first that
I must be hallucinating because my thoughts were full of my
Korzec childhood. I continued to sit on the floor, motionless,
until I heard a female voice telling a man, in Yiddish, that they
should hurry and finish their work before the devils returned.
I had thought the Yiddish language had died with the Jews!
Was I dreaming? I raised myself from the floor and went to
stand near the window, waiting tensely for another police visit.
Through the window I saw a young woman dragging various
boxes behind her. My curiosity got the better of me and I asked
her, in a whisper, about the remaining Jews in Troitsk. She was
astounded, but recovered enough to come close to my window
to see if there was anyone else in the room with me. I told
her quickly that I would like to talk to her about the Jewish
holocaust, but she had to know that I was masquerading as a
Christian and she must not put me in any danger.

For the next seven days I had a connection with some of
Troitsk's few remaining Jews. Naturally enough, our main
topic of conversation was the tragedy that had befallen the
Jewish people. Troitsk, too, had witnessed the slaughter of its
Jewish population and, in June 1943, only ten Jews remained
there. There was no place for them to run and hide and they
were forced to work very hard; every day several policemen
led them to work.

The police had established a makeshift restaurant for
themselves, which provided them with free food. The place
was operated by Jews who smuggled out food and passed it
to me through my window, although they risked their lives
in the process. Those poor unfortunates knew there was no
chance of them surviving the war. Still they tried to encourage
me to keep fighting, insisting that I must prove to the world
that the Jewish nation will not be erased from the face of the
earth. They were sure I could survive and live to tell the world
what happened.

Every night throughout my imprisonment, a policeman took me for interrogation. One night something changed. One of my interrogators told me to leave with an armed soldier who had a knapsack and a rolled blanket on his back.

After midnight that night I set off toward an unknown destination. Although I was afraid I would never see another dawn, I had no choice but to acquiesce. The soldier led me through endless dark uncultivated fields; I tried to engage him in conversation and asked him where we were going, but he replied in broken Russian that he was forbidden to talk to me. I realized that he spoke only Romanian but tried to convince him that I was honest and incapable of even harming a fly. He did not respond, which I thought was ominous.

Eventually we neared a dimly lit site that turned out to be a train station. We then traveled for many hours on a filthy, overcrowded train; even the corridors were packed with people and the congestion was almost unbearable. Late the following morning I saw the mass of people moving towards the exit. The soldier ordered me to follow the crowd.

It was wonderful to be outside again and breathing clean fresh air; I hoped it would help me overcome my dizziness. It took me a while to regain my equilibrium, and I was very cold. The soldier was surprisingly patient; I suspected he felt sorry for me.

We arrived at a prestigious part of town, comprising elegant neighborhoods and attractive houses. The peace and quiet in this tree-filled town helped me relax. The soldier led me to a big old office building, staffed by people who spoke only Romanian. The soldier quickly performed some tasks and left. After a while, I was taken into another room where a man was sitting behind a desk; from the beginning he made a positive impression on me. I still didn't know where I was or who these people were but I had every reason to assume that I was in the presence of an important man. Later, I discovered that he was the chief prosecutor and I only saw him once. The prosecutor asked me the same old questions: How had I succeeded in crossing the border without official documents? Why had I moved to a place where I couldn't speak the language? He kept asking me about my family and friends and wanted to know what I knew about Romania.

I wondered if I should make up a few useful stories. These people seemed to be trying to help me and even dropped hints as to what I should tell them. I conjured up an imaginary uncle in the city of Tiraspol, and an older sister who lived in Ananiev. Hadn't I already learned that if I was to survive, I needed to lie? I had to cultivate some good solid *chutzpah*! In fact there was a grain of truth in the Tiraspol story, because I had been acquainted in Zhitomir with a large family of Moldavians who had come from Tiraspol. They had come to Zhitomir before the German invasion to visit relatives. Then, when the Germans occupied Russia, a new border was created between Germany and Romania and the Moldavians couldn't go home. This turned out to be advantageous for me, because I could now tell my interrogators a story that sounded true! Fortunately, I remembered the name of the family and even their address in Tiraspol and once I started, I got quite carried away with fabricated stories about all my so-called relatives. In the prosecutor's office I passed from table to table, until the clerks had all filled out forms for me.

After some effort, I discovered that the soldier had brought me to the Ukrainian city of Golta, where I was held in a camp for illegal border crossers. Once all the paperwork and documentation had been taken care of, I was taken by a group of soldiers into a large courtyard, at the gate of which stood a Russian-speaking Romanian soldier. The courtyard was surrounded by a tall fence with barbed wire along its top.

I was very tired and very hungry; all I could think about was food. I kept my eyes on the gate, waiting in vain for someone to bring me something to eat. I tried to believe that there had been a misunderstanding. How could they keep me under arrest without food? A few days later I realized that the people in charge of this camp thought I had no need for food!

Meanwhile, it was nice to rest under the blue sky and breathe fresh air. I soon found out that I had found the very best spot and began to sleep in the yard, even though I shivered all night from the cold. I often wept silently and suffered extreme tension and sleeplessness.

I thought of the clothes I had left behind in Zhitomir and yearned for something warm to wear. As for the Grigorevich family, I was torn by conflicting emotions. I had been absolutely devoted to them and defended them to myself and to others. I still felt connected to this family and wanted to help them, but now I was very angry with them.

I couldn't understand it, nor could I understand why I couldn't see Ira as she was—a devious, conniving, selfish woman with strong criminal tendencies, who callously exploited others to serve her own interests. She never seemed to care about me. So why did I always want to help her? Why did I allow myself to see only the good in people and allow myself to be manipulated? Why had I given Ira my gold coin that I needed so desperately now? Why did I always forgive her, no matter how badly she treated me?

With all the other prisoners or 'detainees' I was confined to a camp that included two large rooms devoid of all furniture. It was so crowded that no beds or other furniture could be brought in, even if we had wanted. The walls were permeated with the stench of sweat and urine; but worst of all were the bugs and lice. I was terrified of catching lice because of my long, heavy hair; I had nothing with me with which to keep myself clean, not even a comb or a bar of soap. I was horrified at the sight of the women working hard to rid themselves of the offensive lice, under awful sanitary conditions. Lice were everywhere—on our bodies, in our hair and in our clothes.

The people who were brought to the camp at night had evidently been taken off coal or freight trains. They were inevitably young, able-bodied and full of life; there were no children. The jumble of languages indicated the presence of people from Moldavia, Romania and Russia. The noise in the camp was unbearable, especially the shouting and the weeping.

All the detainees said they wanted permission to get to Odessa in order to reunite with their families. I was worried. If the Romanian government was making it so difficult for people who only wanted to reunite with their families, what chance did I have? I had no idea what was happening. How could this government prevent unfortunate refugees from joining their families? Many of my fellow detainees were Romanians and the Romanian gatekeeper told me in a whisper that I shouldn't feel sorry for them. He was sure that they were scavengers wandering from place to place, trying to get rich quick. They were all heading for sites where Jews had been murdered, in order to lay their hands on left-behind Jewish property. The preferred destination at that time was Odessa, where a lot of Jewish wealth still remained. It had nothing to do with family reunions.

I actually heard detainees say that in Odessa the Germans had locked up Jewish houses containing vast fortunes and there were no guards to keep the scavengers out. In June and July of 1943 I had witnessed a stream of people on their way to Odessa and rumors had quickly circulated that certain Romanian officials had to be bribed into issuing the coveted permits to enter that city. Some of my fellow detainees had brought with them money and valuable jewelry and were prepared to pay any price to secure a travel permit to Odessa; all day and all night they talked about nothing else.

I had heard of this back in Zhitomir. Indeed, the Grigorevich girls had also planned to travel with the Koch family to Odessa in order to lay their hands on Jewish wealth. It was an ugly fact that people everywhere saw themselves as the legitimate heirs of the murdered Jews, only because they had breathed the same air on the same accursed planet.

I soon learned that where the detainees were concerned, there was no equality before the law. Everything depended on how much silver or gold you had in your possession. It came as a surprise that the norm in Romania was to pay bribes for everything. For me, this was a new world. I watched the way many of the detainees did very well for themselves in that ghastly place; in return for a handsome sum of money, they received a permit and settled in Golta. I was most upset by the fact that everyone else in that camp had some source of food from the outside; while some of them received baskets full of the finest delicacies available on the black market, I had nothing! No one cared that I had nothing to eat. I was just a young girl and did not need much food, but I was starving!

I was on good terms with the gatekeeper, but didn't have the nerve to complain to him about anything. He understood my circumstances and may even have taken pity on me because once every day he gave me a slice of bread that was so dry, it looked like the sole of a shoe; sometimes he even added some pig fat. Perhaps he was given food for me, but never passed it on, except for that piece of dry bread. There was a nationwide food shortage in 1943 and, anyway, many years have passed since then, but I have never forgotten the bitter taste of starvation.

Every day a group of women, including myself, was taken to the city to clean offices. I didn't know whose idea it was to organize this detail, but I thought it was a good one. First, we were all young and able-bodied. Second, we were all happy at the opportunity to leave the squalor of the detention camp, to walk outside and be able to look around. For me, work also provided an opportunity to befriend fellow detainees, who passed on information and news.

I wanted to know what was going to happen to everyone in the camp and my new friends told me that many people were granted permits to live in a place where they had family, but sometimes people were handed over to the Germans.

Golta was on the Romanian side of the border and a bridge
from the city extended to nearby Pervomaysk, which was
under German rule. Sometimes, the Romanians would take
detainees as far as the center of the bridge and then leave them
to the mercy of the Germans. More than anything I feared
being turned over to the Germans. A Jewish girl with forged
documents could expect nothing more than torture at the
hands of German interrogators. It was ironic, therefore,
that I was happy to remain under Romanian detention; no
amount of hunger, lice and cold could compare with falling
into German hands. I tried unsuccessfully to devise a scheme
to extricate myself from my predicament, so all I could do
was wait for a miracle.

Whenever I wanted to escape the terrible noise in the
detention area, I would climb up the wooden fence and
gaze enviously at the lovely view beyond; how quiet and
peaceful it was. On the opposite side of the road a residential
neighborhood extended towards the river. I had always loved
rivers and now I took advantage of every opportunity to
watch the changes and reflections in the deep, wide body of
water that was known as the Southern Bug River.

I was sitting on the fence one day when I saw a large woman
leaving the chief prosecutor's office. Although she was not
young, her clothes and her bearing seemed to indicate a person
of importance. She looked familiar; I vaguely remembered
having seen her before, after my arrival at the detention camp.
She noticed me on the fence and quickly walked over to look
at me. The woman appeared older than my mother and there
was something very friendly and welcoming about her. For a
long moment she stood motionless next to the fence, gazing
directly at me. I was discomfited, wondering what she was
thinking. My distinct impression was that I reminded her of
someone dear to her. Later, the gatekeeper told me she was
the chief prosecutor's wife! After that, she made a habit of
'visiting' me every day; she stood near the fence and gazed at

me wordlessly and I became used to this rather extraordinary daily ritual.

One day, a soldier came and ordered me to follow him. We walked to a neighborhood of detached houses and I realized when we entered one of them that this was the chief prosecutor's home. My biggest surprise was being welcomed into the reception room by the prosecutor's wife herself! She exchanged some words with the Romanian soldier and I understood from her gestures that she had herself asked the soldier to bring me to her home. A tall, elderly man with a well-tended moustache and white hair was sitting on the porch; he was very handsome, despite his age. The gentleman noticed us and rose from his chair, pacing the room nervously. What was happening? Why did he sound so angry? The prosecutor's wife banged her fist on the table and raised her voice, as if she were presenting a case. The elderly gentleman then appeared to agree with her every word. I felt I was watching a play in a language I did not understand; at that time I knew only the few words of Romanian that I had picked up in the camp. Although I didn't really understand what was happening, my impression was that this woman was acting as my defense advocate!

I stood in that living room like a block of wood until they told the soldier that we were free to go. Suddenly, I plucked up the courage to ask permission to bathe in the Bug River that was not far from the house. The prosecutor's wife came over and looked at me with eyes that were full of compassion. It took her a few minutes to shake herself back to the present and she said quickly, "Yes, of course. Take as long as you need."

I was happy as a lark, putting all my problems aside, able to enjoy a few minutes of freedom in this beautiful area so full of green trees, flowers and water. At last I was able to wash my long, heavy hair, even though I didn't have such luxuries as soap, a towel or a comb. At first the soldier refused to leave me for a second, but I convinced him that I needed a secluded spot where I could wash the clothes I was wearing. I ran barefoot down the bank of the river, my long hair flying in the wind. I was thin and light and felt like a feather blowing in the wind.

I don't remember how long I stayed in that camp but I'll never forget my last days there. Every day, all the detainees were assembled in the camp's large courtyard. This included people who possessed permits to live in Golta as well as newcomers. Every day, we were reminded that, for us, judgment day was nigh. We all shared a similar fate and were bound together by the fear of what lay in store for us.

One day seventy judges and their assistants were brought to Golta in order to determine our fate. I wondered why one detention camp required so many judges; after all, we were hardly dangerous criminals or espionage agents who threatened the state! In the end it turned out that even more than seventy judges had been brought from all over Romania to decide which of us would receive a permit to live in Romania, and which would not. It appeared, therefore, that the Romanian government related to our detention camp with considerable seriousness.

Some prisoners claimed to be very experienced and mentioned the bribes they had paid in return for their permits. According to them, they had already submitted bribes to a specific clerk who had connections with the camp commandant. I doubted this system whereby one clerk, however corrupt, was influential enough to broker such deals. Anyway, my 'advisors' tried to help by advising me to insert a large sum of money or jewelry into an envelope alongside the special request for a permit. They said that if I had no money or jewelry, I should offer a valuable gold object. But I had nothing—neither money nor jewelry—and I had already given Ira my gold coin. It looked as if I had no chance of ever receiving a permit and I was afraid they would hand me over to the Germans.

Finally, judgment day arrived. All the detainees were ordered into the camp courtyard, as usual. This time, however, the tension was palpable; but since I was the only one who had no hope, I sat myself in a corner to avoid the others and didn't even hear my name being called out. As it happened, I was among the first to be taken into the office. The three rooms contained long narrow tables laid out from wall to wall. The judges sat close together, while their numerous assistants rushed back and forth.

I was asked to pass slowly between the rows, so that each judge could get a good look at me. Next, I was ordered to enter another room. The man there was evidently the chief judge. He examined the papers they placed before him and he signed them quickly. He then handed me a large envelope containing documents and said I was free to go wherever I wanted! I was overjoyed; this was the miracle I had prayed for.

The man was clearly very busy, but he was patient with me and waited to hear anything I had to say. I was unable to utter a sound. The judge may have noticed the emotions that were written across my face, so he explained gently that the envelope contained everything I needed to become a Romanian citizen. "You must take these to a police station as soon as you have found a permanent place to stay," he added.

The doors of Romania were now open to me and I was overwhelmed, standing there in the middle of the street, free at last. Had the prosecutor's wife been responsible for this good fortune? I wondered, but I could never be certain. In my heart I thanked her. As to the fate of the other detainees, I had no idea. Then I started to come back to earth and realized that I was in dire need of food and shelter. I remembered that the Ukrainian villages were better off economically than the cities and therefore I decided to start my search for work in the rural areas. Admittedly, I still spoke very little Romanian, but I knew I'd get by on my German and Russian.

Dressed in a sleeveless summer dress I wandered from one poor, downtrodden village to another. I wondered if it was just my bad luck, or were all the villages in Romania in such dire straits? I thought of looking elsewhere, but before anything else, I needed to eat. Besides being constantly ravenous I suffered from pains in my liver and the occasional dizzy spell. I thought these were the side effects of malnutrition.

I noticed some women standing at the roadside gossiping and decided to approach them. "I am hungry," I said simply. "Can anyone around here give me food in return for work? I am quite willing to work anywhere, in the house or in the field."

Without missing a beat, one of the women said she had temporary work for me. Later, I discovered that she lived alone and was therefore happy for me to move in with her. I remember the hot corn porridge she made me that tasted exactly like ambrosia.

Always one to appreciate help from someone else in times of trouble, I decided to do something special for this woman so she would not regret helping me. I had noticed that her garden appeared neglected and nothing seemed to grow in it, although there was plenty of water available. So I set to work from dawn until dusk and after just a few days the garden began to show signs of life.

My employer kept her bed right inside the hearth, even though the house was very well heated. The hearth was wide and clean, but still it seemed to me a strange place for a bed, as it was the upper part of the baking oven that the woman used all day to cook her rather sparse meals. She offered to make space for me to sleep next to her in that hearth, but I declined politely. Instead, I was given permission to sleep on a wooden bench near the wall.

One morning I opened my eyes and everything was blurred. I asked for water, but was unable to pronounce the words correctly and no one could understand what I was saying. My tongue was of no use because it was completely dry; I was very weak, as if all my body fluids had been squeezed out of me. I didn't even know where I was at first, but then I saw that I was surrounded by a large number of women, looking at me, crossing themselves and whispering something before leaving the room. My employer and her friend did not leave my side for a moment and were obviously happy to see that I was alive. When I began to feel better, the women told me that I had lain unconscious with a high fever for two days and chattered deliriously in a foreign language that no one understood. She had been very worried and had brought in her neighbors, who managed to make out the word "mama" and realized that I must have been telling my mother something. They were all convinced that I was dying. My employer felt an obligation to provide me with the last rites before I died and had sent someone to fetch the priest, who lived a long way off.

Very slowly, I began the long road to recovery, but I was incapable of working and I didn't want to be a burden on this very caring woman; how much longer could I expect her to feed me?

I discovered that there was a town nearby called Ananiev and the name immediately rang a bell. A year earlier I had met Vera, one of the Grigorevich daughters, who had married and moved to Ananiev to be near her in-laws. I felt I had no choice but to ask for her help. But how could I do something so humiliating? All I had left was my self-respect and self-worth. I didn't have Vera's address, her husband had died a long time before and I didn't even know her marital name. But I remembered Vera telling me what a lovely town Ananiev was, with fields and orchards, and plenty of fruits and vegetables—a veritable paradise. And now that fate had brought me so close I decided to make my way to Ananiev and try to find Vera. I would ask her to help me find domestic or agricultural work and make a point not to impose on her. I was extremely grateful to the woman who had nursed me through my illness and thanked her profusely before taking my leave.

I reached Ananiev on foot and made straight for the marketplace with its abundance of fruits and vegetables, just as Vera had described. In the marketplace, I soon found someone in charge and offered to work in exchange for food; I was willing to sweep the street, wash windows, clean floors; in short, I would do anything. When that didn't work, I made my way determinedly from stall to stall, asking for work—but to no avail. I was very tired and depressed when suddenly, behind a stall with a lovely pyramid-shaped display of fruits, I saw Vera Grigorevich and her sister, Liuba. They were busy counting money, probably their day's takings and didn't notice me at first. I couldn't believe my eyes; as far as I knew, Liuba had stayed behind in Zhitomir when her sister Ira had spirited me away to Romania on the coal car. All of a sudden I understood that even then the Grigorevich sisters had been weaving their plans to leave for Odessa, to lay their hands on Jewish loot.

The two sisters looked up and saw me and in a flash they welcomed me and invited me to join their business. They noticed I looked sickly and quickly decided leave the market and take me home. I was so happy to have found friends at that difficult time; I felt infused with new hope and courage.

I was very grateful to Vera for allowing me to stay in her home for a few days and making it possible to recover and regain my strength without having to go out and look for a job. Vera saw that I had nothing but the clothes I was wearing (and my documents) and gave me a few useful gifts—an old, small suitcase, a towel, some underwear, a brassiere and a white summer dress that fitted me perfectly. I really liked that dress—the fabric and stitching were in the best of taste. In fact, everything Vera gave me was clean and in good condition. I was grateful for her generosity and concern in my hour of need.

When I felt better, I told Vera and Liuba that I really liked the village and wanted to look for work and lodgings there. But I was disappointed to discover that Vera did not like the idea and used the excuse that no appropriate work was available in the town for young people. But I knew the real reason: she didn't want me around, as I was a living witness to the Grigorevich girls' indiscretions in Zhitomir. She must have been worried that I'd let slip something inadvertently. So I accepted her 'advice' with understanding, but reluctance.

When I look back at this with the wisdom of hindsight, I know that Vera could have saved me much needless suffering if she had only agreed to my staying on in the same town as her. If only I could have remained in Ananiev until liberation! I was usually very careful about what I said and kept all the Grigorevich girls' secrets, but on one occasion I did allow myself a slip of the tongue that changed the family's attitude towards me. In a moment of weakness I asked Niusia, "Does Anatoli steal from the Jews, too?" This single comment was very damaging, because after it, the girls whispered among themselves to be careful what they said in my presence.

It was time for me to move on and I decided to try my luck in the big city, where it might be easier for me. It was only polite to share my plans with Vera and I told her that I wanted to join relatives in Tiraspol. I gave my thanks, said goodbyes and left Vera and Liuba.

On a hot, late summer day in 1943 I arrived in Tiraspol and walked around the streets looking for a much-needed job. I didn't have a penny in my pocket and I looked for people to talk to; I also planned to look for the Moldavian family I had known in Zhitomir. Luckily, I remembered their address by heart, as I had long since thrown out the piece of paper on which the address had been scrawled. It took no time to discover that the house was in the center of town.

Happily, my Moldavian friends gave me a warm welcome. My hope was to secure work in Tiraspol and support myself, while staying close to these friends. But things were more complicated because I couldn't find any work, no matter how hard I searched. I felt guilty about living with relative strangers and eating their food; how long could I stay with people who weren't even relatives? But I had no choice.

Tiraspol looked like a ghost town. Everywhere I went, I saw large homes that were boarded up and abandoned, silent testimony to the Jews who had lived there before they had been taken away to be murdered. It became gradually apparent that even in the neighborhood occupied by my Moldavian friends, most of the houses were empty and few people lived on the same street. By now I was living there legally and according to all the rules I was entitled to register at the police station and requisition an apartment, which I could then live in, as did many others who wanted to improve their standard of living. But I just couldn't do it. I still believed at the time that I was the only Jewish survivor and if I were to move into another Jew's home I would be haunted by all my horrendous memories; I might even be driven to insanity. It was for this reason that I continued to live with my Moldavian friends who were so kind to me. I also continued by extensive search for employment, but it seemed as if the world had closed itself to me. I was at the end of my tether and didn't know where to turn.

One day, on a walk beyond the city limits and looking in all directions in the hope of seeing someone I knew or who could give me a job, my eyes alighted on a charming river. I went and sat near the water, depressed and mentally exhausted from the constant fight for survival. After uttering one final scream I entered the water at the deepest spot I could find, so as not to allow myself a chance to change my mind. I had to get this over with as quickly as possible, to join my family in the next world. Most of all, I wanted to be released from all the pain and sorrow, the grief and the yearning for my lost loved ones. But, as with so many of my other plans, this one failed, too.

Somehow I found myself on the riverbank, next to a young man who was gazing down at me with the deepest compassion. He cared for me carefully and gently and then extended his arm. I took his hand and walked with him wordlessly, although this behavior completely contradicted the upbringing I had received in my parents' home. My savior, a young man I had only just met, led me to a nearby hill, sat me down on the ground and pointed out the lush, green vegetation that covered the hill leading down to the river. It was the first time in my life I had ever seen peanuts growing (I had believed that they grew on trees or bushes, like walnuts or hazelnuts) and the young man said to me, "Look how big these peanuts are, why don't you try to pick some for yourself?"

I asked myself how this young man had found me in the water. There's no one else here! He was very handsome; perhaps he was a student. When he saw that I was beginning to recover from the shock of being found, he said. "Look down at the wonderful view and see for yourself how beautiful the world is."

He was right; everything looked different from above. Listlessly I looked down at the River Dniester and the many happy holidaying people on its banks. They were there to swim and get suntanned, to enjoy life.

And it was only then that I noticed that the river did not flow in a straight line, but took a curvy, meandering route. About two kilometers from the spot I had chosen to divest myself of this cruel world there were a number of twists and turns in the river; no wonder I didn't see all those people earlier. This young man must have been watching me from up here, at the top of this hill.

He asked gently what had induced me to take such desperate measures. I told him I couldn't find work and hated the thought of being supported by my acquaintances. He said, "Work is no problem! Just outside Tiraspol there is a large canning factory that operates all year long. But you'll have to wait two days until Monday, since the managers don't work on the weekend. I'm sure you'll get along very nicely there."

What a relief! It had been a very difficult day and my rescuer would not leave me on my own for a moment because he must have felt I needed company. None of my excuses or arguments had any effect on him; he insisted on escorting me home and even befriended my landlord. The two spoke Moldavian, a language I was not familiar with. It was not difficult to guess that my rescuer was asking my host about me. Luckily, the family had first met me in 1942 in Zhitomir, when Ira Grigorevich had, for some reason, introduced me as her sister. My suitor obviously made a good impression on my hosts, who accepted him warmly, and he knew how to take advantage of this. As for me, I didn't know at the time that his wealthy family occupied a grand villa in a prestigious neighborhood. He invited me to go with him to a play and my host insisted that it would be very beneficial if I were to allow myself to have some fun and to trust this young man. Whenever we returned from some outing or other, my host would be waiting at the gate, to meet and chat with the young man who was so interested in me.

It seemed at long last that I had a chance at a normal life, with normal relationships and even a boyfriend. My problem, however, was that the German occupation had caused me to lose my faith in humankind and I had learned to fear and suspect everyone I met. After everything I had suffered, I did not believe there was such a thing as a time friend. I was filled to the brim with appalling memories of destruction and carnage, the fruit of human brutality. And on those rare occasions when anyone did reach out to me in kindness, as did my rescuer and all those people in Zhitomir, there was always a voice inside me that asked if they would still be like this if they knew I was Jewish, or would they promptly hand me over to the Nazis without a second thought?

In those days, when my life was in danger, all I wanted was to be alone. I didn't want to have real friends because I couldn't describe to them the tragedy that had destroyed my family. I believed that any friendship I had would be based on a lie; any friends I had would be Lida's friends, not Anna's. Looking back today, I think I may have made a terrible mistake, one that would affect the rest of my life. I should have allowed myself to make close friends when I was younger; I should have allowed people to touch my life, to help me. How much pain and grief this could have saved me and it would have made my life so much easier.

Thus, in spite of the fact that I desperately needed a real friend from among the local community, who would be able to help me when I needed help, and although I was fond of my rescuer and appreciated the friendship he offered me, I couldn't continue the relationship. So, at the first chance I had, I broke off all contact with the young man, although I couldn't even provide myself with a decent reason for doing so.

As fate had it, I was to meet my savior again in the spring of 1944, two days before the liberation of Tiraspol, under circumstances that were singularly embarrassing. But more about that later.

CHAPTER 10

Fatal Attraction

As I approached the canning factory in search of work, I noticed a young woman standing near the main gate, her eyes darting nervously in all directions. I asked her for directions to the personnel office and whether she knew the name of the person with whom to discuss work. Realizing she didn't understand me, I switched reluctantly to German. I explained to her that I had come from Poland and was here visiting relatives. The delay unnerved me slightly, but the German woman reassured me that there was no need to worry, since any time we spent talking would be recorded as time on the job. I was sure this was a joke and we both laughed. Wanting to say something nice to her before parting I said, "What a shame you don't have any influence in the personnel department!" In response, the woman moved closer to me and said that she was actually the factory's personnel manager!

"I am also responsible for interdepartmental work," she reassured me, "so you have nothing to worry about at all." She promised me she'd hire me immediately and seemed very pleased to have met me. She then asked me to speak in Polish.

It later transpired that the woman I had met unexpectedly at the canning factory's main gate was none other than Rosalia Rosenberg who, I was soon to learn, was the mistress of the managing director, Richard Richter from Berlin.

Richard Richter was a prominent industrialist who had been sent to Krakow after the occupation of Poland to run a chocolate factory. Richter took his mistress with him and they lived together in unmarried bliss. Gossip had it that Rosalia made the most of this posting to have a clandestine affair with a Polish gentleman who taught her to speak his language. But the affair came to an abrupt end when Richter was transferred to Tiraspol to manage a canning factory and Rosalia went with him. Richter, whose main job was to ship merchandise back to Germany, also managed a few other factories in the occupied territories.

It was extremely opportune of Rosalia to have taken an immediate liking to me, enough to have given me a job in the factory. As well as a job, I asked for and received accommodation close to the plant. I was assigned a room in a large house that was meant to accommodate only Germans. It was a lovely room—large, clean and full of light. I shared the room with several other girls and we were each given a bed with a blanket and sheets. We also had the use of a kitchen well-stocked with dishes and utensils. I couldn't believe my good fortune; to me this was absolute paradise! I discovered that my roommates were Germans who had been born in Russia because of some kind of entitlement. They all came from around Odessa and were old friends. I was not offended by the girls keeping their little secrets to themselves; I had my own secrets that I could not share with anyone. Most important was the knowledge that I finally had a bona fide job to support myself and a roof over my head. Now, I thought with relief, I could relax a little after all my nomadic trials and tribulations.

Once again, I hoped and prayed that this time I would be able to remain in this factory until the end of the war. Rosalia was responsible for my job description and I did everything she asked me to. I typed the labels that were pasted on the cans and, when necessary, I also worked in the various departments.

I tried to excel at whatever I did and was eternally grateful to Rosalia.

One day at work, a stocky, middle-aged woman came over to tell me that the factory manager wanted to see me in his office. It seemed suspicious and I went, full of trepidation, to learn what I was being accused of now. I was led to an unfamiliar office; behind a big desk sat a tall handsome young man I had never seen before. "I know quite a lot about you," he said and I waited tensely to hear what he wanted. The man was Valeri Liunev and he was one of the locals who had been appointed to his position by the Germans.

Valeri told me that, since my roommates were engaged in prostitution, he had found me a new place to stay. He then instructed one of his assistants to show me to my new accommodation. Of course I was grateful to Liunev who appeared to be trying to help me, but I was also more than a little suspicious. It was not hard to guess that he'd taken a liking to me but I decided that, no matter what, I would never ask any favors of this man, so as not to be indebted to him.

The room I was given was part of an isolated, two-family house in the factory yard. It was very small and clean, only one and a half square meters, with a large window overlooking the center of the yard. But it lacked a bed so I went to the stable to look for a sack of straw on which to sleep. Luckily, the very kind stable hands helped me and, to my delight, they soon provided me with a small bed and a clean, straw mattress. All I needed now was a blanket and some sheets, because the nights were cold and I had nothing to cover myself with. Needless to say, I didn't dare approach Liunev, but I was on good terms with Rosalia and considered asking her. But, perhaps this would upset Liunev. I didn't want him to think I was ignoring him after he had singled me out so kindly. He had told me specifically that he'd be happy to help me with anything I needed; and then he sent me to live in a room without a bed! In the end I slept without sheets or a blanket and froze. I awoke numerous times during the night, trying to think what I could wear to keep myself warm. I was already using my one towel as a sheet to cover at least part of the straw, but in the middle of the night I pulled it out from under me and covered myself with it. I had to buy myself a blanket, so I could at least get a decent night's sleep.

In those days the Germans provided the local population with nothing and there was a dire shortage of all basic commodities. On the other hand, everything anyone needed was readily available on the black market. Most of the things sold illegally had been stolen from the Jews. If you had money, you could lay your hands on anything you wanted. I was shocked to see that German army personnel, too, were involved in this dirty business. I couldn't believe how in 1943 German officers, who had been so arrogant right after the invasion, were seen in Tiraspol openly buying and selling all kinds of black-market merchandise to anyone with money to spend. I still didn't have a penny to my name and was glad that no one was asking me for rent money. I hadn't eaten any bread in what seemed like ages, or even drunk a cup of tea. I survived by sneaking out fruit or vegetables delivered almost every day to the canning factory; I managed somehow to get by on this.

At long last, I received my first salary and the first thing I did was to buy a gray blanket from a German soldier. I borrowed a fashion magazine from Rosalia Richter and sewed a beautiful fashionable coat out of that blanket. It didn't have a lining, but still looked elegant and expensive and I also slept under it at night. With my second pay check, I bought a large new sweater that was made of excellent quality wool. I fashioned a pair of knitting needles out of an old bicycle wheel, unpicked the sweater and knitted myself a gorgeous suit from the yarn, following instructions from that same fashion magazine. From time to time I introduced some change or devised a small accessory to match the suit. Women looked at me enviously and asked where I had managed to find such lovely clothes!

After a while I dyed the suit a different shade, to make it look like new again.

A large family by the name of Marciano arrived from Bucharest and moved in next door. One day I saw little children playing outside and I understood that they belonged to my next-door neighbors. My heart broke to see those adorable little creatures playing so happily; they reminded me of my brothers and sisters. Their mother noticed me and came out of the house to invite me to join her guests. It was nice to have such a friendly, good-natured neighbor but it soon became apparent that she spoke only Romanian. She hugged me tightly and said she was sad that we didn't have a common language. But I was relieved in a way that we had separate entrances to our apartments; I couldn't bear the sight of those happy children.

I worked hard at my job and did my best to excel at whatever was asked of me. At night I went back to my room, where I slept all alone; it was disconcerting, but I got used to it. One night I left my room and went to the bathroom in the hall and who did I encounter but Valeri Liunev! He was dressed in a robe and slippers and smiled at me as if we were old friends. My heart sank; I felt as if I had received a sudden blow. With my heart thudding, I ran back into my room. Unable to fall sleep, I stood by the window until dawn. Only then did I understand that this so-called empty house actually belonged to Liunev, my boss, and he had given me a room in it. Clearly, I was now totally dependent on this man's whims; he could throw me out on the street whenever he wanted.

What was I to do? The very thought of starting from the beginning, of taking to the road again, looking for new work, trying to find food and a new place to stay, made me weep. No, I decided I wasn't going anywhere. There was no choice but to keep an eye on Liunev's movements, to discover at what hours he was home so as to know when to avoid him. It transpired that Liunev and my new neighbor, Marciano, were best friends and Liunev visited him every evening. I therefore took my shower and did everything I needed to do out of my room in the hours when Liunev was not there. Whenever I absolutely had to leave my room, I stood tensely by the door to listen if Liunev was in the hall. I tried to be as unobtrusive as possible.

One day, I returned from work to see a young village woman in the kitchen. This was Liunev's Russian housemaid, Marusia, who had returned from a visit to her village. Marusia, whose husband was on the Russian front, had a five-year-old son, Kolia. I envied the way this woman seemed to have adjusted so effortlessly to life in these crazy times of war. She was nimble and daring and knew how to take advantage of all her options, whether these were in the factory, in the village she occasionally visited, or elsewhere. She never seemed to lack food or other essentials. I could never understand, though, why she insisted on remaining in the house, where she and her son slept in the kitchen. Even later, when Tiraspol was liberated and there was no government and no law and order, Marusia and I were among the few who stayed on in the factory when its doors were flung open.

Admittedly, I was very happy to meet Marusia that first time in the kitchen and was relieved that another woman shared the house; I hoped her presence would make things easier for me.

But that is not what happened. Liunev continued to stalk me like an infatuated schoolboy. One morning when I was about to leave for work, Liunev was waiting patiently beside my door. He held out a large glass carafe and asked me politely to bring him wine from the company's wine department in which I worked. I understood immediately that he was looking for an excuse to be alone with me. Marusia, who had been following this little incident, walked into the corridor and said, "That's my job; I'm the one who brings you your wine every day. You don't have to bother Lida with this."

Liunev was very angry with Marusia for interfering in his private life. He looked at me and said, "It's about time you stopped evading me, Lida, and get used to having me around. I need to talk to you about an important matter and I'd appreciate it if you would come to my living room after work."

It was exactly what I had been dreading; I was utterly dependent on a man who was enamored with me, even though he knew nothing about me. I tore at my hair thinking that my hard-won, new-found security could be taken away from me in a moment. But I could only try to hide the storm raging within me.

That evening I went to Liunev's living room with the wine he had asked for. I stood by the door, reluctant to go inside and take a seat, at his invitation. There was a victorious smirk on his face. However, he was my boss and I was dependent on him, so I had no choice but to enter the room and give him the wine. I asked him in a serious tone of voice, "Why have you invited me here, Mr. Director? You do have an office after all." Liunev did not reply but walked over to a cupboard from which he removed chocolates, cookies, liqueurs and various other treats I had long forgotten existed and did not need. He then accused me of avoiding him and denying him the chance to express his good intentions. Deep inside, I was quite happy to hear that he took me for a Russian-born German. He thought I was a good friend of the Richters. He then insisted I tell him everything I knew about some of the people I worked with; I defended and praised them all. I felt very pressured and worried over how this meeting would end. Fortunately, Marciano from next door heard I was there and helped get me out of there, albeit very discreetly.

Marciano was a fun-loving man who never missed a chance to have a good time, even though he was married and a father of four. In the factory he was in charge of all the machines. I hoped and prayed that Marciano would be able to keep Liunev away from me. But then I had an idea. I would conjure up a German boyfriend; the thought of a rival might put him off me. And in the meantime, I was very careful to keep out of his way.

I was so worried I couldn't sleep and started to read books all night, but I couldn't concentrate and would float off to another world, where I was with my family in the ghetto. My nights passed and I didn't sleep. Fortunately, I was young, healthy and adaptable; my sleepless nights did not prevent me from working normally during the day.

One night, I lay in bed staring out the window, when I thought I heard some movement outside. I got up to check who was there and was surprised to see a pretty, blonde, blue-eyed girl outside the window. She was shivering and hopping about in an attempt to warm herself; all she wore was a short flimsy skirt and a sleeveless, low-cut, see-through blouse. The girl asked to be allowed into my room, to warm herself up a little.

I was in a dilemma. On the one hand, I felt sorry for her standing there in the cold. On the other, I found her outfit quite suspicious; she was hardly dressed at all. I then thought she might be all alone, hungry and exhausted, having arrived at the factory with the last of her strength to search for work. But how could I allow someone I didn't know into a room that wasn't mine? Supposing Liunev threw me out, together with her? I went out to bring her, quietly, into my tiny bed. I whispered that she could sleep until the morning. Who was to know what tragedy the poor thing had endured!

But life is full of surprises, including unpleasant ones; I was so wrong about my little 'guest. ' The first thing she said when she entered my room was, "You're the cause of all my problems!" It turned out that she was no innocent little girl. Everyone in town knew her by her nickname, Valka; everyone knew her in our factory, too. Her full name was Valia Volkovska, a Russian girl of about seventeen, the only daughter of a wealthy family that lived in a fancy villa in Tiraspol. She lacked nothing and was probably used to getting everything she wanted. As soon as she met Liunev, she decided he had to be hers. She crept through his open window and into his bed, where she waited for him to return from his night out! When he discovered her, he tried to drive her away but it was not easy.

Liunev told her that one of the rooms in his house was occupied by the girl he loved and that she, Valia, did not interest him. He was obviously referring to me. Valia told me that Liunev felt rejected and humiliated by the way I treated him; he yearned for me and thought I was the most intelligent and most beautiful woman he had ever seen; of course, he had hardly ever spoken to me! But Valia continued to look for opportunities to climb through Liunev's window and, each time she did, he would promptly throw her out. He was cruel and merciless to her, but she wasn't angry with him; I think she was used to having men reject her. But Valia was cunning and worldly-wise. She had devised a plan to help Liunev by telling me how much he loved me, and that's why she was at my window in the middle of the night.

I assured her that I wasn't interested in him and would be quite happy if she would attract his attention away from me. In an attempt to befriend Valia, I told her that although a man like Liunev is the stuff of dreams, I myself had a German boyfriend who was just waiting for the right time to marry me. I told her a myriad of wonderful things about this fictitious boyfriend, the most important being that he was very protective and jealous of me, and capable of killing anyone who tried to court me. Of course, I told her all this in 'secret' as one friend to another and she was not to repeat it. Then I waited impatiently to see the effect this would have on Liunev; I had no doubt she would pass on my 'secret' and he really did seem to cool down a little. But the Liunev saga was far from over. Of course, I had no way of knowing that one day Liunev would wreak his revenge on me.

Meanwhile, life went on as usual in the factory, and Rosalia continued to seek me out; I was the only production worker Rosalia took any interest in. She said she was bored and insisted that I stay close to her.

Once, when there was a day off work, I made plans in advance in order to take advantage of my free time. I had decided to wash my prized hand-knitted outfit that day. I waited all morning for everyone, especially Liunev, to finish using the bathroom and leave the house, when suddenly I had a guest. It was Rosalia Richter with a phonograph and some new records she had brought from Berlin. How ironic it was for a pampered German woman to be seeking out the company of a Jewish girl on the run from death! We sat on my bed, placed the phonograph on the stool and listened to music.

Rosalia described a wonderful period, when the Germans were just beginning to occupy other countries. In those days of glorious military triumphs, German soldiers were welcomed everywhere with open arms, as heroes. In those days the German army had seemed truly invincible. But things had changed suddenly; the German army suffered one defeat after another and began retreating from the front lines. Many people were changing their attitude towards the Germans, Rosalia told me in confidence, and were trying to sabotage German interests in every possible way. "We can no longer collect agricultural produce from the villages, even by using force," Rosalia sighed sadly. "Why, just this week the goods we received from Bulgaria were mostly substandard, or downright spoilt!" Clearly the Richters were finding it increasingly hard to ship containers of food to Germany.

That day was the first time I visited the factory's new building; I had not even known about it previously. It contained huge refrigerators stuffed full of rare and expensive delicacies— choice cuts of meat, chicken and beef; quantities of smoked food; cooked fish and fancy cheeses I had never seen before.

I was astonished by the sight of crates upon crates full of eggs, fruit preserves, jams and jellies of all kinds; all this in the middle of a horrible, long, drawn-out war that continued to cause food shortages across Europe. As I wandered around the warehouses and looked in wonder at all the delicacies, I thought I was dreaming. In one of the warehouses there were puddles of broken eggs and I couldn't stop myself from thinking how delighted our children in the ghetto would have been to lap up these spills, as they would have licked ice cream.

One day, in late summer 1943, I thought I heard people speaking Yiddish at work. I thought there were no Jews still alive in the entire area of the German occupation. I pricked up my ears at the sound of a Yiddish conversation beside the giant refrigerators and made up my mind to conduct a meticulous search outside, after which I came across a hall that was closed with a steel door. Inside the hall men were stoking a fire. The men looked at me in fear and asked each other in whispers, what does this German lady want from us?

I had not forgotten my own origins and felt immediate solidarity with these people who were so afraid of other human beings. Happy to discover that other Jews had managed to escape the jaws of death, I did something stupid and extremely dangerous—I went into the hall.

The stokers were young people with sad, frightened eyes. They looked so familiar it broke my heart. I wanted so badly to tell them that I was a Jew, also living in fear, and that our common language was Yiddish. In a trembling voice I asked, "How many Jews are still alive? Where do you live? Where are you from?" The men froze and exchanged horrified glances. When they understood who I was, they burst into tears. They didn't dare touch me, but surrounded me in a circle so tight that I couldn't leave. I was terrified in case their overseers returned and saw us there; they would certainly suspect me of being Jewish, too. In those days, the slightest suspicion was reason enough to kill someone.

Apparently there was a small ghetto, containing thirty-five Jews on the main street of Tiraspol. My heart bled for them, knowing that they could be murdered any day. I was unable to sleep that night and a day later I went looking for them again; they were made to do the most difficult, dirty and dangerous jobs in the factory. "How can I stay in contact with you without endangering myself?" I whispered. "Take a pair of shoes with you and ask for the shoemaker in the ghetto," they told me. "The Jews will do what has to be done."

After searching for the location of the Tiraspol ghetto, I discovered that it was near the house of the Moldavian family I had lived with. All the houses in that area were single-story. The armed Romanian soldier who stood at the entrance to the ghetto treated me very respectfully and permitted me to enter. I walked into the house and saw the men from the factory; it was obvious they had been waiting for me. The house had only three rooms and all the windows and door were tightly sealed despite the hot summer weather. Nothing could be seen of the outside and the inside of the house was like a tomb. The inhabitants were all single survivors of entire families, who were still alive by pure chance. From the corridor someone quickly led me into a small room. Here I met the only woman in the group, Mrs. Abramov, who was older than the others. We fell upon each other like a mother and her lost daughter, separated for a long time. We had both accumulated enormous pain under the occupation and it now poured out as we wept bitterly on each other's shoulder. Briefly, I described the murder of the Jews in the Ukraine and the circumstances under which I had survived.

The survivors told me that they were natives of Bucharest. Before the war, they had all had reason to travel with their families to the city of Iasi. But the Germans had advanced quickly and captured territories in Romania, leaving no way for the Jews to return home. In Iasi, the Jews were forced into a ghetto and sent to do forced labor in the local quarry. The Germans then rounded up all the able-bodied Jewish men and later they collected the remaining Jews and murdered them. Mrs. Abramov, who had also come from Bucharest, told me her husband and children had been among the Jews murdered by the Germans in Iasi. The others then told me that following the massacre the ghetto leaders had sent the few survivors to the Tiraspol ghetto deep inside Romania.

I tried to maintain contact with these Jews for as long as I could, until one day, they and the ghetto simply disappeared. I searched for them and asked about them, but was never able to discover what had happened to them.

By late summer 1943, there were a number of people still living on the grounds of the canning factory who all knew each other. One day I noticed two young men I hadn't seen before. I was told they were engineers. After work they remained in the factory yard and whenever I saw them they were sitting motionless on a bench. They had all the proper documents and at first their behavior did not arouse suspicion. They seemed to want to strike up a conversation with me and I thought there was nothing odd about them wanting to make friends in a new place. The two engineers knew several languages, but with me they spoke Russian. One was blonde and blue-eyed, the other, who was called Viktor, was dark. They told me they were from Lvov, which had once been under Polish rule, and they had an apartment in Tiraspol. Once I had learned their last names, which were typically Ukrainian, I decided to avoid them; but made sure not to hurt their feelings.

A month later something happened that I didn't understand until later. After work one day I went as usual to visit the Jews in the ghetto and I suddenly met the two engineers from work. Although tired and emotionally drained, I stopped to exchange a few words with them, to avoid suspicion.

Later, on my way back to the house in the factory yard where I lived, I noticed a man lying on a bench near the main gate. It was late and all I wanted was to crawl into bed. I approached and saw that the man's upper body was covered with newspapers; it was Viktor the engineer. Without removing the newspapers, Viktor asked what was happening outside the factory gate. He then pleaded with me not to leave him, because this would be the end of him. I stopped for a while as he asked, but then he started plying me with a myriad of questions that I did not understand at the time: Where had I been? Who had gone with me? Who had I met on the way home? How dare he interrogate me in this way, I thought!

Not far from the bench on which we sat, two women appeared to be taking an evening stroll. One of them was a local German woman from Odessa who was employed in our office as a clerk. She was young and had been given the nickname "Gorilla." The other was older; she was Romanian and came from Bucharest and worked as a nurse in the factory clinic. As far as I knew there was no reason to suspect these two women and there was nothing untoward in their taking an evening stroll in the street. Other people kept their distance from these two women, but I never understood why. It was only later that I learned these women hunted Jews, officially, and were now spying on the new engineers, hoping to hand them over to the SS. Unfortunately, however, I only discovered this after the event.

I casually mentioned the two women nearby and Viktor started to tremble like a leaf in the wind. I advised him to try to get some sleep, because he wasn't looking well. But he straightened quickly and asked me to sit next to him; he said he had something important to discuss with me. In retrospect, I believe he was trying to buy time until darkness fell. He rested one arm on the back of the bench, just behind my back, and I felt very uncomfortable. Was he trying to court me? He mumbled something I didn't understand; something that sounded like, "You are the only one who can help me." I asked him, "Where is your friend?"

"He ran away," Viktor replied. "I have to make a decision, and I'm really struggling. I can't decide if I should tell you what my main problem is." I had no idea what he was talking about, but couldn't help thinking that I had to avoid encouraging another would-be suitor to make my life miserable.

"I don't need friends," I said brusquely. It was late and I wanted to get back to my room; I certainly didn't want to raise his hopes. But Viktor begged me to stay beside him on the bench a little while longer, until he could leave the yard. I capitulated reluctantly, but left as soon as I could.

I didn't sleep well that night and kept mulling over the strange conversation I had had with Viktor. I felt guilty for not having been more attentive and for not having the patience to listen to his confession. Maybe he wasn't just another frustrated suitor after all?

My answer came the following day when everyone was talking about a couple of Jewish engineers who had managed to dodge the authorities and escape at the very last moment! People were amazed to learn that there were still some Jews alive. Painfully I realized that this probably wasn't the first time these men had been forced to run away and I knew how they had to be feeling. I was sorry I hadn't shown more compassion to Viktor the night before. Nor did I ever discover what happened to them. However, my association with the two engineers, however superficial, was sufficient to bring down unexpected and lethal suspicion on my head, too.

After the two Jewish engineers escaped, the factory was visited by members of the secret police, who made a thorough search of the place. Anyone would have thought they had been in the underground, threatening to topple the regime! They arrested me at the beginning of their investigation and wanted to know where the Jews had escaped to. The interrogator told me they knew I had come to work at the factory in order to prepare jobs for other Jews. "We have witnesses who saw you with those Jewish engineers," they said, intimidatingly. "And we now know that you, too, are an escaped Jew from Poland." They threatened to torture me until I revealed my secrets.

The tenuous personal security system I had built over the past few months dissolved in a moment. All the accusations they levied at me confused me and rendered me speechless. I tried to project an image of calm composure; it took all my strength to face them with my back straight. My silence clearly enraged the interrogators, who then listed the various forms of torture I could anticipate at the hands of the SS.

Something inside me rebelled and insisted on fighting for my life. I invited my interrogators to check the records to see that I had moved to Tiraspol from Golta. I admitted having entered Romania illegally, "but the honorable Romanian judges saw fit to release me and signed all the necessary documents to allow me to live anywhere in Romania. Even here, in Tiraspol, I have friends, local Moldavians, who know me from Zhitomir." They immediately asked for and received the address of the Moldavian family, before I added, "And apart from that, you'll be interested to learn that my family has decided to move back to Odessa, where they lived before the war. I intend to go to Odessa myself to join them; I'm tired of living on my own."

They continued to ask me further provocative, intrusive and irritating questions that actually alarmed me. In the end I said, "How dare you accuse me of having sex with those engineers? I have never in all my life had sex with any man." They brought in two physicians to examine me, to see if I was telling the truth. To me this was more humiliating than death. The entire interrogation lasted three whole days, until, to my great relief and surprise, they said I was free to live and work in the factory, on the condition that I did not leave the premises.

They finally released me, but the German clerk and Romanian nurse continued to harass me. "You won't get away from us," they hissed at me. "We're on your case and you may as well know that your days in this world are numbered."

During that period, Rosalia Rosenberg instructed me to work in the office; I was the only one who was trusted to type up the labels that were to be stuck to the cans. When the lunch break arrived I joined the others and left the office. I saw from afar that Rosalia was standing next to her house, surrounded by a number of German officers. The German clerk and Romanian nurse stood nearby, staring at me with unmitigated venom. They watched me approach and I understood that they were testing my reaction. My first instinct, of course, was to run away, but I knew that to do so would have been the worst thing; they had set me a trap. I told myself to relax; that I was no better than my fellow Jews, my family. I had no choice, I was walking towards my death, but I wouldn't lose my dignity. Even in those critical moments, I knew I had to hang on to my humanity. I could barely drag my feet as I walked along the path leading to the Richter home, praying all the while for my death to be immediate, that I would be spared the torture.

Nadia Shevchuk, the Richters' maid, stood on the steps, as I calmly I walked over to Rosalia and hugged her affectionately, as if nothing had happened. I greeted everyone, especially the German soldiers, and stifled a yawn, as I said, "How boring everything is these days." Rosalia replied, "Then here's your chance to do something interesting, at long last! These young men work in the SD Headquarters [security service of the SS]; what interesting lives they lead." The officers laughed at this, each trying to impress me with a different story. Rosalia hugged me again and whispered in my ear, "Look at that nurse, walking circles around us; she's desperate to hear what we're saying. What a revolting woman she is. I hate her! And look over there, that's her friend; she's also spying on us." I realized how lucky I was. Clearly Rosalia, who had just returned from Odessa, was completely ignorant of what had happened in the factory over the last few days! She knew nothing of the Jewish engineers and my interrogation. What a stroke of luck!

We stood in the yard for a while, passing the time. The whole thing seemed quite surreal. On the one hand, I had been held under house arrest by men from the secret police; on the other hand, these men from the SD headquarters were actually flirting with me in the middle of the factory yard, which was full of workers on their lunch break. I was gratified to see Liunev there, too and tried to impress everyone with the fact that I was very friendly with German military headquarters staff. Then the German officers climbed into their army jeeps and I joined them. There wasn't much space in those jeeps and some of the officers had to travel with their legs stuck out of the doors and the windows. Without further ado we sped off.

After a drive of about 60 kilometers we arrived on the outskirts of a town called Dubasari. The town had experienced tremendous destruction and I soon noticed signs that there had once been a flourishing Jewish community here. The jeeps stopped in a part of town that appeared new, with pretty private houses and well-tended gardens. The neighborhood was full of Germans and gave the impression of a small village in Germany. A man of about thirty, dressed in civvies, came to greet us. "We've brought a guest," the officers cried. "See she gets everything she needs." And everyone left.

I was shown into a large house that looked like a hotel and was given a room. I was so tired I could hardly move and felt that this was only the beginning of new torments for me. I had no doubt as to where I was, right inside the lion's den, a place where only Germans lived, a place where no foreigner dared enter. It was clear the SD would never employ me before conducting a thorough examination of my profile.

When I left the room to look for the lavatory I noticed a man in civvies, who didn't leave me alone for a moment and even accompanied me inside. I caught a glimpse of numerous stalls, but most of the doors were closed. I wished I could spend some more time in that corridor, to see what the windows faced, but I didn't want to get into trouble. I returned to my room and stood by the window until dark. I had neither eaten nor drunk all day, not so much as a sip of water. But more than the hunger, it was the uncertainty that tortured me.

Suddenly, a pretty young woman stormed into my room. She told me her name and promptly plonked herself down on the bed. "This room used to be mine," she explained, "but I left about a month ago to visit family in Germany and some other countries. I'm back now, and I'm really glad to be home!" She must have noticed the expression on my face because she said, "I'm so happy to be sharing my room, I hate being on my own." I had no doubt she was simply following orders and that anything I told her would be reported word for word to the Germans. She talked incessantly, mostly nonsense, and when I finally managed to get a word in edgeways, I told her I wanted to sleep. Only then did she tell me that we had to get ourselves ready for a splendid party. This was not what I had in mind! I tried to explain that I was tired from the long drive, that I had brought no luggage and had nothing appropriate to wear, but my excuses fell on deaf ears. It was the department manager's birthday and we were required to attend a banquet in his honor.

At the party I was given a formal welcome and a German army general shook my hand and said, "We are glad to have you here at my birthday banquet." A beautiful girl stood beside him, who I assumed was his daughter. She placed her hand on my shoulder, brought her face close to mine and asked me to tell her my name. I was then ushered to a table, where I was seated between two SD officers. Beside my plate was a beautiful place card with my name on it.

That meal, at which a variety of imported delicacies were served, was truly spectacular. Detailed explanations were given of all the various dishes and, after the first and second courses, there began a fabulous display of cakes, specially shipped in from Germany. The general's many relatives outdid themselves in their sycophantic congratulations, while I didn't forget for a moment that I was in the lion's den. My roommate was very friendly and wanted to know everything about me; she particularly wanted to know how I could have left my family and gone off to a place where I had no one. I told her that I always wanted to live in a place like Tiraspol; I described the wonderful fruits and vegetables that were so readily available in the town and the fascinating job I had managed to find in the canning factory, and the new friends I made who were always there to help me.

The girl insisted I tell her about my family, so I said that although it had been possible to bring my family to Tiraspol and they would have enjoyed a comfortable life there, my sisters decided they wanted to live in a big city like Odessa; and it was for that reason I had to go there, to see if any of my relatives had already arrived. "Now you know all my problems!" I told her confidentially, before asking for her help in finding transportation, because I was in a real hurry to get to Tiraspol. She promised to do her best for me; and I was certain that every word I had said would reach the ears of those who had sent her to spy on me.

I spent a few days there, in that lion's den, anxiously waiting for a signal that I could leave and resume my life. One day I was taken to an office in which only officers worked, and I was asked if I wanted to stay there and work with them. Telling them I needed time to consult with my sisters I tried to devise a way to leave. They told me in the office that there was no transportation for me, and that I would have to wait for "an appropriate opportunity" to leave. I suspected that it was just a ruse.

But, eventually, I did manage to return to the canning factory, surprised and happy to still be alive. I then discovered that an unexpected but welcome consequence of my trip to SD headquarters was that Liunev, who had seen me laughing and joking with the German soldiers in the factory yard and then leaving with them in their jeeps, now seemed to believe my "German boyfriend" story and no longer bothered me. Little did I know that the time would come and he would take his revenge.

The Richters wanted to know if I had 'enjoyed' my visit to SD headquarters and I described the wonderful time I had had with their friends; I was particularly grateful to Rosalia for all her help and told her about the helpful people who had offered me work, which I 'regretfully' was unable to accept since I had decided to go to Odessa to settle some family issues. Rosalia immediately jumped in with, "Oh, but we visit Odessa every week; we'd love to take you with us to visit your family."

My heart dropped; the last thing I wanted was to go to Odessa with the Richters. But the damage was done and I couldn't get out of it. I racked my brain to remember the name of someone I knew in Odessa, fully aware that Richard Richter would ensure that I really did have relatives there. And then I remembered some people I had befriended in the factory, who mentioned having family in Odessa.

I had met these friends one summer's day in 1943, when I thought of checking all the gates in the factory yard to see where they led. One of the doors I knocked on was opened by a couple of about forty. We struck up a very pleasant friendship and I made a habit of visiting them occasionally. The man, who was tall, broad-shouldered and handsome, came from a large well-established Greek family. When they married, he and his Romanian wife had decided not to have children and to live only for themselves. They bought a horse-drawn caravan and set out to see the world, wandering from place to place. They visited foreign countries and lived in the open, rather like gypsies. Whenever their money ran out, they would go to work in a factory for a while and save some money for the next leg of their journey. The couple was happy with their chosen lifestyle and, for many years, had no desire to change it.

They had once told me that they had family in Odessa and, knowing I could trust them, I asked for a huge favor, to which they readily agreed. What I needed was a letter of introduction to the wife's sister in Odessa and a few nights' lodgings. I was touched by their willingness to help me.

On the designated day, I met Richard Richter and his personal chauffeur, but was disappointed that Rosalia would not be joining us. We stood around for a long time beside the expensive car and I noticed uncomfortably that my fellow workers were watching me enviously. They obviously thought that, as a good friend of the Germans, I had influence in high places. But the truth was that I was fighting for my life; I knew the Richters were suspicious of me and it was for this reason that they were taking me to Odessa.

I could never have imagined the day, after liberation and the downfall of Germany, when I would suffer for the false impression I had created; that I would be accused of collaborating with the Germans and rubbing shoulders with the cream of German military society. I was Anna, the Jewish girl who did whatever she did in order to survive.

When we arrived in Odessa Richter insisted on driving me straight to my 'relatives' and asked for their address. I gave him the address I'd received from my Greek friends and prayed for my ruse to work and Richter to leave me in peace; but I was wrong. We reached a charming, quiet neighborhood and the car stopped in front of a one-family house. The driver sang out, "We're here, we've found your relatives!" I knew that these were simple, poor people, and that I had to shake Richter off quickly so he wouldn't discover that my 'relatives' had never met me before. I knocked on the front door and a pleasant woman in her late thirties came out; she was very like her sister in Tiraspol. I introduced myself as a good friend of her relatives and gave her the letter that her sister had written in the Romanian language. I was reserved about telling her I was looking for a place to sleep and that I hoped she would pretend to be a relative of mine. I prayed she would read the letter immediately and understand what was happening, but she didn't and I noticed out of the corner of my eye, that Richter and his driver were inspecting the whole house. My heart sank as, alarmed and embarrassed, I watched the contempt and disdain with which the Germans treated these lovely, simple people. Richter then informed me that he had decided to stay in that house until his business was done.

I was nauseated by the man's boorish effrontery. If Richter, a well-educated man and a wealthy and respectable industrialist behaved this way, what was to be expected from ordinary working-class Germans! I felt so sorry for bringing these Germans into the home of people I had never met and involving them in this subterfuge. The couple was clearly not happy with these uninvited guests and when Richter realized this, he said, "Very well then, the driver can stay at a hotel for Germans." Richter gave the driver instructions as to the tasks he should take care of; and didn't leave me alone for a minute.

I had seen Richter at his most charming, with Rosalia in the Tiraspol factory, and now I was seeing a totally different side to him, a side that was nasty and cunning; as well as behavior that was nothing short of disgusting. He was furious at these simple people for having taken advantage of the annihilation of the Jews by appropriating Jewish property. According to Richter's world view, all property left behind by the murdered Jews belonged exclusively to Germans like himself. He was incensed by the way indigenous populations in German-occupied areas took advantage of Germany's defeats in the battlefield by stealing Jewish property. Throughout the years of the Third Reich, Richter had been a successful manufacturer, wearing elegant clothes and expensive leather gloves, symbols of the superiority and loftiness of the educated German. But now, the real Nazi hoodlum under the smart clothes was revealed for all to see.

My plan was ruined; Richter understood I'd brought him to the home of strangers, and I knew that I had to recreate the impression that I had relatives in this city. What was to be of me, I wondered? I sneaked out of the house in the early morning hours, before anyone else had awakened, made my way to a streetcar, chose a comfortable seat and stared through the window at the streets passing by. So engrossed was I in the sights of this city that I became completely oblivious to what was happening around me. Suddenly, someone was embracing me tightly and smothering me with tearful kisses. A head was resting on mine so I couldn't budge to see who was weeping so bitterly on my face. Someone must have mistaken me for someone else, I thought and said, "Stop this at once!" To my enormous surprise, the person before me was none other than Ira Grigorevich!

I was sure I'd never see this woman again and, what's more, I never wanted to see her either, after all she had done to me. I remembered how cold I had been, and that she hadn't even told me to take extra clothes with me. I had suffered so because of this woman. But I couldn't deny what a stroke of luck this was, meeting her here after telling everyone that I had relatives in Odessa. I was surprised by Ira's appearance; she had changed so much I could hardly recognize her. She had aged and looked unhealthy. Yet I realized that in spite of myself, I still loved her. We hugged and cried without inhibition, each for her own reasons. Ira refused to talk about herself; I couldn't even tell how she supported herself. Where Ira was concerned, I was still that same innocent girl she had brought to the Romanian border. Then on the streetcar, Ira announced that we were going home.

We reached a neighborhood of new-looking houses and Ira, who held a large bundle of keys, opened a door and we walked into a marble stairwell. Ira's building was magnificent and divided into numerous large apartments. All the windows had beautiful curtains and the furniture was probably all in the exact position in which the original owners had placed it. I noticed a large crystal bowl full of different kinds of wristwatches. Ira saw me looking at the bowl and promptly picked one out and handed it to me. I hadn't forgotten Ira's indifferent and hurtful response to my gift—my valuable gold coin—and I reacted in the same way. I didn't care what she thought!

Ira gave me a penetrating look, noting the apathy with which I accepted her gift. She had a sly, cunning look in her eye when she said, "Remember how you said when you gave me your gold coin that you had planned to use it to buy yourself a watch. Well, there you are, now you have a watch in return for your coin." As usual, I said nothing, but saw that Ira was very satisfied with herself for having outwitted me yet again. I looked up and saw dresses and blouses made from the fabrics I had left behind in Zhitomir in the package my mother had prepared for me before I left the ghetto. A sharp pain pierced my heart. How could she have stooped so low? "What nice clothes you have," I said coldly. Ira must have been uncomfortable at being confronted by her duplicity and, after thinking for a moment, she offered me a much-used, worn-out blouse made from one of my materials.

What was her game and why was she playing it? Even Ira couldn't pretend to disregard everything I had done for her and her family, or could she? I had believed the Grigorevich family would never forget everything I had done for them and was horrified at the way Ira could rob without a qualm; although I had learned to shrug when my possessions were stolen, I still could not forget how Ira had dragged me away from Zhitomir on that coal train, dressed in no more than a light summer dress. She had allowed me to suffer and freeze while she herself had taken the trouble to dress warmly; and my own warm clothes had remained behind in Zhitomir. Yet somehow, despite everything, I found it in my heart to be happy to see her.

Ira went for a shower and change of clothes, leaving me alone in the living room with my sad thoughts. Then, who should appear before me out of nowhere, but Mrs. Dusia Koch! In Zhitomir the Kochs had taken an immediate liking to me and had tried to convince me to move in with them, at a time of severe food shortages and there was hardly anything for me to eat in the Grigorevich household. But they had a hidden agenda—they wanted me to marry their son, Anatoli, who was seriously infatuated with me. I was unwilling and had fended off all of Anatoli's advances even when he threatened suicide. Now, I wondered, how would they react to me?

Dusia had not forgiven me and neither had the rest of her family. Mrs. Koch passed her penetrating gaze over me from head to toe and I had the distinct feeling that she was sorry I looked so good. She appeared more than curious about me and clearly wanted to know more about me beyond that revealed in my brief description of my job at the Tiraspol canning factory. And I wanted them all to know that I no longer needed their help and that I could get along on my own. "I have some highly-placed German friends, one of whom brought me here for this visit," I announced. "They have been very good to me in Tiraspol. If you like, I can introduce them to you." Ira swallowed the bait and looked very pleased with my offer; she always wanted to meet people she could take advantage of and said slyly, "Odessa isn't a good place for you, you shouldn't be alone here. Today, I'll take you around and show you the city and then we can go and meet your German friends."

I enjoyed my little outing with Ira, seeing the sights of Odessa and, for the first time, seeing the ocean. Then, late in the evening, we returned to the home of my friend's Romanian relatives. My hostess whispered to me that Richter had spent the day standing by the window, waiting impatiently for my return. I thought this was strange; didn't he say he had urgent matters to deal with in Odessa? Why was he wasting his time waiting for me? Was he afraid I would disappear?

I walked straight over to Richter. "I spent the day with my Odessa family," I said happily, "and now I've brought my big sister Ira to meet you." Richter scrutinized Ira from top to bottom; I could tell from the way he looked at her and from his body language that he was not happy with what he saw. But I thought: It doesn't matter what he thinks of her; the important thing is that I have a prominent German witness who can vouch for the fact that I have relatives and friends in Odessa!

I returned to Tiraspol in a much better frame of mind than when I'd left. Now, no one would dare harass me and accuse me of being a Jew. Yes, indeed, this trip had been the best thing that could have happened. How lucky I was to have met Ira again.

My Greek friends in the factory, who were afraid they might never see me again, were thrilled to see me, especially since I had brought them warm regards from their relatives in Odessa. They were pleased with my account of their relatives' warm and hospitable welcome and said it was time for them to talk to me about something important that they hadn't dared mention earlier.

They told me they loved me as if I were their own daughter; that only after meeting me did they begin to regret never having had children of their own. They realized they were getting older and couldn't continue their nomadic lifestyle indefinitely. In short, they had decided that it was time for them to return to Greece, the husband's homeland, to settle somewhere permanently and begin planning for their old age. But they found it hard to leave me and literally begged me to go to Greece with them. They asked me to move in with them, saying they would care for me as they would their biological child. They told me they had educated, well-placed relatives who could help me get along in life; they offered me everything they had; they said they couldn't leave without me.

I was heavyhearted, knowing I couldn't go with them, tempting as their offer was and I tried hard to explain, as gently as I could, that it was inconceivable for me to go and leave my family behind. The couple decided to postpone their move back to Greece in order to continue trying to persuade me. And I, for my part, was happy they were still nearby. I was extremely fond of them; it was wonderful to have such friends, people who were almost parents to me, who really cared and did their best to help me.

On December 31, 1943, the canning factory held a party to welcome in 1944. The workers waited impatiently for the festivities to begin and there were rumors of lavish food and free liquor. I would have preferred to avoid this party; I knew that when the liquor runs free, there are always people who drink too much and then say and do all kinds of dangerous things. But my friends couldn't understand how I could even consider passing up a fabulous meal and plenty of free alcohol. "You can just eat the food and leave before anyone has a chance to get drunk," they reassured me. I knew how suspicious it would seem if I did not make an appearance, however brief, and agreed reluctantly to go to the party with them. Moreover, the party was to be held in a building near my room so I wouldn't need anyone to take me home when I wanted to leave.

On the day of the party we were all ushered into large halls that were used for special functions. The party was luxurious, as if there were no war and no shortage of food. Many of the guests did not work in the factory and included German military personnel who strolled around, drinking heavily. I began to feel uncomfortable and my friends suggested we put some distance between ourselves and the hall. We found a secluded bench away from the crowds and sat down together. To be honest, I was quite happy to have a decent meal and to be able to eat as much as I wanted. It had been a very long time since I'd had a proper cooked meal.

While still at the table, I noticed a tall, good-looking young man enter the hall. He scanned the room, as if looking for someone. Suddenly, he picked up a chair and came to sit opposite me at the narrow table. I felt acutely uncomfortable but forced myself to ignore him and finish my meal. But he was very persistent and insisted that I drink a toast with him. He introduced himself and started asking me questions. My Greek friends tried to maintain a conversation with me, to show this insolent pest he was not welcome. I knew that if I got up and moved away the man would simply leave with me. In the end, my Greek friend turned to the man and asked, "Why don't you just go off and look for someone else who would really like to be with you? You can see that this girl is not interested in your company and doesn't drink." When there was no reply, he said, "Please leave us alone. Stop harassing this young lady, or you will have to deal with me." The man said nothing and just continued drinking vodka out of a large glass, as if it were water. I was very frightened because he was obviously drunk.

I was even more upset when I discovered that he was the factory's chief engineer. He refused to leave and began telling horrendous stories about his crimes during the German occupation, because he was sure it would continue forever. He was a Russian who had once been a member of the Communist Party and then turned fascist. He had no qualms about betraying his homeland, his family and his friends; indeed, all he wanted was to live an easy life, so he quickly joined the Germans. But by the beginning of 1944, everyone knew about Germany's defeats on the battlefield. Traitors who had crossed the lines and collaborated with the Germans were terrified of falling into the hands of the Russians who had started to liberate some of the occupied cities. This engineer was panic-stricken and said he had to run away before the German army started to retreat back into Germany. I looked at him with utter contempt.

Eventually, our unwanted guest rose from his seat and stood on unstable legs, looking all around him. I hoped and prayed that he was looking for another table to sit at, that he would leave us in peace. But no; suddenly he began to shout at the top of his voice, "My dear friends, we have an enemy among us and she is here to celebrate the fall of the German Reich! This woman is a member of the Communist Youth League, a Komsomolka and she is spying for the partisans. We have to eliminate her before she escapes!"

That foul-mouthed, evil traitor didn't know if the Germans understood him and looked around to see the other guests' reaction. I knew I dared not move and waited in terror for my sentence. But salvation came from an unexpected source: my Romanian friend faced the Russian engineer shouting, "You drunken lout, you worthless piece of trash! How dare you stand here and insult my daughter!" Immediately her Greek husband rose to his feet, grabbed the man by his hair and pulled his head back to expose his bulging neck. The Greek then unsheathed a terrifyingly large homemade knife out of his boot, and roared, "I've sat by and watched you harass my daughter even when I asked you politely to leave us alone and I kept my silence. But this is going much too far, you have humiliated her and now you'll have to deal with me. You are nothing but a common criminal; I should slice open your neck and cut you into little pieces, but I wouldn't want to taint everyone here with your poisonous blood! Just get out of here, you snake, before I finish you off!"

The engineer fell to his knees and, with trembling hands, grabbed my friend's boots and begged for mercy, saying he had drunk too much and didn't know what he was saying. Meanwhile, the drama was being watched by an ever-growing audience, as word quickly circulated about the brave father who had defended his daughter's honor. People came running in from all the rooms to get a glimpse of the excitement, and the 'event' turned into part of the evening's entertainment. People gathered around to support my Greek friend, who was still holding on to the Russian traitor. Everyone shouted, "Kill him, teach him a lesson, kill him!" But my Greek friend was obviously unhappy with the situation; maybe he feared the consequences of killing a friend of the Germans. In any case, he seemed to have loosened his grip on the drunken engineer, who then managed to pull free and scamper off.

I knew that my quick-witted friends had saved me from certain death. I loved them dearly, these true friends, who really cared about me and came to my rescue; not like the Grigorevich family, who cared only for what I could provide them, or the Kochs, with their not-so-hidden agenda. I shall never forget that threatening, homemade knife and the things those people said in my defense. And I knew in my heart that I was truly fortunate to have such patrons; I would never have survived otherwise.

Sadly, our friendship was to be too short because the couple left the factory straight after the New Year party and returned to Greece, as they had planned. I really wished I could join them, but was simply unable to do so. Germany was on the verge of defeat and liberation was on its way; I would return to Korzec, to find out what had happened to my family. Also, my mother had made me promise to take care of my brother, Leon, once the war was over. Parting from them was painful, and I have never forgotten those wonderful people.

The canning factory ceased to operate in early 1944, shortly after the big party. Huge German trucks drove into the yard and took away all the merchandise from the warehouses. The machines and equipment were next to disappear from the factory's different departments. Finally, experts arrived to work around the clock dismantling anything that could be taken back to Germany. A little later the company's director, Richard Richter and his mistress, Rosalia, left quickly.

All at once my life took a turn for the worse, when my job and its attendant security were taken from me. During that period of instability and uncertainty there were no jobs to be had and I had nothing to live on; I had no food and lived only on water, tormented by constant hunger. I knew that liberation was nigh, but in the meanwhile I had to find something to eat. Then one day, as I passed through the market, I realized that I had luck, after all. The market was where I would look for blemished or rotting vegetables to keep myself alive.

At least I had a place to stay. I still had my room and Marusia and her son Kolia continued to live in the kitchen; they, too, probably had nowhere else to go. Marusia continued to visit her relatives and bring back baskets of food. The woman always seemed to have money and food and was the only one to use the oven.

We continued living in that house that had once been used by the director, Valeri Liunev. Unfortunately for me, that man did not run away like the others, although he did at least move into the Richter's house. But I was still wary of him and gave him a wide berth; especially now the factory was deserted. I tried to avoid Liunev and prayed he wouldn't have the nerve to enter my room; he hadn't done so before, after all.

I returned from the market one night at midnight with some vegetables I had managed to forage. My mind was working furiously, planning ways to survive until liberation. Suddenly, there was gentle knocking on the door; this was most unusual as no one ever came to visit me. I got up from bed to open the door. Liunev was standing there in the corridor, smiling at me like an old friend. I had a very bad feeling.

The crafty fox was grinning like a bashful schoolboy, as if he felt bad about bothering me at that time of night. I glared at him; what did he want from me? He was very polite, even apologetic, but he had some important German visitors who were in need of a translator and begged me to come to his new house for just a few minutes. What could I have done? I wanted to refuse and slam the door in his face. But we both knew that he could throw me onto the street any time he wanted. I had antagonized him enough with my stories of a German boyfriend. Now I knew I had to watch my step. I had no choice. With a sigh, I followed him to Richter's house nearby.

Outside the house I could see no sign of any visitors, but in the living room, I was introduced to a tall, barrel-chested young German major, who proceeded to converse with Liunev. He was the only guest. I translated everything they said, then the major smirked at me. It occurred to me suddenly that the man understood Russian and that they had prepared a trap for me. I tried to excuse myself, but the two had clearly set this 'visit' up well in advance. It transpired that Liunev and his German friend had been spying on me collecting rotten vegetables in the market and ravenously eating wilted cabbage leaves; they knew how hungry I was. Now they showed me a table groaning under the weight of delicious food, but insisted that we begin our meal with some wine.

They must have been sure that someone as hungry as I was would fall on their food, but they were mistaken. I still had my pride and my self-respect. I was strong, with a great deal of self-control and no amount of hunger was going to break me in front of these German beasts. I didn't touch their food or their wine and racked my brain for an elegant excuse to get out of this situation and continue living in my room.

Suddenly, Liunev sprung up and raced out the door, locking it behind him. That contemptible villain had known me for quite a long time, but he did not see fit to spare me. He had gone out and left me locked up inside his house with a drunken German officer. But I was determined not to let that creature see any evidence of the tempest raging within me; I tried to relax and think clearly. Having visited Rosalia in this house on many occasions, I was familiar with every room, every nook and cranny. I searched for an excuse to leave and make an escape through the bedroom window. But, despite his drunkenness, the German officer had his wits about him and did not leave me alone for a minute. For the time being, he even continued to treat me politely. He stroked my hair and asked me to sit next to him. I pretended to be patient and civil with him, stalling for time. When I asked where he'd learned Russian, he told me that everyone in the intelligence service had to learn foreign languages. As I tried to devise a plan to get out of there, he mumbled something about spying.

He then held my head between his hands, and sniffed at my hair as if I was a flower.

This was when I made my exit, saying, "I'm terribly sorry, but I absolutely have to use the lavatory, immediately." In the bathroom I closed the door and opened the tap, then started climbing out through the small window, impressed with my own ingenuity and tenacity.

Once outside, I ran like a mad woman through the factory's many departments looking for a place to hide, but finding nothing. Where was I to go now? Suddenly, in the corner of one room, I noticed a narrow staircase leading to a loft. I raced up the stairs and found a nut-processing plant that I'd never seen before! By now, only nutshells remained, but the floor was littered with piles of apricot kernels and tools for cracking them. For me this was a golden opportunity – I had found shelter and food to quiet my hunger. Then, I noticed that this loft had a large wall-to-ceiling window overlooking the middle of the yard; perfect for keeping track of all the comings and goings below.

I continued hiding in that nut-processing plant, all the time trying to think of my next move. Obviously, I couldn't spend the rest of my life in hiding. Hopefully that vile Liunev and his German friend had forgotten all about me and were entertaining themselves elsewhere. I decided to run back to my room before dark and was relieved to find Marusia and her son Kolia in the kitchen. Marusia was happy to see me, but her news troubled me. "Some German officer is looking for you," she said casually. "Oh, and another thing, Liunev told me to stop locking the front door from the inside. He wants to be able to come and go as he pleases." This was a very bad sign, but I said nothing. I was very tired, but where could I sleep? At first, I got into bed in my clothes, listening carefully to any unusual sounds. As soon as I heard steps, I ran quietly into the kitchen and hid under Marusia's bed.

This nightmare continued for several days and nights. The German officer returned a number of times looking for me, and my nights on the freezing floor under Marusia's bed, with no sheets or blankets, continued. I was even afraid to change position so as not to irritate Marusia, who occasionally glanced at me under her bed. I knew that curiosity was preventing her from getting much sleep, but I was afraid to tell her about Liunev's involvement in my predicament.

Marusia realized something was going on and confided in her friend, Nadia Shevchuk. The two had known me since my first days in the factory and we were on good terms; they had also been aware of my earlier trouble with Liunev. When the German officer came looking for me day and night and I took to sleeping under Marusia's bed, they connected the dots and understood that I was in trouble. Without my knowing it, they decided to join forces and help me. Having lost my faith in mankind, I didn't even confide in them. I also tried to hide my hunger and suffered in silence. Every morning I would leave to spend the day hiding in the nut-processing plant, eating apricot kernels and drinking water. My stomach began to swell and I developed stomach pains, which after a few days had become unbearable. I knew I needed help, but where could I turn?

Then I remembered the Moldavian family who lived in Tiraspol. They had helped me in the past and were always happy to see me. I mustered all my courage and paid them a visit, taking with me the watch I had received from Ira, which I decided to offer them in exchange for their help.

On my way over, I was aware of Liunev and his German friend stalking me. I was horrified to see how low these men had fallen. Was I the only woman in the world that they had to make my life hell? Had they nothing better to spend their time on, than stalk me day and night? Had I survived the entire German occupation only to fall victim to these repulsive creatures, with liberation just around the corner?

This had to end, somehow. But I had few options; I dared not continue to the home of my Moldavian friends because these scoundrels would then know where they lived. I also dared not go back. On the verge of despair, I looked around for some kind of refuge.

Suddenly, I saw a girl I had once been friendly with in the factory. She was the oldest child in a refugee family, who had taken a liking to me and had sometimes invited me to her home. She was about 17, pampered and good-spirited; her family lacked nothing. She had tried to persuade me to join the German club and go out with her in the evenings. It was from her that I learned about the anti-Jewish atrocities in the Crimea. She was quite open about the carnage her father had carried out in the city of Kherson and bragged of his successes under the occupation and the lavish lifestyle her family enjoyed as a result.

Here on the street, the girl was happy to see me and hugged and kissed me, as if I were a long lost friend. She immediately invited me to her family's new home, which I saw as an excellent opportunity to rid myself of those persistent German leeches. But, as soon as the visit was over and I left the house, I noticed them still lurking outside.

I was nearing the end of my tether, but I had a plan. I would go straight to Marusia's room and play with her son. Then I'd ask her to help me slip outside unseen. The factory yard had an exit to an open field that had a path leading toward the home of my Moldavian friends. But, of course, nothing went according to plan.

As soon as I opened the front door I saw Marusia and her son waiting for me, together with some unexpected visitors. It had been a month since I'd seen or heard from Nadia Shevchuk and here she was, together with a German soldier. They seemed very happy to see me and sighed with relief that I had finally returned. I had no idea what it was all about.

The German soldier, whom I was seeing for the first time in my life, told me he had been waiting for me all day and that I had to pack my bags quickly because we had to leave. He appeared worried and said he had been absent from his factory for too long and he really had to be going. I was astonished and no one was about to explain! The soldier suddenly remembered a sandwich he had brought for me. It consisted of two slices of bread on either side of a large meat cutlet and an enticing smell that can't be described in words. Still, despite my hunger, I looked at that sandwich with indifference. Everyone begged me not to be ashamed to eat it, but I just stood there motionless. What was going on?

The soldier must have realized I was in shock because he became very solicitous and treated me like a sick child. "I run an abattoir," he explained patiently. "We employ a large number of German soldiers, as well as many Russian-speaking locals and we have been unable to find an interpreter. Which is why we need you."

How had this happened? How was he connected to Nadia? Apparently, when the canning factory closed, Nadia had married an engineer and gone to live with her husband's family. He and his brothers worked in the abattoir and had heard that their boss was looking for a translator. Nadia remembered me and made the connection, telling the Germans about a friend who had been a translator at the canning factory and was now unemployed. The general manager had actually left his busy factory and come in person to offer me a job and discuss my terms of employment. This was how Marusia and Nadia helped me, although I never asked them! I was extremely touched.

Anyone else would have jumped at the chance, but I was in no hurry to accept. Instead, I wanted to take advantage of the offer to ask for work in the abattoir, rather than in the office. I could see the three looking at each other angrily, wondering how it was possible to reject an office position and ask instead for hard dirty work on the factory floor? Suddenly, the German soldier straightened himself to his full height and informed me in no uncertain terms, "We have enough production workers; what they need is a translator, and you have to help them." I understood that I had better not push my luck.

CHAPTER 11

Still No End to the Suffering

The abattoir was only four kilometers away from my room in the canning factory, but still they sent a soldier with a wagon drawn by two horses to collect me and my luggage. Nadia and I sat side by side in the wagon, our arms around each other, talking quietly. She told me she thought about me all the time and really wanted to help me. I had always been very fond of Nadia and enjoyed being her friend; I loved her self-confidence and her stories. However, I was terribly reserved about expressing my feelings and was never able to tell her outright how much I loved and appreciated her. Nadia was intelligent and quick witted, with a natural ability to take care of herself as well as others. I must admit that I quite envied her social skills and talent for always being in the center of things and thoroughly informed on current events and local gossip. Before the war Nadia had been the canning factory's head bookkeeper. Under the German occupation, however, she had opted for a less responsible job that provided more access to basic commodities. She accepted the post of housemaid to the Richters and it was there that I met her; we became instant friends. When Rosalia and Richard were frantically liquidizing their interests and transferring products from the factory to Germany, clever Nadia took advantage of the chaos and confusion to take home numerous packages of food. Quite naturally, Nadia had no existential problems.

We soon arrived at the village Kolka-Tova-Balka, which Nadia called home. I was taken to a beautiful home owned by the Semionov family. The yard, which was surrounded by a fence, contained a large storage shed, a cowshed and a pigsty. I was quite surprised to see that the owner and his wife, Klara, were a young couple with two small boys. They seemed overjoyed to have me live with them and I was delighted with my large, very clean room. Just across the road from the Semionov home was the abattoir, where each night, large numbers of livestock were brought; the German laborers worked at an extraordinary pace, but the work was never-ending. Whenever the German army was forced to retreat from a specific area, soldiers were sent to rob all the livestock in that area and brought it directly to this abattoir, which was also a meat-processing plant. They shipped the finished products to Romania in trucks, and then on to Germany. I noticed that sometimes the soldiers brought eggs, chickens and even pork to that abattoir; perhaps it was for the workers.

On my first day at the plant, I was met by Captain Neumann, who escorted me to work every morning and then back home at the end of the day. I discovered that this German officer had no connection whatsoever to the factory. After walking me home after work, he'd sit with me on the porch until the Semionovs turned on the lights inside, then we'd go into the kitchen and chat with the family, even though none of them spoke German. At first, I assumed that Neumann was happy to spend time talking to the Semionovs because he missed his own family but I soon learned that I, not the Semionovs, was the true focus of his attentions and that he had serious intentions toward me.

One morning, when I was leaving the house, I ran into Mr. Semionov who was about to shovel snow off the path. All of a sudden, my watch fell off my wrist, right into the snow. I quickly bent down to look for it, but Mr. Semionov laughed and told me not to worry, I could go to work and he would return the watch later, when he'd finished shoveling the snow. I didn't really believe him and suspected that he was the kind of person who would never relinquish anything of value that had fallen into his hands and, unfortunately, I was right. Despite all his promises, I never saw that watch again. This incident was very painful. How could I have let such a thing happen to me, when I was always so careful and responsible? And how could my charming landlord steal something so precious from me and then continuously lie about it?

I had treasured that watch because knowing that someone like me, alone and living on my wits, needed at least one item of value that could be sold in return for food, if necessary. If I lost my job, I would have nothing to eat until I found another one and that watch was my guarantee against starvation. Even when I was really hungry, after the closing of the canning factory, I did not sell the watch because experience had taught me that I might one day have to face even worse times; if, for example, I was forced to leave my present accommodation. I was very distressed at having 'lost' my only item of value.

I was aware that Captain Neumann did not like my landlord and suspected him of being less than honest and when he heard that my watch had 'disappeared,' he was so outraged that he took off his own watch and placed it around my wrist. Of course, I refused at first to accept such an expensive gift from a man who was courting me, but he tried to convince me by saying, "If my intentions towards you were not honorable, I wouldn't be so quick to part with a new watch that I bought only two months ago in Switzerland."

I gave the matter some thought and came to the decision that I could not afford to miss such a rare opportunity of acquiring something as valuable as this. I knew all about hunger, exposure and bitter cold, and I needed to avoid needless suffering in the future. So it was, with a heavy heart, that I agreed to wear the German officer's watch, despite the guilt and self-blame it caused.

A few days later, before I'd even had a chance to quiet my conscience. Captain Neumann surprised me with several necklaces. I was dismayed and thought sadly that after I had accepted his watch he must think I'm one of those women who takes advantage of men. The thought burned like a fire inside me, and I said quietly, "Oh, how lovely these necklaces are, but I don't wear jewelry; I'm not mature enough." He was wise and intelligent and understood me perfectly. Once again he assured me that his intentions were nothing but honorable. I knew that after the German withdrawal we would never meet again and I didn't want to leave him with a bitter taste from our relationship. On the other hand, I didn't want him to remember me as one who exploited then ran, because I really wasn't like that. Still, the awfulness of my life overrode everything and I knew that if I stayed alive, I could expect more suffering. I accepted the necklaces sadly. For years afterwards I was sorry I had.

CHAPTER 12

The Germans Retreat

Six kilometers from where I worked, to the back of the village of Kolka-Tova-Balka, there was a hill, surrounded on all sides by wasteland. It was in this mountain that the Germans stored the munitions they used at the battlefront. Captain Neumann was in charge of these munitions and he often took me with him when a shipment was due to be dispatched. One day, when he was on his way home, a jeep full of soldiers stopped him and asked him to hurry and provide them with some urgently needed ammunition. Instead of tending to them immediately, he went to pick me up from the abattoir and took me with him. He spoke to me in his usual soft, relaxed voice, as if nothing unusual was happening. Within minutes I found myself in the jeep looking at the frantic soldiers and I began to understand a few things.

Neumann drove quickly and I sat quietly, listening to the men discussing defeats and casualties in the battlefield. We reached the hilltop and while the soldiers were busy loading the ammunition, I stood gazing at the beautiful view below and the myriad of colorful sparks rising up from the earth. It looked as if the sparks were covering the entire hill, literally beneath my feet. I was sure that Neumann had already removed the explosives from the part of the mountain on which we stood; I knew he'd never allow me to walk around here if it was dangerous.

At long last, the soldiers finished loading their truck and drove off, heavy-hearted, toward the front. Those unfortunates didn't even try to hide their fear. It was the winter of 1944, the Germans had withdrawn from Crimea and on the eastern front the war was becoming extremely vicious, with heavy losses on all sides.

At work one day, someone noticed a long convoy of wounded German soldiers making its way past us. Everyone rushed to the window and, transfixed, watched as the miserable parade made its way back from Germany's latest defeat on the battlefield. It was a horrendous sight and it was not hard to imagine the hell from which they had returned. I have to admit that although I did not lose sight for one second that they were my enemies, the same people who had destroyed everything that was dear to me, and that my own life was still in danger, still it pained me to see the suffering of those German soldiers and I knew that if I could have, I would have helped them unhesitatingly.

How strange it was that I could pity those German soldiers, when they had had no compassion for my family and my nation? But what I now saw were young men who had unwittingly been transformed into unfortunate, wretched invalids, barely able to stand up. We stood there gazing in horror at that string of broken men; how low had those false heroes fallen? Many were barefoot and bareheaded, although it was winter and very cold; their uniforms were torn and filthy, like rags pulled out of the garbage; some of them were missing a sleeve or part of their pants, while others wore only bandages on their naked chests. There were those who had both eyes bandaged and had to be led by others.

How hard it was to believe that these were the same Germans I'd seen at the beginning of the occupation, when they had been arrogant and puffed up with pride and hubris, bragging about their omnipotence and invincibility; masters of the universe. I never thought I would see with my own eyes how the mighty German army would roll gradually into the abyss.

The Germans I worked with in the abattoir were clearly jealous of Captain Neumann and were constantly making fun of him for behaving like a love-struck schoolboy. My employers were displeased with Neumann because, at a time of national crisis, he appeared to care only for me. When I discovered that Neumann had told them about his serious intentions toward me I understood why the Germans treated me as if I was one of them. On one occasion I heard them surreptitiously accusing Neumann of being insensitive towards his fellow Germans who were less educated than he and had no profession. Neumann was the only son of a highly respected, well-to-do professor in Berlin; he, himself, was a renowned lecturer with an international reputation. According to factory gossip all he cared for was his girlfriend and was planning a future away from his homeland.

Whenever we were alone together, Neumann spoke about the present situation and about himself and his family. I didn't even look in his direction and was as silent as a lamb. What could I say to this German who had fallen in love with me without knowing who I really was? Naturally enough, he expected me to talk about myself or to ask him about himself, but, seeing no reaction, he said sympathetically, "I understand. You feel that wartime is not the right time for us to discuss each other or make plans for our future." Neumann talked about his military service and his disappointment at having to remain in Kolka-Tova-Balka until the end, when the place would be evacuated of all the Germans. Captain Neumann was convinced that he and I were kindred spirits and sought every opportunity to be alone with me, when his face would light up with happiness. I sometimes wondered what Neumann's Hitler would have to say about this forbidden passion for a Jewish girl?

Neumann told me this was his last army job and if everything went well, he'd soon be free to spend all his time with me.

"I plan to take you to London," he whispered. "Everything will be wonderful, I promise; in London, we'll forget all our troubles." I had the impression that England was his second home and that he felt comfortable there.

Neumann was worried at the thought of my leaving Kolka-Tova-Balka alone; the area was full of partisans waiting for the chance to attack the retreating German forces. He told me the partisans were very likely to avenge themselves on me because I had worked for Germans. "Even others, like your landlord Semionov who collaborated with the Germans, are likely to attack the retreating Germans in order to curry favor with the new Russian rulers." This was something new to consider: that I might be singled out as having been sympathetic to the Germans, the people who murdered my family.

Of course, I said nothing.

One day, Neumann came to tell me of a plan he had for me. Apparently, his commander had managed to escape from Crimea with his Russian wife and they were now resting in Neumann's house. Very cautiously, he told me, "I would like you to come to my house tonight to meet them." I gave him a questioning look and he told me his plan. "I want to send you away from here with these friends of mine. I want to spare you the dangers of the official German retreat." I didn't know where Neumann lived and didn't ask, because I had no intention of going to his house or escaping anywhere with his friends. It was totally inconceivable that I, a Jew who had survived the Holocaust, whose life was still in danger, could escape with the Germans. I had to get myself out of this situation, but how? In the end I had no choice and Neumann took me to his home, which, I was surprised to discover, was quite near my own. The beautiful new villa was surrounded by a well-tended garden. A young woman received me at the door, angrily telling me that there was no room to include me in the journey because of all the luggage. I was very relieved for her help in extricating myself elegantly from an impossible situation.

Neumann listened to our conversation; of course he expected me to discuss my personal issues. For the first time, he asked me what my reason was for not wanting to leave this place. He was sure I had parents and that our relationship was very deep. I saw how sharp and clever this man was and I was afraid of him. I weighed thoroughly the answers that ran through my mind, knowing that this time I would have to provide a special response. I told him that I had always been an only child and that my parents now lived in Siberia. Neumann said happily that this was not a problem, that we could turn to international organizations, which would help us find my parents; I had nothing to worry about, so long as I realized that I had to be evacuated together with the Germans. He tried to persuade me that things under the Russians were extremely grim and that before retreating from a region, the Germans did their best to cause as much damage as possible to the infrastructure, which has terrible consequences among the local population. He informed me that they destroy sources of energy, bridges, factories, rail tracks; they even take away all the local horses so as to leave behind no means of transport. He explained that this was the best way to cause havoc within the enemy ranks and painted a very bleak picture of what was likely to happen to me if I stayed on alone in Kolka-Tova-Balka, without work and with no source of income. He warned me repeatedly not to trust my landlords, the Semionovs. Once we are gone, he warned me, these people will throw me into the street.

I knew he was genuinely concerned about me, I also knew that he was right and I was at risk in Kolka-Tova-Balka; it was time for me to quietly leave the town for good. I would take with me the expensive watch, which I would sell in order to put food in my mouth until liberation. I was careful, though, to keep my face impassive; Neumann was watching my reactions and facial expressions closely. But as usual, I had nothing to say. I didn't want him to be angry with me, nor could I tell him the truth.

Neumann had told me of the decision to blow up the arsenal he was responsible for and that he was very sorry he would be unable to be with me during those difficult moments. He begged me to join the Semionovs in their basement while the explosives were going off. He also advised Mr. Semionov to remove all the windows and doors and store them in the stable, wrapped in hay, so they would not be damaged.

At the designated hour, when everyone else was in the basement waiting for the nightmare to be over, I insisted on staying in bed, in the house that was now exposed on all sides, listening apathetically to ear-splitting explosions. My mind went back to the distant past, when I was still surrounded by a large, devoted family. I told myself that the long-awaited liberation was just around the corner, and soon I would be free again.

But there was nowhere and no one for me to return to. I knew that my family was lost to me forever. There was nothing left for me to live for. The long-awaited German defeat had come and there was nothing else to keep me alive. I was so immersed in my thoughts that I did not notice a jeep pulling up beside the house and someone running along the path. Suddenly, Neumann was in the doorway, drenched in sweat and barely able to stand up. He seemed utterly exhausted and unable to speak. We exchanged glances and he smiled at me. There was something very moving in his glance and it was then that I finally understood something—this man really loved me. His visits were not just a way to while away the time; he wanted to marry me. I felt a sharp, stabbing pain. But then I thought, what would he say if he knew that I was one of those people his government had vowed to annihilate?

I jumped out of bed and ran to the yard and then to the street. In the sky three Russian fighter planes were spewing fire. Neumann ran after me and tried to calm me, pleading with me to come back in before I got myself killed. He didn't understand my crazy behavior; in all honesty, neither did I. Suddenly, he shouted up to the skies, "Are you insane? Are you trying to get yourself killed or seriously wounded?" I had always been afraid of injury and this warning immediately returned me to sanity.

We sat on the open porch, as shrapnel fell onto the roof of the house. I understood that Neumann had decided he had to desert his job in order to become my guardian angel. At the first opportunity, Neumann invited me to tour the area we lived in. Next, he took me to Tiraspol and went straight to the elite residential neighborhood. I saw places I had never seen before. Then he told me that he wanted to visit some fellow German officers. We went from house to house and were told, each time, that the Germans had all run away! In the middle of a deserted street Neumann, disappointed and dejected, stood and chain-smoked. From the corner of my eye, I noticed people peering at us from behind closed curtains. It was as if they had imposed a curfew on themselves to allow the Germans to retreat quietly, unnoticed. Neumann waited for a miracle; for a lone German to materialize. I still had no idea why Neumann had brought me there; it was only about seven kilometers from where I lived. At that moment, however, we were both deep in our respective thoughts.

Suddenly, someone appeared on the street; I recognized him immediately as the young man who had saved me from drowning myself in the river, when I was new and depressed in Tiraspol. It was he who dragged me out of the water and suggested I ask for a job at the canning factory! He had tried to befriend me, but I had brushed him off and we had parted ways because I was too stupid to understand the value of friendship. And now, here he was again, as if from nowhere. He was standing on the steps to his house; when he saw me he froze as if he couldn't believe his eyes. He obviously couldn't believe he was seeing me in such an upper-class neighborhood accompanied by a German officer. He may even have regretted saving my life. I stared at him, unable to move. Only a few meters separated us; his accusing look said more than a thousand words. That look hurt me and I wished I could have defended myself, but how could I, when I was clearly with that German officer, who was beginning to suspect something, too.

Again I wondered how I could have rejected such a valuable friendship, one that might have prevented so much hardship. I was very upset by this sudden encounter and wished I could run away; but I was not alone. Eventually, the young man turned his back to me and walked into his house.

After a long pause, Neumann started to talk; this intelligent, tolerant and sensitive man was furious. "For years," he told me, "we were convinced that the German soldier was incomparably courageous and heroic, but it's a fake, a lie; it's become apparent lately that German officers can't face defeat and difficulties, they are only good for parades! Look at how these officers have behaved; they are the first to run away in terror. And if that's the case, what can be expected of the rank and file?"

We returned to Kolka-Tova-Balka and Neumann stayed a while, lit a cigarette and looked at me piercingly; he was pleased with me for my stoic behavior. Later, I thought about that strange excursion, and concluded that Neumann had intended to send me with his German friends, but had left it too late. He then wanted to test my stamina; perhaps he wanted to take me away with him on foot. I knew I had to do something to avoid having to leave with the Germans, but what?

Neumann spent every moment he could with me and was informed of everything I did. As the withdrawal approached, the Germans were edgy and suspicious, so I had to be extremely cautious. I knew that if I were to secretly leave, Neumann would be very upset and insulted. He would suspect me and he was not the kind of man to give up easily. Having no better plan, I decided to simply go up to the attic and hide in the hay, until an opportunity arose to quietly disappear. If worse came to worst, they'd search and find me in the attic, and I could say I was unwell and had wanted to rest. But, as usual, nothing went according to plan.

One evening, Neumann informed Mr. Semionov that he would be spending the night in his house. My room was large, with a number of windows on both walls. Two large, heavy wooden beds stood in an L shape, but there was still some space between them. Neumann opened the two doors of my room and there, in the adjacent room, slept the landlord and his family.

The officer then removed his boots and lay down on the unoccupied bed in my room. But he didn't sleep all night; I heard him sighing and tossing about nervously from side to side. I pretended to sleep but instead, I watched secretly as he chain-smoked, tiny bulbs of light illuminating his worried face. I wondered how he would react to the kind of humiliation and severe beatings I had experienced, and having to live every day under the threat of death. Occasionally, Neumann went out to the yard and spoke quietly with men there. I tried to listen, but I heard only snippets of conversation. I understood that the house was being guarded by soldiers.

Even before dawn he was pacing around the room before finally announcing, "You're not sleeping either, let's go outside." He took me to his villa, which was lit up by numerous lamps. The place was crammed full of military personnel; no one seemed surprised to see me and accepted me as one of them. It was obvious that they, too, had not slept all night. The officers were examining maps and documents; occasionally they consulted with Neumann. I was glad he was busy, while I was in the entrance hall with the soldiers, considering my options.

Oh, what a strange world; I didn't know whether to laugh or cry. Here was I, the Jew who escaped the ghetto, waiting for the right moment to get away, with Germans who had wreaked destruction on my own family! I thought if Father were to see me now, he would throttle his beloved daughter with his own hands. I hated myself for my stupidity and for not anticipating in time where it would all lead.

But, unfortunately, it was too late to do anything to change the situation. My mind was working furiously to devise a plan for getting out of there. Neumann was busy and I said to some soldiers that I couldn't bear sitting in one place for so long and that I would love to step outside, to breathe some fresh air for a little while. The soldiers had no objection and kept the dogs away, to allow me to slip out.

Once outside, I knew it was important that none of the other Germans noticed me from any of the adjoining rooms. It was very early, all the locals were still asleep and the street was empty. I fled from yard to yard like a bird on the wing, with no plan or destination. I had to avoid meeting anyone. Suddenly, Nadia Shevchuk came out of the stables across the road and ran toward me. The last thing I needed was for a neighbor to testify to having seen me making off in this or that direction, but there was nothing I could do. Nadia and her engineer husband worked for the Germans in the abattoir and she was always abreast of the latest gossip and knew everyone. I decided to tell her that Neumann wanted to take me abroad with him. Nadia immediately responded that no one could take me anywhere because she wouldn't allow it! I thought she was joking and started to move away, but Nadia grasped my arm and said it was dangerous outside and that I should go to their stables. She told me that Neumann had lived in her area for quite a while and everyone knew him. He had a girlfriend with whom he'd had a close relationship, but when we met, he tried to keep that fact from me.

At that early hour Nadia's large family was already congregated in the stable; they all looked worried. Nadia told me that her brother-in-law had been taken prisoner by the

Germans at the beginning of the war and, fortunately for him, had managed to escape and make his way home. However, to the German authorities, his escape had turned him into a criminal. The family, fearing that the neighbors might inform on him, had sent him to stay with relatives in another village. Now that the Germans were retreating through the villages and pillaging every house on their way, it was dangerous for him to stay there and he was brought back home, despite the risks involved.

Throughout the night, the family had been busy digging a large bunker under the spot on which their cow stood, that would serve as a hiding place for the escaped prisoner. By the time I arrived, they were closing the bunker with wood planks and covering the area with dirt and straw. They then returned the cow to her place and now no one would be the wiser. The only problem was that they didn't know how to dispose of all the dirt they had removed from the ground. But they were all happy that I would be staying in the shelter with their dear brother. All my life I have found myself facing *faits accomplis*, which have always come as a complete surprise. This time was no different.

Inside the shelter, I could hear the heavy breathing of the animal above. I couldn't see my 'roommate's' face, but his behavior was unbearable. He strode up and down the confined space and lit one cigarette after another; I thought I was going to suffocate from the smoke. I became dizzy and nauseous and held my hand over my mouth so as not to start coughing.

Deep in the shelter, I could hear loud blasts of explosives. I knew immediately that the Germans were blowing up houses. I also heard shots being fired from German rifles.

Although much older than me, the man broke down and completely lost control; his behavior was embarrassing. He kept grinding his teeth, stamping his feet, banging his fists against the walls and even smashing his face into the ground. I think the shelter was too small for him and he was looking for more space. I was worried he'd start screaming and run outside. There were moments when I thought our end had come. I knew there were men walking around outside; I could hear the sound of their army boots. Someone opened the stable door and removed the cow that stood above us. For some reason, I thought they were capable of setting fire to the straw and wood in the stable. They were very tense moments, but luckily everything ended well.

I must admit that I was proud of myself for being able to stay in control and maintain my human instincts. I won't insinuate that I was a hero, but, if it was impossible to change the situation, at least I could prevent myself from reaching rock bottom.

It was after midnight when members of Nadia's family arrived to open the shelter and let us out. We learned that there were no more Germans in the vicinity. Nadia told me that they had come to look for me before they left. I looked at Nadia's large family enviously.

I remained in their yard, not knowing where to go at such a late hour. It was no longer possible to start walking to Tiraspol, looking for people I knew. In our area, everything was in chaos. I looked terrible; there was no way I could appear like this among people who didn't know what I had been through during the last twenty-four hours. But I had a plan. Once I had washed and changed, I decided I would approach a Tiraspol family and offer them my expensive watch in exchange for food and lodgings, until such a time as Zhitomir was liberated. I would then rejoin the Grigorevich family in Zhitomir.

But right then, I needed a place to stay for the night and I had no choice but to return to the dishonest Semionovs. Mr. and Mrs. Semionov were stunned by my appearance; in fact, they looked at me as if I was a ghost. They asked me where I had been and told me that Neumann had burst into their house brandishing a gun, looking for me. I explained vaguely that I had stayed with neighbors for the last few hours. They didn't even ask if I'd had anything to eat or drink.

I couldn't wait to shower. I had lived in this house for quite a while and got along well with everybody in it, so I didn't suspect a thing. I was shy and felt very uncomfortable when Klara kept walking around me, under various pretexts. When I stepped out of the shower I couldn't find the expensive watch Neumann had given me to compensate for the one Mr. Semionov had picked up and kept after it fell in the snow. No one was able to say where it had disappeared to during those minutes that I had been in the shower. And, as if to add insult to injury, they had the nerve to pretend to be offended by me. Semionov said in a somber voice that it was inconceivable for something to simply disappear in his house. I felt distinctly unwelcome in this house and now I was facing a new set of unexpected problems.

How could I ask acquaintances for food and shelter, when I had nothing left to offer them in return? I knew that my troubles were just beginning, but they were actually worse than I thought. But I was so tired that I couldn't think of a solution.

I didn't dare enter my bedroom and searched for somewhere else where I could he down. Suddenly, a huge battle broke out and the air was filled with the ear-splitting noise of explosions. The Semionovs raced into the cellar and I went to the yard to see what was happening. I wanted to witness with my own eyes the arrival of the first liberating Russian forces; it was a moment I had waited so long for. The Semionov house stood on a hill overseeing much of the town and there wasn't a soul on the streets. I watched the shells cutting through the sky, lighting up the heavens and knew that no one would be able to sleep on a night like this.

After a while, Klara and her husband joined me and behaved as if nothing was wrong. Mr. Semionov explained that the Germans had dug themselves in on the other side of the Dniester River and were fighting to prevent the Russians from entering the Tiraspol area. The young Semionovs were a happily married couple and they stood beside me embracing each other; occasionally they kissed. They had every reason to be happy; they had stolen my expensive watch.

As I was about to re-enter the house, I noticed a soldier striding toward me. He came closer and I noticed that he was young, very short and dark and wearing the uniform of the Russian army. He was bareheaded and very dirty; he looked exhausted. To me, he represented liberty; freedom from the German occupation. I wanted to kiss his boots and scream at the top of my lungs to release the pain and suffering of all those years.

The Russian soldier asked where the Germans were. He was hunched over and trembling with fear; I tried to reassure him by saying that the Germans had left long ago and he had no reason to worry. As I looked at this poor soldier I thought, if he can be of use to the army, so can I, and decided there and then to seek the first opportunity to volunteer for work at an army hospital. It might even be a solution to my own existential problems.

I ran into the house to fetch some water for the soldier; I wanted to do something for him as an expression of my thanks to the Russian army for liberating us. Suddenly, I remembered something I could give him; when my job ended, the Germans had given me a small gift as a token of appreciation for my dedicated work. I'd received 100 grams of chocolate, 200 grams of salami and one candle. I hadn't touched any of these things, although it had been years since I'd tasted anything so delicious; I'd wrapped them into a small package and hidden them in the attic. Now I went to get the package, to bring it to the soldier. I am not usually one to do things on impulse; I always try to calculate my actions in advance. But somehow, in my excitement at seeing the first liberating Russian soldier, I lost my good judgment and rushed to bring him my little gift.

Unfortunately, his response was not what I had hoped. At first, he couldn't believe what he was seeing and then he shouted threateningly, "How dare you have eaten chocolate and salami when I was risking my life. You will now accompany me to my commanding officer and explain to him where you obtained all this during the occupation."

It had been a terrible mistake; I knew that immediately. I also knew it would cost me dearly. Terrified, I wondered where this soldier could take me in the middle of the night. I was afraid he'd attack me and couldn't forgive myself for getting into such a mess. I wept bitterly and begged him to leave me alone, telling him that my intentions were good; I said I'd go with him in the morning, but not in the middle of the night. But he was adamant and threatened me with his rifle, saying that if I made trouble he'd simply kill me on the spot. It would be easy enough to cover his tracks later.

I had no choice but to follow him in the dark to somewhere unknown. On the way, I saw houses blown up by the retreating Germans. The soldier stopped to look at them and then, when a sudden explosion rocked the remains of one of the houses, he became agitated and shouted hysterically that the place was full of bombs. He ran off hysterically and I took my chances and escaped in the opposite direction.

I turned around; yes, I was free of that poor excuse for a soldier, but where could I go now? Afraid to return to the Semionov house, I decided I had to leave the area as fast as I could. I had suffered quite enough trials and tribulations over the last two days!

I had to reach Tiraspol. However, instead of taking the main road all the way there, I chose to walk through the fields. I thought I knew the way; I had taken those dirt tracks many times before and had never seen other people on them. I'd be safe this way, or so I thought.

Heavy hearted, I ran as fast as I could, my feet barely touching the ground. I saw no one, but heard dogs barking in the distance. How I envied those dogs—even they had someone to care for them, whereas I had no one, not a soul to help me, to care about me.

I should have reached Tiraspol long before. Why was I still wandering around those never-ending fields, with no sign of a way out? I was exhausted and hungry and afraid of losing consciousness and no one finding me. I regretted setting out in the middle of the night through these accursed fields. It occurred to me that I must have lost my way and walked in circles. There was no longer any point to this, so I decided the best thing would be to just lie down and rest, before my heart exploded.

I looked around me, searching for a good place to rest, when suddenly I noticed a very dim light in the distance, first flickering, then disappearing. When it next shone, I started walking in its direction. Maybe someone had opened and closed a door? I couldn't see a house anywhere but I wanted to believe there was one there. This hope injected me with energy and I continued to move toward the mysterious light. Then I saw it: a house in front of me, on a three-way intersection. From a distance I saw the burning tip of a lit cigarette; this, evidently, was the light that had led me out of the tunnel.

At the fence, I was met by a man who had been watching me approach. He opened the gate cheerfully and ushered me inside. Then he offered me water from a bucket beside him. It was embarrassing to be seen in my present condition; I was barely able to stand upright and couldn't say a word, or even swallow water. The man said nothing, just poured water over my head and helped me into the house, where a group of women of all ages seemed to be expecting me, which I found strange. Without saying a word, the girls took care of me and put me to bed.

The following morning I awoke in a large, sunlit room. The sheets on the double bed looked brand new and I was wearing a snow-white nightgown. Everything was clean and shiny in that house and even my clothes were already dry. My hosts were seated at the table, waiting for me to join them; only then did they eat breakfast. They acted naturally, as if they knew everything about me and were overjoyed to see me.

Eventually, when we finished our breakfast, the man of the house said he had to talk to me. I was very grateful for their warm welcome, but I was wary of telling them the truth. After struggling with my conscience, I told them that I lived in Kolka-Tova-Balka and on my way home from visiting some friends I had lost my way.

The family looked at me with unconcealed emotion. Something was up, I could tell. Then they told me, excitedly, that the Germans had mined the fields I had run through. According to them it was a miracle and they had witnessed it with their own eyes. They had learned from the Germans that even a rat would never be able to cross through that field unharmed. I remembered Neumann's warnings and was sure that he had been behind this minefield. My hosts stared at me with deep admiration and pure joy. These good people had been unable to sleep all night out of worry for me; wandering around in that minefield that was so close to their home. They had no doubt that others had been killed or crippled in the minefield.

How long was death going to breathe down my neck? Was I destined to spend the rest of my life keeping one step ahead of death? It was a frightening thought.

Since my troubles were not yet over, I wasn't even in a position to rejoice properly. As I suspected, I had been walking in a circle and now, in order to get to Tiraspol I would have to pass the Semionov house. It was time to collect my clothes and suitcase and leave the Semionovs forever. Fortunately, I had at least eaten a good breakfast with those wonderful people.

At the Semionov house I learned that my old room was already taken; a Russian officer was resting on what had been my bed. He was clearly an important person because hordes of aides were milling around him and the house was full of Russian military personnel. The doors of the house were all wide open. I was very tired and would have liked to rest a while, but I grabbed my meagre possessions and made to leave. Instinct told me that I should get out of that house as quickly as I could.

The Russian officer surprised me and ordered me to follow him and his retinue of soldiers. He looked terrible, as if he'd slept in a garbage dump. He wanted to know where I kept my clothes and jewelry and refused to believe that I owned only one small suitcase. This was ominous. The German retreat was replaced by anarchy, there was no law and order. I had good reason to worry. I discovered later that this man's mistress had worked with me at the canning factory and had been jealous of me. It was she who persuaded the officer to steal my possessions.

It was a lovely spring day in 1944, full of light and sunshine. I looked up at the blue skies, sure that I was seeing them for the last time. But I was no longer afraid; I was tired of the unremitting struggle for my miserable life; of spending over two years under an assumed name. There was nothing left for me to lose; there would be no one to mourn me. I looked at my drunken Russian executioner, lolling about unsteadily on his feet, his head dropped down over his chest. But, however drunk he was, he still managed to grasp my small suitcase as if it contained a priceless treasure. It made me very sad to dunk that my life was in the hands of this thieving drunk.

A block away from the house I had lived in, we entered a yard. In one of the corners was a wooden outhouse containing a latrine, and they forced me to stand beside the back wall, my face very close to the bowl. On the officer's orders, the men cocked their guns ready to shoot me in the back. The officer stood near me facing the soldiers and said, "You see? This is the place for you. That's where we'll put you, because we don't have the time to dig a pit for you."

I shouted, "Quick, quick, don't torture me!" For some reason, they were in no hurry to kill me. I stood stock still, but he kept telling me not to move or look. I had every reason to believe he would carry out his threat to kill me and throw my still-alive body into the filthy latrine. The thought of such a cruel death drove me crazy.

The tension was worse than death itself. I remembered miserably how, at the beginning of the occupation, I had been dragged by the Germans to my death together with other Jewish victims; then, too, I had prepared to depart from this world on a beautiful sunny day. But what did they want from me now that we were liberated? Didn't I have the right to live, just like anyone else? What was going on here? How had I sinned, that they still wanted to kill me after I had managed to survive the German hell?

My thoughts must have wandered off into the nether world, when suddenly I felt someone shaking me roughly by the shoulders. The Russian officer was shouting at me angrily, "What's wrong with you, are you deaf? Can't you hear us talking to you? Turn around this second and face the yard!" I felt my ears ringing; I was sure my time had come and he wanted to shoot me in the chest. I watched the murderer apathetically; I no longer had the strength to suffer.

The first thing I saw when I turned was a large group of Russian soldiers, their rifles pointing at me. But something was happening, because they were in no hurry to kill me. Next, I noticed I was in a spacious and clean yard; an elderly general stood at the entrance; he was a heavyset man, who appeared very tired, but he watched me with considerable interest. In a deep, hoarse voice, he ordered the drunken officer to set me free immediately before banishing all the soldiers from the yard and leading me into his house.

The general sat me down on the edge of a bed and took a seat opposite me. In a surprisingly matter-of-fact way, he asked me how a nice girl like me could have agreed to collaborate with those murderous German monsters. I told him that all the factories had been run by German managers and I was happy to be given any kind of work, because that was the only way I could eat. I explained that after the canning factory had closed down I had had nowhere else to turn and, for a while, I had literally starved. Fortunately, I then obtained work in the abattoir; which was also run by Germans. I wondered if he wanted to punish me for that; whether that was considered collaboration with the enemy. I wanted to understand what my crime had been, since it was quite obvious to me that I had become a victim because I was alone in the world.

The general stopped looking at me, stood up and began pacing the room. He told me that he was the first and only general to have arrived recently with his men to liberate the Tiraspol area. "In the absence of a formal government, there is a tendency for hot heads to try to take the law into their own hands in order to feel strong and influential. But what are we supposed to do with these criminals, when the war is not yet over and the army still needs soldiers?" I dared not tell him about my difficult circumstances—I had nowhere to live, nothing to eat and I needed temporary work until Zhitomir was liberated and I could return there. I don't know how long I sat there, but I remember to this day that I sat there tensely waiting to learn how it would all end. I was happy when the general told me I looked tired and should get some rest. Relieved, I walked out of there without lifting my head, my gaze fixed to the ground.

I had covered about half the distance home, when I heard the drunken spluttering of the Russian officer I was so afraid of. Not far from the road a large farm wagon harnessed to two handsome horses was full of the same soldiers who had been about to shoot me that morning. Their commanding officer, a captain, descended heavily from the wagon. Weaving from side to side, he shouted, "You won't get away from me! What do you think, that a general can save you? He'll never know what I've done to you. I'll kill you in such a way that no one will be able to identify that pretty face of yours."

He grabbed me by the neck and dragged me to the wagon. Every few minutes he pulled a bottle of alcohol out of his jacket pocket, taking swigs from it as if it was water. Now I understood why this monster didn't sober up during the day. From the moment the cart drove off, he began hitting me, delivering murderous blows to all parts of my body. Tears streamed down my face and neck. I bit my lip to stop myself from crying out, afraid of angering him further; he was a cruel sadist and continued to torment me mercilessly. He saw me writhing in pain and laughed in my face. The soldiers who sat around us kept silent and tried to look elsewhere. The murderer felt omnipotent, no one could stop him, and he proudly took out a revolver and played with it in front of my face before aiming it between my eyes; when he got tired of that game he pressed the gun against my temple, proudly announcing that his finger was on the trigger. Then he started hitting my head with the barrel of the gun. Blackness filled my eyes and I felt the world spinning. A stream of blood flowed over my eyes and mingled with my tears and I screamed with pain.

We passed places I didn't recognize until we reached a densely populated neighborhood. The soldiers received permission to leave the wagon and disappeared. I was now left alone with the murderer, who didn't stop threatening me. Finally, the wagon reached a large yard and a woman came out of the house and ran towards the officer as if he was her husband. I could not believe my eyes. I knew that woman; it was Niuska. Niuska was the name everyone called her, somewhat derisively; she had worked in the canning factory. Admittedly, we had never been friends, but we knew each other. She was unmarried and had a reputation for being rather free with her favors and choice of male partners. She didn't even look at me, just asked the man quickly where my things were.

I was confused. This odd couple seemed happy; they grabbed my suitcase and rushed into the house. They sat me in a room with an old woman who stared at me wordlessly but with considerable interest. Before I could understand what was happening, there were loud sounds of heavy objects being hurled about in the adjacent room. A furious Niuska was going berserk, shouting loudly and accusing me of fraud, of deliberately denying her my expensive clothes. It's true that people always had the impression that I owned beautiful clothes, because no one really knew how hard my daily struggle was to exist.

The sadistic officer emerged from the bedroom, furious, and pushed me in the back with his pistol. He ordered me out of his house so as not to contaminate it with my blood. He dragged me to the outdoor lavatory, to kill me there. The old woman in the other room screeched wildly and tried to hold onto me; even Niuska was panicking, not knowing how to protect me. She clearly regretted having brought me to this state and claimed she never wished me dead. At the very last minute, Niuska embraced her lover and smothered him with kisses, trying to convince him that he'd already taught me a lesson and I had been punished enough. The drunken couple raised hell all night; but I was saved from certain death. I had no idea why he wanted me dead; he didn't know me and I had never been involved in any conflict.

How strange our world is. I have often wondered why people develop a profound hatred for each other for no reason; but then, nor could I ever explain love at first sight. But this apparently is what happened to me. The old woman, who had seen me that day for the first time in her life, called me "my child," kept inviting me to lie next to her in her bed, and promised to keep me safe from the two drunks. She covered my head with kisses and licked my tears, calling me affectionately "my dove" and "my angel." This woman's love for me knew no bounds, even though she was Niuska's mother.

My mind was blank and I was unable to sleep. It was dawn, but still dark outside. The drunken officer burst into my room, ordering me out and pushing me roughly, intent on hurting me. He continued the violence of the previous night. Niuska expressed her regret for having incited him against me during the night; she must have realized now that she could not prevent the murder. She and her mother ran into the street shouting hysterically for help. Within minutes, numerous people came running, many in a state of undress. They came from all over the neighborhood and pressed themselves against the fence, straining to see the show. Many entered the yard and formed a circle around us. The officer sobered up immediately, shocked by the number of inquisitive witnesses to his violence. Having no other choice, he walked me to a nearby neighborhood and into a house, of which two rooms had been let to newly arrived officers of the MGB.[3] The drunk told them I was suspected of collaborating with the Germans and promptly left me there.

I was a prisoner again, though they treated me decently enough, which gave me a little courage. I told them what had happened to me since liberation and described the cruelty of the captain who had brought me there and how he had robbed me. My story upset them visibly. The MGB officers talked with me without pressure, but still I broke down. I was so tired I couldn't concentrate and spoke uncontrollably; I was on the verge of insanity. My guards brought in a young woman doctor who gave me some medication, but my condition did not improve.

I was being held prisoner by heartless people. After midnight one of my interrogators left for the night and I remained alone with the second officer, who was in excellent spirits. Even though he knew what I had been through and how bad I felt, he didn't care if I died on that chair. Suddenly, he grabbed me like some inanimate object, threw me on the bed and raped me. A large family lived in that house, there were a lot of people, but not one of them came to see why I was howling and weeping. I don't know what that bastard was thinking. He stood near the

---

3   The Russian National Security Agency, renamed the KGB in the 1950s.

window and waited for dawn. In the morning he couldn't look me in the eyes, maybe he regretted what he had done, maybe he was even afraid of me, because he described the solidarity among the MGB men, the fact that they always looked out for each other. He made it clear that it would be unwise to report him. After this warning he took me to the office building nearby and said merrily, "This building used to be SS headquarters, we're in control now."

He handed me over to the only other person in the closed building. It was a magnificent building that was still decorated with Nazi flags and symbols, filth that no one had been in a hurry to remove. A young man in civvies, holding a large bundle of keys, opened the front door. He led us into an enormous room. On both sides of the room the walls were lined with filthy, empty cages with doors made of steel net. Immediately, the two placed me in one of these cages, as filthy as a garbage dump, and locked me up.

After the events of the previous night, I felt my world had collapsed; the ground had been pulled out from under me. I was in shock and desperately needed to rest, but the floor was filthy and it was impossible to lie or even sit on it. I was the first and only prisoner in this building. I was held without a drop of water or food, and no one checked if I was still alive. I realized that I couldn't survive very long under such conditions, and thought this was my end. I was reconciled to my fate and dreamed of eternal peace.

After about two days, they took me to be interrogated in a clean and tidy, light-filled room. The three young soldiers in the room treated my case with exaggerated importance, as if I was suspected of a serious crime. I knew these cruel people could fabricate a criminal record out of thin air, but I was in no fit state to concentrate and defend myself. There were silent pauses between each question they asked and they scrutinized me from every possible angle.

One of the men asked why I looked so young in comparison with the age listed in my passport. They wanted to know why I had come to Tiraspol; they wanted to know if it was true that I had risked my life and hidden from the Germans who wanted to take me with them. I didn't know whether to laugh or cry; I, who had yearned for liberation, had become a prime suspect in some crime I hadn't committed. But of one thing I was sure—this was neither the time nor the place to tell them who I really was.

In the end, they ran out of questions. The high-ranking officer gave me my documents and apologized for all my unnecessary suffering. He treated me with respect and told me that although the MGB installation was still not functioning properly because they hadn't hired suitable staff, he still tried to get to the truth. For that reason he sent his men to interrogate Semionov, my former landlord, as well as the neighbors. Apparently, his staff had visited many of the locals who had worked with me and they had accumulated a lot of information. He looked into my eyes and said, "I have reached the conclusion that your life has been that of a Jew. Only a Jew could behave as you do." He asked if there were any Jews in my family and even offered me a job.

A lump of bitterness blocked my throat and I could not utter a word. Here was my only chance of help, in my tragic situation. But a victim who has undergone so many calamities turns to stone. I was in desperate need of employment, but I felt compelled to flee these dangerous people at all costs. I could do nothing else. It is hard to believe that at such a critical juncture in my life I actually turned down help from the MGB director. This attests to the emotional state I was in at that time, and my personality.

In fact I had nowhere to turn. My feet took me to my only remaining friend. With a broken heart, I went straight to Nadia Shevchuk's home on the hill; I could no longer control myself.

The suffering, the shame and the outrage were just too much. I fell to the wet floor and burst into bitter tears.

Nadia tried to comfort me and I described to her my disastrous last few days. She was horrified by what I told her, because she genuinely loved me. This truly courageous and fearless woman was always willing to fight for justice. But this time she was unable to help me because she had problems of her own. Apparently, Nadia's brother-in-law, the man I had hidden with in the shelter under the cowshed, was being accused of betraying his country during the time he was imprisoned in Germany. This was utterly outrageous because he had escaped from prison, but his interrogators continued to insist that he had been released in return for collaborating with the Germans.

Nadia and her family, who were aware of my financial situation, were furious with the Semionovs. It was no secret that they were seen traveling around the countryside trying to peddle the two watches they had stolen from me. Semionov had been offered two cows, but he wanted more. Nadia took some of her relatives to the Semionov house and tried to force the man to return the watches. He and his wife eventually admitted to stealing the watches from me, but refused to return them. In his defense, Semionov said, "I have two young sons who need milk and the Germans stole my cow." Anyway, he told his neighbors, "Why make a fuss; she's just a foreigner who can get along anywhere. It won't be such a tragedy if we use her watches for the good of our children." And that was the end of it.

The Russians had erected Katyusha rocket batteries right next to Nadia's house and the soldiers who activated them ordered everyone out, because the building could collapse on them. According to them, the safest place to stand was directly below the rockets. To me this sounded like a joke, but I said nothing. The soldiers explained that the Germans had dug themselves in so well on the other side of the Dniester River, that it was impossible to move them. Curious onlookers started to gather by the Katyushas. I was in desperate need of rest and finally

I found myself a clean space in the yard, beside the stable. But my heart was so heavy that I was unable to relax or rest and instead I nervously scratched at the dirt with my fingers. I paid no attention to the roar of the rockets until suddenly there was an ear-splitting explosion and the earth shook violently under me. Pieces of shrapnel flew in every direction and people were shouting hysterically. I jumped up and ran towards the house; and, instead of Katyusha batteries, what I saw were random pieces of machinery and injured people begging for help. Soon, people were rushing to administer first aid to the wounded and everyone else left the area as quickly as possible.

Nadia joined me in the yard, sat down beside me and, in order to break the silence, she started to tell me about her problems. Recently, she had been investing considerable efforts in ingratiating herself with someone, anyone, with influence in the newly-appointed Russian local authority. She had managed finally to befriend someone who fitted the bill—a young woman whose Jewish parents had for many years been neighbors of her family's. This woman had succeeded in escaping the death pits in which the Germans had murdered her family and all the region's other Jews. She had somehow made her way to the partisans and had even gained a reputation for her courageous anti-German activity. With the liberation of Tiraspol, the partisans had received important positions in local government and Nadia had tried hard to renew her acquaintance with her former neighbor who had returned from the partisans and now moved in important circles. Unfortunately, however, another neighbor got there first, waving her Communist Party membership card and claiming she had suffered under the occupation. In fact, this so-called communist had collaborated with the Germans and worked for them as an informer. She had searched for Jews under every stone and then handed them over to the Germans for rewards, such as salt or matches. Nadia Shevchuk was furious that people from her town were capable of changing overnight from communists to fascists and then back again and continue to cynically flash their Communist

Party card, which they had kept well-hidden during the German occupation.

I was very keen to meet this Jewish girl who, like me, had miraculously survived the Holocaust. But for some reason, she didn't return to her home. I was sure that she'd appear one of these days in Kolka-Tova-Balka, the place where she had been born and grown up until her family was murdered. But I was unable to continue waiting for her, however important it was to meet her. Because I was constantly hungry and had nothing to wear, I had no choice but to turn to a wealthy local family whose daughters had worked with me in the canning factory. Two of the girls had been office clerks and had often invited me to their home where I was made to feel a welcome guest.

I stood near their front gate like a starving predator, about to pounce on the food that was laid out on tables in the garden. The only people who can understand how I felt are those who have experienced real hunger. But the family that had once pretended to be my friends now ignored me entirely. I saw I was not welcome in that house, but still, I went into the garden and waited for an opportunity to talk to the girls. I noticed suddenly that the family was following me from the window. My heart broke, but somehow I mustered enough bravado to walk into the house. I was very keen to know if there remained the smallest spark of hope for improving this sorry situation. Unfortunately, this family wanted nothing to do with someone who had witnessed their behavior during the occupation. To me it was a stinging blow and I swore never to humiliate myself again, even if the alternative was death.

I decided to leave Tiraspol and went to say goodbye to Nadia Shevchuk and her family and the Semionovs, although they were responsible for my current plight. They even invited me to visit them in the future. And they all asked me to write to them and jotted down their addresses on small pieces of paper, so I wouldn't forget them. But none of them offered me so much as a piece of bread.

CHAPTER 13

Back to Korzec

I decided to make my way to the main road in search of a ride; I had no real idea of the route I would take and there was nothing in the way of organized public transport. Every now and then a small, rather old army truck would drive up with two soldiers in the cabin. People would pay for the drive with liquor, German cigarettes or a slice of pig fat. You couldn't move anywhere without those commodities and people were trying to get away at all cost. I had nothing to offer and just had to adapt myself to the situation by climbing on the backs of the trucks as they started to drive off. If the driver noticed me, he would throw me off the truck in the middle of nowhere, where there was no sign of human habitation. Drivers would stop in isolated spots to let people off, who would then disappear down dirt tracks off the main road. I discovered that most people were traveling for short distances only; the drivers appeared to be locals, exploiting the situation for profit or to visit relations. At some point a driver pulled up abruptly and ordered me out of the truck, before disappearing down a side road. I was stranded in the middle of a deserted road, waiting a very long time for my next ride.

I was alone at night in the desert; there were no more trucks and I was terrified. There was a wooded area ahead and I made for it, hoping it would lead to a village. But it was an impassable forest, full of wild animals. I lost consciousness, until the driver of a military truck found me and drove me to the city of Zhmerinka.

I made straight for the central train station, where I walked along the tracks waiting impatiently for a train to run me over. In those early days after liberation, there still was no organized train schedule and some soldiers nearby were eying me suspiciously. Understanding that I was planning to commit suicide, they ran over, grabbed me and took me, wordlessly, to a long convoy of military equipment and vehicles. They then brought me to their commanding officer and told him that I had tried to kill myself because the Germans had murdered my children. I was too tired to care what they said about me. The car we were in was terribly crowded, but the soldiers made room for me to sit and were very caring toward me.

The Russian military convoy I had just joined did not move off because the Germans were still only a few kilometers away. The soldiers clearly had nothing else to do, so I was soon the main topic of conversation. The commanding officer was a tall, handsome young man called Piotr Prokhorov, who before the war had managed to graduate from university with an engineering degree. Before being drafted into the army he had married a fellow student. But although they loved each other dearly, his wife ran away with the Germans. He had never met me in his life, knew nothing about me, but immediately offered to marry me. I thought, what a crazy, capricious world this is: they saved me from death in order to bring me under the wedding canopy. Piotr went out of his way to cheer me up and told me about his family and especially about his physician father. He wanted me to live with his father until his release from the army and gave me his family's address and the number of his regiment. I had no address of my own to give him.

Piotr and I reached Berdichev, where I had to stay for a while because there were still Germans in Zhitomir. Piotr found an army truck waiting for an opportunity to leave for

Zhitomir and the driver promised to bring me to the town center. Piotr's convoy set off in a different direction, I think to Belorussia, and we parted ways.

I reached Zhitomir eventually and discovered that the battlefront was still too close to the city to allow me to continue on my journey to Korzec; I had no choice but to remain in Zhitomir and decided to visit the Grigorevich family, with whom I had lodged earlier. On Gunchara Alley I was spotted by neighbors who immediately ran through the gardens to inform Anastasia of my arrival; it was like the return of the prodigal daughter.

So excited were Anastasia and her daughters to see me that they ran to greet me, semi-dressed and barefoot with their uncombed hair flying across their faces. I noticed that their house had been partly destroyed. They told me that only a short time earlier, the Germans had blown up many of the town's houses and many people had died from the shrapnel, including their relative, Evgeni Koch. I was very sad to hear the news, because Evgeni had been kind to me and had wanted me to marry his son.

I had survived and was able to witness the long-awaited liberation. At long last, I was a citizen with equal rights. But my troubles were far from over. I learned that the MGB office in Zhitomir was searching for me; this time for having worked under the Germans as an interpreter; also, my old friend, Zoia Spiegel, was in prison. I had tasted the bitter taste of imprisonment in Tiraspol and could not allow myself to go through that hell again. It was not the right time to return to my real identity.

Many reasons led me to the decision not to tell people I was Jewish. Although the German murderers had retreated, I was shocked to see how many locals—murderers, robbers and traitors—had been willing collaborators during the occupation and were now ingratiating themselves with the new regime and exploiting their 'connections' in high places.

No, this was neither the time nor the place to admit to being Jewish.

It was painful to be made aware, yet again, of the fact that so many of Zhitomir's Jewish inhabitants had simply disappeared, as had the Jews of so many other cities; and that others had simply moved into the homes the Jews had left behind. The Germans had plundered what they could, but even they had been unable to find a way to take all the abandoned Jewish real estate back to Germany.

There was no time to feel sorry for myself because I desperately needed work. At least in the Grigorevich home I had a secure roof over my head again. After their previous house had been destroyed by the Germans the local authorities had provided them with alternative accommodation. I was advised to seek work in the local hospital and went straight to see the director. There was a serious lack of workers in the hospital and everything had to be re-organized—it was perfect for me. I joined a small group of people who were familiar with every inch of the city and we canvassed the different neighborhoods collecting beds, linens and dishes for the hospital. I was horrified to see warehouses full of furniture and other possessions, all stockpiled by the local population, and all once belonging to the city's murdered Jewish community.

As soon as the necessary medical supplies arrived a flood of wounded soldiers arrived at the hospital. The hospital now housed in excess of 600 patients and there was a severe shortage of nurses. I joined an accelerated nursing course arranged by the hospital's director and managed to juggle my studies with full time work in the hospital. The program suited me and I found refuge in caring for others, which alleviated my inner turmoil and emotional distress. I worked eighteen hours a day non-stop and had no time to think about my own problems. It was good to have a job again and to be able to support myself. I was completely dedicated to my work.

Sometimes I was too tired to walk home after my shift and slept in the hospital's treatment room. To me, those wounded soldiers were kindred spirits who had fought the Germans to avenge my family. Admittedly, I was young and naïve and I set aside my own needs in order to help others. That is my nature, and I was not able to change it.

The people I worked with treated me with great respect and admiration. I was touched and grateful, hoping to remain in the hospital until the end of the war, but as usual, things did not turn out according to plan.

I had to know if my younger brother Leon was still alive. More than two years earlier, when he was about five years old, my parents had paid a Ukrainian family to save his life. I knew the name of the family and the village they lived in, but I had no way of getting there. The village was in western Ukraine, an area that was now overrun by criminal gangs, murderers and robbers who had collaborated with the Germans. Now wanted by the Soviet regime for having been traitors, they were in hiding, at war with the new government. I was told that the area was extremely dangerous for foreigners.

However, if I couldn't go to the Ukrainian village, I knew I should go back to Korzec and speak to former neighbors; maybe someone there would know what had happened to my brother. I also needed to know what had happened after I escaped from the ghetto and waited for my hometown, Korzec, to be liberated. At the first opportunity, I made my way there.

It was very hard to return to the place of my birth, which held so many painful memories. I hated having to face my parents' Christian friends, my Ukrainian teachers and others who had turned their backs on us. But it had to be done.

Wandering through the neighborhoods of Korzec I observed the great destruction wrought by the Germans. I could find no Jewish survivors in Korzec or in Rowne, but there was still a glimmer of hope that someone else had, like me, managed to survive.

My father's large and prosperous family had lived for many generations in the environs of Rowne, where they owned land. My grandfather, Efraim Rubinstein, had lived in Koritz and inherited his parents' wheat fields and orchards. My grandfather had owned several flour mills. He was a wealthy man and did business with many of the local Christians. In his old age, my grandfather gave his land, fields and mills to his oldest son, Ben Zion Rubinstein, who worked them with his own sons. My relatives had owned land and valuable real estate; out of this entire clan no one survived, the Germans had murdered them all.

I walked aimlessly through the town and reached the spot where my father's store and workshop had once been. There remained no sign of it now; it had been destroyed in 1941, after the German occupation. After the Germans had murdered the town's entire Jewish population, the local clergy took advantage of the catastrophe and burned down all the surrounding Jewish houses, wiping them off the face of the earth as if they had never existed. My father's store and workshop had been among them. It was hard to believe now that until 1942 so many Jews had lived there for so many years.

I recalled my father's store. There were several large steps at the entrance, leading to two big sunny rooms, one of which contained items for sale: sewing machines, phonographs, scales of all shapes and sizes, various kinds of bicycles that Father himself had assembled from parts purchased direct from the manufacturer. The second room contained objects and instruments people had brought to be repaired, as well as all the necessary tools. On the walls, arranged neatly like an art exhibition, were all the framed documents relating to my father's patents and inventions. Beneath the store was a huge room with two barred windows, which served as my father's locksmith's workshop, filled with state-of-the-art tools. From that room a door led to a small yard, in which father had stored merchandise.

With a broken heart, I forced myself to walk to our house. I was destitute and had nothing; now I would be able to get my family's beautiful house back. But the house was no longer of any significance, because nothing could ever bring me back my family. I had no way of knowing then that the local council would later erect a multi-story building on the site of my family home.

I don't know how long I stayed there, immersed in my memories, but I was suddenly overcome by dizziness and almost fell. Forcing myself back to reality, I ran away as if from a fire, not looking back. After that first visit I returned to Zhitomir, but went back to Korzec frequently, almost every week. Sometimes I could spend little more than a couple of hours there, sometimes longer. I was torn in half: in Korzec I trembled at the very thought of those hobnailed German boots on the stone pavement, suffocated by the air that still seemed permeated with blood and death. Whenever I visited my hometown I felt sick and I'd rush to leave that accursed place. I'd go back to Zhitomir, where I had lived and worked, and slowly returned to myself. A few days would pass; I'd recover from the visit and then feel the pull of Korzec, which had turned into one big cemetery. It was a pattern that continued for quite a while. But I could never spend the night there.

One day I was wandering through the market in Korzec when I ran into some acquaintances, who crossed themselves, amazed to see me still alive. Some of the neighbors were afraid I was there to settle accounts and ran off quickly. And then I spotted a Polish widow, a former neighbor of ours.

This woman had lived among the Jews, who had taken pity on her and had helped her open a business, providing her with the income necessary to support her children. This woman had been genuinely grateful to her Jewish friends, who were her major clients. But, influenced by her new German customers, she took to robbing the Jews, beating and threatening them, at times even killing them. Her sons, too, wanted to get rich quick at the expense of the Jews. Over two years had passed and now I saw this woman peddling her homemade pies and cakes.

She noticed me and froze to the spot. Our eyes met and she threw down her basket and started to run away, sure I'd follow her. Her merchandise was scattered on the ground and bystanders started to collect it, competing with each other. They were all laughing, although they knew the woman. Oh yes, I remembered the way these people had behaved during the occupation. I expected no better of them. Sadly, I am not a vengeful person. I understood how that widow felt; she had lost both her sons, who had tried to escape with the Germans and were killed on the way. So I followed her to her home, to visit her and reassure her that she needn't run away from me in fear; that I'm not like her. Later, I learned that she was convicted of serious war crimes and sent to a labor camp in Siberia.

During the early years after the war, I nursed the hope that those who took part in the annihilation of the Jews would be brought to justice and made to pay for their crimes. Indeed, some collaborators were convicted by the communist regime but, unfortunately, whereas many innocent people like myself were hounded by the MGB, many thieves and murderers got away scot-free.

Although I never stayed overnight in Korzec, I did go to Rowne fairly frequently to visit a wealthy Jewish family. I had known the parents, both doctors, since I was born, as they had lived in Korzec. Whenever we discussed the past, they would mention my father warmly, as if he had been a beloved relative. These conversations gave me a warm glow inside and drew me to them like a magnet. They wanted me to do something for them; to befriend their spoiled, empty-headed daughter, who had never worked in her life and wanted only to have a good time. They hoped I would be a good influence on her and encouraged our friendship. This Jewish family was exceptional in that they had spent the war years in Russia, where they managed to preserve their wealth and had returned to Rowne after the war. They were truly fortunate.

One day on my way to the doctors' house, I met a young man who, as a boy, had lived near us in the ghetto. His older sister had been protected by her Russian lover, who also saved her brother. The boy had somehow managed to graduate from university and was now interning in a hospital. I introduced him to a female friend of mine, whose father was an influential senior consultant and might help the struggling intern. This meeting led to a very successful match when the young intern married my friend.

One evening, I was visiting them when the neighbor's brother entered. Apparently, he had seen me in the yard and decided to secure an introduction to me and walk me home. He took advantage of the short walk and proposed marriage, even though it was the first time we had ever met. I am unable to explain why strange men are drawn to propose to me at first sight. It seems I possess a certain kind of good fortune that I have never been able to take advantage of. Without giving the matter much thought, I told the young man that he wasn't my type. He was persistent, but I didn't want to see him again and told him his efforts were futile.

He was a handsome, well-educated young man from a good family; he dressed nicely and was popular with the ladies. As we were saying goodbye he told me that if I ever needed a true friend, I should not hesitate to contact him. His name was Aharon Podgajecki. Aharon lived in another city at the time and visited his brother, the only member of his family to have survived the Germans, in Rowne twice a year. After our meeting, Aharon would make a point of calling me on the telephone. I was not interested in him at all and did not want to see him. Still, he maintained a casual relationship with me. Three years later, he would reappear in my life. But that belongs to the future.

It was early summer 1944. I was tormented by yearnings
for my dead family and desperately wanted to know what
had happened to them. I tried to find comfort in the fact that
no proof existed that my younger brother Leon had been
killed; perhaps he would still appear one day in Korzec, so
I continued to visit there. Whenever I could get off work early,
I'd run to the road looking for a ride to my hometown. There
was always that feeling that somewhere, somehow, a relative
had survived and was waiting for me. But every time, I would
return to Zhitomir broken-hearted and disappointed.

On one visit an acquaintance told me about Leon, whom
my parents had given to a Ukrainian family for safekeeping
in return for a handsome sum of money. She told me that
Leon had spent much of his time in the fields watching the
family's livestock, until it was discovered that he was Jewish,
when he was immediately killed. It sounded true enough,
so I decided to visit the grave and see for myself. I received
detailed travel directions and ignored any potential dangers
on the way; I wanted to be alone, to see that small grave with
my own eyes and I lay spread-eagled on that grave in the
field, desperately wanting to reunite with my dead brother.
Cursed was the day I escaped from the ghetto; I had been so
selfish. There no longer seemed any point to my life or to my
endless struggle.

My life changed the day I believed I had discovered my
brother's grave. There seemed no further reason to visit
Korzec or to remain nearby in Zhitomir. That day I returned
to Zhitomir and made straight for the War Ministry where
I enlisted; my new life had begun.

Two years later, I discovered that the grave did indeed
contain the body of a small Jewish child who had worked
as a shepherd; but it wasn't my brother Leon. The body was
that of a neighbor's grandson.

CHAPTER 14

A Nurse on the War Front

The clerks in the War Ministry eyed me suspiciously and exchanged be mused looks, trying to determine if I was quite normal. After considerable deliberation, they jotted down my address and promised to contact me as soon as I was needed.

However, I was still committed to the hospital and I was late for my shift. Since I had already wasted valuable time, I looked for a short cut, walking quickly through alleyways and ending up in a neighborhood I'd never known existed. It was lovely and clean and I found it hard to remain indifferent to all the trees and flowers. I slowed down to examine the lavish houses with their large, high-ceilinged rooms. The neighborhood looked quite old and well-established and I noticed in one of the windows a notice, saying in very large letters, "Needed immediately: Volunteers for a military hospital at the front." Not wishing to miss this golden opportunity, I walked right in and signed up. I was greeted by an elegantly dressed, well-groomed young woman who ushered me into an enormous room and looked me up and down, clearly trying to understand my motives for volunteering to serve at the battlefront, when I could lead a normal life at home. I later discovered that lunatics like me were quite a rare commodity.

I described my plans to the Grigorevich girls, who were horrified. Why, they wanted to know, was I so keen to put myself in danger now, when I was finally safe. They tried to convince me that this kind of work was totally inappropriate for me because I'd have to spend too much time among men.

Admittedly, the Grigorevich family had known me for several years, but they knew nothing about my family tragedy and, of course, they had no idea that I was Jewish.

At the train station I made the acquaintance of a certain Major Rappaport, a heavy set older man who was a native of Zhitomir. He had served in the army from the beginning of the war and was a senior physician in a field hospital at the battlefront. He explained that the hospital was constantly on the move, as the battlefront advanced. He was now spending a few days in Zhitomir visiting relatives as well as recruiting volunteers for his department. Rappaport seemed happy to confide in me and told me that he was a well-known expert in internal medicine, but his private life was a mess. He had never married and felt duty-bound to help his large extended family; as a result he was very lonely.

We eventually arrived at a lovely vacation town called Truskawiec (Truskavets in Ukrainian), where we were met by a medical team that had worked with Major Rappaport during the war. They were very welcoming, accepting me immediately, and although they knew nothing about me, they liked me and tried to befriend me. All the senior doctors tried to convince me to join their respective departments with offers of better conditions. Major Rappaport treated me like an old friend. I was the youngest of all the women there and the doctors told me that my youthfulness had a positive effect on the patients. Even Rappaport said he felt younger in my presence.

In the end, I didn't work with Major Rappaport although we remained friendly and after the war I visited him in Zhitomir. He lived in a large, well-appointed apartment but he was alone and unwell, and made bitter by his lack of success.

I was the youngest of all the girls who worked in the hospital in Truskawiec and we were forever surrounded by young men. So I suppose it was no wonder that I began attracting serious attention almost as soon as I arrived. The girls envied me and couldn't understand why my success with the opposite sex left me cold, so they used me as bait. They were full of *joie de vivre*, trying to leave behind the horrors of war. When we were off duty, we would all congregate in my room to chat, gossip and laugh together. They used to come with their fancy shoes and clothes and force me to choose something for myself to wear to go out with them. But the German occupation had destroyed my youth and with it my desire to live. I had a tormented, grief-stricken soul that was in perpetual mourning for my murdered family. All I wanted was to be left alone, but when I ran out of excuses I agreed reluctantly to join in, if only to remain on good terms with the people I lived and worked with.

During that time, large numbers of soldiers congregated in Truskawiec. However, although the town was very crowded, there were very few girls. The local community center contained a library and a games room, and entertainment was provided for soldiers on leave, including dances, concerts and parties. While competition was fierce to attract the attention of the few available girls, the girls themselves were interested in finding a serious relationship that would lead to marriage.

Suddenly, the order came to pack up the hospital and move on. Closed army trucks arrived, the equipment was loaded and we were on our way. We drove through the Carpathian Mountains, where battles were still being waged, until we reached the city of Ungvár (Uzhgorod today), and billeted with the local people. Ungvár had a large monastery, a multi-story building with storerooms and basements, as well as a large courtyard. Someone decided that this was a perfect location for the hospital, so the monks were quickly ousted to make room for hospital beds and medical equipment. Each department was housed on a different floor.

This hospital treated only Air Force personnel and I was very soon being courted by men in blue, including some who waited for hours outside the building in order to escort me home. Some were in a hurry to ask me to marry them, although they knew nothing about me. It was wartime and they had no time for lengthy, old-fashioned courtships and, as they were mostly high-quality men and promised me a good life, I knew I was very lucky to be offered the chance to choose a husband to take care of me; who could tell what the future had in store for me if I decided pass up this golden opportunity? But for some reason, I turned them all down. My common sense rebelled against my instincts; I knew that I was being foolish, but I simply couldn't do otherwise. I wanted only to be alone.

There was a nurse in our department called Bogacheva Ekaterina Gavrilovna. She was a small, lonely woman with a sad expression on her face, who enjoyed the respect and praise of her colleagues and patients alike. It was said that she had the knowledge of a doctor; it is no wonder, therefore, that she felt more comfortable among her patients, and didn't like to leave the ward.

She saw that I, too, avoided people and tried to convince me to share a room with her near the ward. She needed someone to talk to and she explained to the hospital director the benefit of having us near his ward. I was that person and I gave up my comfortable conditions to go and live in a tiny room, and to share a narrow bed with Bogacheva.

Bogacheva had grown up in an orphanage and the man she had believed to be the love of her life took advantage of her and abandoned her. I, on the other hand, under the harsh circumstances in which I was forced to exist, when I remained on my own, had managed to survive independently. From an early age I had been accustomed to care for creatures that were smaller and weaker that I, so that it must have been second nature to me to take care of this woman. I did everything I could to sweeten Bogacheva's life; I sewed and knitted pretty clothes for her; when I could, I bought her better quality shoes and clothes from the locals. I cared for her as I did for myself.

Bogacheva was delighted by the change in her life; the grim expression on her face took on a happy radiance. She wanted everyone to know what kind of person I was and what I was capable of and made it known that even on a modest salary such as hers, it was possible to live a respectable and enjoyable life. She knew me well and was sure that I would never desert her. She was wise and experienced and wanted the best for me; she wanted me to have happiness and wealth and understood that I was in a position to find myself a good husband. Bogacheva was unable to understand why a poor young girl like me, with no family, would repeatedly reject marriage proposals from financially secure, well-established, educated, high-caliber men. It just didn't make sense.

But Bogacheva and I had become very close and got on extremely well. Our friendship lasted three years and our eventual separation was very painful for us both. In fact, Bogacheva was not alone in caring for me. I was lucky; I had many girlfriends who loved me unconditionally and when I look back I know what a shame it was that I didn't take advantage of the many opportunities offered to me. But my broken heart and unhealed wounds led me to make many unfortunate mistakes.

Two senior doctors worked in the hospital. Both were tall and handsome but not young; both were successful and influential in their work, but not in marriage. Fiodor Gavrilovich Turkov headed the department in which I worked and Piotr Naumovich Dimitrov was responsible for another department in the hospital. They were old friends and always had plenty to talk about. Sometimes they invited me to join them in their office. They would sit side by side on a sofa next to the wall, while I was given a chair behind a desk, facing them. We discussed everything under the sun and they told me about themselves and their families. They were obviously curious about my life, but didn't dare ask me.

Sometimes the two would sing their favorite aria from the opera *Eugene Onegin*, which is about true love that transcends age. I was a shy young girl who felt foolish and uncomfortable around men and always looked for excuses to avoid the company of the two doctors. For their part, they claimed there was something about me that attracted others like a magnet. I wasn't offended; I knew they cared and wanted the best for me. In a place like that military hospital in wartime, there were no secrets. Young men who were interested in me knew they had to go via Dr. Turkov, as if he were my father.

One day, a young doctor named Alexander Sashkin arrived at the hospital, took one look at me and decided I was the girl of his dreams and moved heaven and earth to court me. When I did not respond he appealed to Bogacheva who tried a ruse: she gave me something to take to Sashkin's apartment. He was overjoyed to see me and begged me to come in. A large table stood in the middle of the room, covered by a white tablecloth with hems that swept the floor. The table was covered with so many delicacies and liqueurs that my eyes couldn't take it all in at once. I was so surprised that I stood open-mouthed and motionless. I wondered what this man was planning to do with all these expensive smoked meats and was indifferent to his superhuman efforts to show me the elegant lifestyle I could expect if I were to make him my husband. It was wartime, but his patients still supplied him with enormous quantities of quality food. Poor man, he was mortified by my indifference, although even in my dreams I had never seen so many delicacies. He tried so hard to tempt me with chocolates and fruit preserves; indeed Sashkin tried to win my heart but he, too, was disappointed.

One day, the head surgeon, Dr. Dimitrov, said he would like to discuss an important issue with me. Dr. Sashkin, he said, was a personal friend and had asked him to speak to me on his behalf. According to Dr. Dimitrov, Sashkin was a good man and would make an excellent husband. Dimitrov tried to persuade me to go to his apartment, where Dr. Sashkin was waiting with a marriage proposal. I appreciated all the good intentions and was thankful to Dr. Dimitrov for worrying about my future. But I didn't go to the meeting, because I didn't want to marry anyone.

Dr. Turkov was a man who could pluck a star from the skies. So popular and respected was he that he was even allowed to break the rules sometimes. Although only official kitchen staff was allowed in the hospital kitchen, Turkov, who loved my cooking, would sometimes send me there to bake the special food and pastries he was so fond of. But his matchmaking efforts made me terribly uncomfortable and on one occasion, when he had thrown a surprise party in my honor and sat Dr. Sashkin beside me at the head of the table, I simply made it clear to everyone that I wanted to be alone. After this. Dr. Sashkin disappeared and I understood him.

I hated myself for my behavior, for rejecting the marriage proposals of perfectly eligible men because I was fully aware of the price I would have to pay for my independence.

In time, however, I learned that other Holocaust survivors behaved exactly like me—they, too, didn't want to marry and bring children into the world. Others had remained alive by pure chance and were never able to recover from the Holocaust. And, truthfully, I could not contemplate bringing a tiny, innocent baby into the world when I could never be sure that I was able to protect it.

I had never forgotten being raped by a monstrous MGB officer, who would have happily killed me in order to keep my mouth shut. I was terribly affected by this act, which caused me to shrink away from men and to see them as repulsive creatures. Rape is an abominable violation that can destroy a woman's life. It is worst of all when the woman who is the victim, is made to suffer and cry in secret and does not always have someone in whom she can confide. After being raped I could never trust a man again and was always afraid that however kind or considerate a man appeared, at some unexpected moment, a monster would emerge. So, although I knew my behavior was self-destructive, my hatred and repugnance towards all men was too deeply imbedded in my soul.

An incident in Ungvár served to confirm my fear of men. I had been nominated for a prize for my good work in the hospital. One morning the hospital director arrived at my department with a colleague to conduct a routine visit. The two, who lived in Odessa, came to congratulate me but, noticing my indifference, told me that my prize—as well as a medal—would be a sewing machine, an expensive top-of-the-line model, inside a cabinet that turns into a sewing table, one that I would have loved to own. Suddenly, as if on cue, the colleague disappeared and the director grabbed me in a bear hug, pinning my arms to my sides. He tried to kiss me, but I spat at him. He released me immediately and started to threaten me as if it was I who had done something wrong. The colleague must have been waiting right outside the door because he walked in with a broad smile on his face. It was clear that this whole scenario had been staged and I was furious. As soon as my hands were free I slapped that criminal with all my strength, wanting to hurt him physically and asked mockingly, "What are you going to do, fire me?" The thugs were taken aback; evidently they could not believe that someone as unassuming and shy could respond so vehemently to their unwanted advances. In the end, the sewing machine that I so coveted went to another woman.

One day, whispered stories about the director circulated throughout the hospital. Apparently, he had been arrested and taken to jail like the criminal he was. I didn't want to know anything about this scoundrel or the list of his crimes that led to his downfall.

CHAPTER 15

First Buds of Love

I dreamed I was in the sunlit courtyard of the hospital-monastery, listening to the chatter of some friends, when two dogs with human faces ran toward me. In my dream the dogs were happy to have finally found me and romped all around me. Then the dark dog chased away the reddish-blonde one and started to dance on his hind legs before me. He performed various acrobatic tricks to attract my attention until suddenly, the courtyard changed and became unfamiliar. I was afraid of the dark dog and banished him from sight. I felt foolish when I awoke in the morning. Although my dreams had come true in the past, this one seemed too silly. I couldn't have known at the time that it, too, was a prophesy of things to come.

One day in September 1944, Dr. Dimitrov asked me to accompany him and his colleague, Dr. Turkov, to the hospital storeroom to fetch some special supplies. In the hallway I heard someone call my name and quickly ran into the giant corridor; it was the head nurse, wanting to discuss a work-related matter. As we stood talking, I noticed two Air Force pilots at the top of the stairs chatting with each other. They looked familiar but I couldn't quite make out where I had seen them before. Both men were young, tall and handsome. One had hair that was a reddish-blonde and the other was dark-haired; the latter appeared quite serious and was more senior in rank. The two stared at me with great interest, as if I was the only woman in the world. I felt awful because their gaze was unflinching.

But I didn't move and stood there pressing at the key in my
pocket as if to justify myself and listened to the nurse who had
called me. My mind was focused on those two officers on the
stairs, racking my brains to remember where I'd seen them. If
it were up to me, I thought, I wouldn't hesitate to choose the
dark-haired pilot. He made such a positive impression on me
that I would even have gone with him to a desert island.

In reality, such a thought was not at all typical of me and
I was ashamed of myself. On the other hand, I couldn't ignore
what I saw. It was a grim and rainy day, but in my imagination
what I saw was beautiful light, a sun-washed field, an endless
field of green grass or grain, its plants fresh and succulent. In my
imagination I drew a large estate behind us with a large two-
story house and a granary in which to store the harvest. In my
blurred vision, I went on to imagine the pilot and I frolicking
like little children, joyfully holding hands and running barefoot
through the grass. I could still hear the echo of our laughter
as I shook myself out of this daydream, hoping that the nurse
couldn't read my mind. I blushed with embarrassment.

I went straight to my room, which was adjacent to the ward
I worked in, and flung open the large window, still musing
about the people I had seen in the corridor. Now I knew why
they looked so familiar—their faces were those of the dogs
in my dream.

There was a sudden knock on the door. I jumped up, sure
that someone was looking for me and picked up my key to
close the door behind me. In the doorway stood the dark-
haired pilot. He had the same the face I had seen in my dream.
He asked permission to enter and, seeing me hesitate, said
that he had something important to discuss with me. I don't
know why but I told him that I was very busy and couldn't
imagine what important matter he had with me, a stranger.
He thought for a moment then slipped into the room, but did
not sit down. He asked me for my parents' address. I said I had
no relatives; my parents had been murdered. He was shocked

and said nothing. He realized that there was no chance of befriending me, but still proceeded to tell me about his life.

His name was Leonid Alexeyev and he was born in the Crimea. When he was six years old, his parents and older sister had died of starvation. Somehow the child made his way to Moscow, where he joined other homeless children, slept in the streets and foraged in garbage cans. When the orphans were caught stealing food they were imprisoned. Little Leonid proudly told the policemen that he had a 16-year-old brother who was serving in the army. There was a ten-year age difference between the two brothers and when the soldier learned that his little brother was being held by the police he went to collect him. The brothers became close and remained together until the outbreak of war. In 1944, when I met Alexeyev, his brother was already a general in command of the armored corps. Leonid's brother had two sons, aged twelve and ten. Leonid corresponded with them and told them about me. He described me as a wild kid who had escaped from the forest and lost her way home. I thought he must have x-ray eyes. He knew nothing about me, but that didn't prevent him from proposing marriage to me.

My response was that I had no such plans and he was wasting his time. But, like me, Alexeyev was a fighter and a survivor; he made it clear that he was not about to give me up under any circumstances because we were so well suited. He claimed that this was a rare phenomenon that should be fought for in order to achieve true happiness. He was full of hope that he would find a way to my heart. He had the patience of a saint; even when I avoided him and was unpleasant to him, he would pretend he hadn't heard or noticed. He was an imposing man, proud and handsome, with his own ways of achieving his objectives. To him, I was the girl of his dreams and he tried to convince me that we were lonely and in need of a family. Over and over he asked, "Why continue this loneliness, when we can live together happily ever after?"

At that time, Alexeyev was a fighter pilot and an Air Force major. He told me that his special status in the military granted him a license to get married immediately and keep me with him. It all depended on my acquiescence. Officers who knew him were convinced that he was destined to become a young general. The problem was that I was an emotional wreck. Memories of my painful past were overwhelming and I was not capable of planning a future. Alexeyev didn't know what I was hiding inside me and went out of his way to prove that he was able to provide me with a very high standard of living. Then, when it occurred to him that I was unhappy with his chosen profession, he insisted that this was not a problem; he was perfectly capable of supporting me by writing newspaper articles. He had friends, he told me, who wrote for a living and made a lot of money at it. In fact, he said he would prefer to stay at home writing articles; that way he would be close to me all day. He had it all worked out and promised to consult with me on every detail.

Alexeyev tried not to upset me and refrained from asking about my past. Instead he opened his soul to me and tried to give me the feeling that he had no secrets to hide. He promised he would always be true to me and really did seem willing to stay by me through thick and thin. In the meantime he exchanged the cigarettes he was allocated by the Air Force for a supply of chocolates for me. Thus, it continued for a few months. I was not blind; I knew he was afraid of losing me and was biding his time until he could uncover my reasons for refusing to marry him and starting a family. Sometimes he even warned me that I shouldn't underestimate a suitor as serious as he.

When Alexeyev saw that he wasn't getting anywhere with me, he asked my roommate Bogacheva to intervene, which is how he obtained a key to our room, which resulted in several awkward situations. Sometimes, I would enter my room to find Alexeyev kneeling next to my bed and hugging my pillow. I was furious and snapped at him. But he swallowed his hurt and claimed that my things smelt like an infant and I, too, was still a baby who needed to grow up in order to appreciate his feelings for me. He even admitted to turning my room upside down, in search of proof that I was interested in someone else. He had managed to obtain a picture of me, which he showed his friends, bragging that it was of his fiancé. I was angry and asked for it back, but he laughed and said he would keep it forever. Instead, he offered me a picture of himself and insisted I had nothing to be ashamed of, with a suitor like him. Suddenly, he extracted something from the pocket of his shirt: he'd fashioned a curl out of a lock of my hair that he'd managed to collect without my knowledge. He kept this curl next to his heart, like an amulet or charm. I had nothing to say.

Alexeyev begged me to be photographed with him, to keep as a souvenir forever. He loved children and talked about having a family, but for me this was a very sensitive topic. The Germans had killed my young brothers and sisters and I felt I would never want to bring children into the world. I didn't even like to see children in my vicinity. I told Alexeyev this and he was so shocked to hear my words that he turned as white as a sheet. Of course, he knew nothing of my background; still I hoped that this time, he would finally leave me alone.

I was mistaken, because Alexeyev was a fighter and didn't give in easily. On one occasion, Alexeyev's plane was hit by a German bomb and he was forced to bail out over enemy territory. His parachute got entangled in the branches of a tree and he was wounded. Germans troops surrounded the area, searching for the missing pilot, and Alexeyev managed to hide among the leaves of the tree. When it was no longer dangerous, Alexeyev dropped down from the tree and discovered that both his legs were broken and he was unable to walk. Nonetheless, he dragged himself by his hands toward his Russian comrades on the other side of the battlefront. There is no doubt that here was an exceptional person in many respects.

It saddened me to see a person of such quality make a fool of himself over someone he hardly knew and had met by pure chance. I begged him to end this futile affair and stop embarrassing us both, but he insisted he was like this only with me and that he didn't want to hear me say that that there was no future for us and that I wanted only to be alone.

Eventually, the hospital had to move again nearer to the battlefront. Alexeyev was worried and warned me that we would be moving to an area of extreme cold; fortunately for me, he was able to find fur-lined pilot's overalls for me. He was indeed right to worry and the overalls really helped. In my heart I appreciated his thoughtfulness but kept silent, as usual.

The freight train from Ungvár was clean; the cars were equipped with bunk beds, so I thought at first that the journey would be bearable. But then, as we traveled toward colder weather conditions, the outside walls of the cars became covered with snow and ice and the inside walls were frozen over. Every member of our hospital staff suffered from the terrible cold and the interiors of the freight train became quite unpleasant. People were irritable and argumentative and some even started fighting over the better seats in the train. All the women envied me for my fur-lined overalls.

Eventually, we reached the town of Bielsko-Biala. Only three kilometers out of town was a large military hospital that the Germans had not destroyed. Once we had established ourselves in that hospital a stream of wounded soldiers started pouring in from grueling battles in the area.

Each department was assigned a separate building with its own lavatories and showers; my department was housed on the top floor, above the ward. Despite our improved living conditions, I continued to share a bed with Bogacheva, though now it was a large and comfortable double bed. In the hospital yard there were piles of mattresses and various pieces of furniture that the Germans had not destroyed. I chose some useful articles and brought them up to our room. Out of three mattresses I created a sofa and covered it with a red blanket. I also managed to find a handsome three-part closet, as well as a round table and four chairs; these were very useful. From a few pieces of broken furniture I created a small dressing table with a large mirror. I took some bits of fabric, from which I sewed pretty curtains. Thus, I gave our bare room a homely, comfortable ambience. Dr. Turkov and Bogacheva sang my praises and I became well known in all the departments. My colleagues sought excuses to visit our room. People joked, "When she marries someone as diligent and industrious as herself, they'll join forces to build an eight-story house in the center of the capital."

I was sitting on the sofa one day, thinking about my life: true, I had seen with my own eyes the downfall of Nazi Germany; I had watched our murderers retreat in fear and disgrace from the places they had occupied so arrogantly; my parents had hoped and prayed I would live to see the day every Jewish victim had prayed for—the Nazi downfall—but I was still wounded inside, still tormented day and night by my heavy burden of horrible memories. My depression made me feel lost; I had no vitality; it was as if I was dead inside and only an outward shell remained.

Just as I was mulling over my pathetic emotional state, Alexeyev walked in. I was so embarrassed at being seen like this that I wished the earth would swallow me up. But Alexeyev only sat next to me and gently wiped away my tears. "What salty tears you have," he whispered. Deep in my heart, I knew what a true gem this man was, but I couldn't stop myself from saying, "I wish you would go away and leave me alone. I'm not looking for a husband." He replied softly that he would go away only when I felt better and had calmed down. I knew how special he was and how modest; it was wrong of me to hurt him and my conscience suffered terribly for the way I treated him.

One day, Dr. Turkov and Bogacheva told me that a party was being planned in the recreational hall, in celebration of the October revolution. They reminded me to dress nicely and be sure to arrive on time. I suspected nothing, but also had no desire to attend the event. The day arrived and Bogacheva stayed close to me, kept checking her watch nervously and begged me to go with her to the party. This woman loved me like a mother and I could not disappoint her, so I joined her, albeit reluctantly. We walked down the steps and were greeted by none other than Alexeyev and his friends who were all in excellent spirits; they even congratulated me. Alexeyev told us he had organized the party just for me. He had written poems that he planned to read in front of everyone, after which he would announce our engagement.

Anyone else would be overjoyed with such a surprise, but I behaved as my situation dictated. In fact I was thunderstruck and didn't know what to do. One thing was clear; I could not let this happen against my will but I didn't want to hurt someone who loved me so much. If only I had met this wonderful man under different circumstances, I would have been happy to marry him. But what could I do? I was still in a period of grief and suffering.

We were surrounded by strangers who knew nothing about me. How could I correct the impression that I was causing Alexeyev a terrible injustice? Surreptitiously, I crept back up the stairs toward my room. Alexeyev was in despair. I said, "You know I have no intentions of ever getting married. Why do you continue to humiliate yourself in front of strangers? You know I've asked you to stop this behavior."

Alexeyev returned to his friends who waited for him impatiently. I don't know what went on in the cultural center, but the festivities continued for quite some time. Suddenly, into my room walked none other than Dr. Turkov, Bogacheva and Alexeyev, who sat down next to the round table in the middle of the room and acted as if nothing had happened.

I served them homemade cake and compote. Usually, I am an easy person to get along with; I've always had an easy going nature, but my heart was broken and it was like a terminal illness eating me up inside like a worm and destroying my life. I had to keep myself busy all the time, so that I would not have time to think. I had to work myself to the bone so that I'd be able to sleep a few hours at night and run to work again in the morning. The people who knew me said I was quick and agile, but in fact all I yearned for was tranquility and peace of mind. I couldn't allow myself to get really close to anyone, to allow anyone into my painful inner world; I couldn't allow anyone to reopen my festering, never-healing wounds. The Germans had taken away my youth and my life. The Holocaust pursued me everywhere and I could not escape it. I suffered from terrible yearnings for my murdered siblings and parents and my heart suffered so much that I became physically sick.

I had excruciating headaches and often felt as if something was exploding in my head. Bogacheva was very concerned about me and Dr. Turkov consulted with other doctors, but they, too, could not alleviate my pain. A patient in the hospital was in very bad shape after undergoing brain surgery and Dr. Turkov decided to invite his colleague, a neurosurgeon, who could then treat me as well. To my surprise, the professor of neurosurgery was young, handsome and very pleasant and unassuming. It was said he was a Jew from Yalta. Of course, he, too, knew nothing about my background, and took my condition very seriously. He said I needed absolute quiet and rest, and only after a few days would he know what direction this illness was taking. Luckily, I started to feel better after five days, although I was weak and had lost weight.

I had many visitors, one of whom happened to be an airplane engineer, who asked to talk to me about something. I was about to invite him to sit down, when Alexeyev burst into my room. The men exchanged pleasantries and the engineer left.

Alexeyev then asked me if I had already converted to Judaism. I didn't know until that moment that the engineer was Jewish, but as soon as Alexeyev asked me I responded with, "I don't have to convert to Judaism because I am one hundred percent Jewish already. I come from a large, wonderful family that was murdered because they were Jewish and that obliges me to remain a Jewish woman for the rest of my life."

I knew it was time I told Alexeyev something about myself. But all he did was burst out laughing. "No one is ever going to believe that you're one of them." He thought I was joking, of course. But then he looked confused, shaken even; I followed the expression on his face and decided here was the perfect moment to tell him all about myself, but he said quickly, "This is silly; whatever's right for you is fine by me." But at that moment a colleague came to look for me and the moment was lost. I didn't attribute any importance to this conversation, but learned yet again how very dear I was to Alexeyev.

Many of the patients in the field hospital were pilots who were impatiently waiting for their recovery in order to return to their units. As soon as they heard that Warsaw was liberated, they immediately organized a trip. I was happy at the chance to join them on their visit to the Polish capital. I had heard that the Germans had destroyed the city during the Polish revolt, but the reality I encountered was beyond any imagination. We all stood aghast at the terrible destruction. It was here that I learned about the Jews who had been deported to the death camps; I would have liked to record the things I heard on that very spot. The blue skies and pleasant weather seemed a cruel contrast to the desolation we faced.

Another time, I joined a group of soldiers on a trip to Budapest immediately after liberation. It was a cold day, with strong winds and a gray sky. I went with a group of young, high-spirited men who wanted to know all about the Hungarian capital. To my surprise, Budapest was almost unscathed, having suffered relatively little destruction. Here, too, we heard about Jewish victims and things they did before being sent to the death camps, including a story about a girl who took out a pistol and killed a German officer.

The next city was Krakow. Even as a schoolgirl, I had dreamed of visiting the city and seeing Poland's historical sites with my own eyes. When liberation arrived, I was fortunate enough to go there as part of an organized group. I was very excited to be walking around the historical museum on the banks of the Vistula River and visiting all the city's lovely tourist sites.

Dr. Turkov and Dr. Dimitrov decided to give all the physicians a special treat to welcome in 1945 by throwing a magnificent New Year party for hundreds of guests. I was charged with the task of organizing it and worked hard to make it a success. Afterwards everyone talked about the success of the party; even the patients in the hospital congratulated me.

Dr. Turkov often discussed Alexeyev with me and even asked what he should say to the man. Bogacheva was also very fond of Alexeyev and tried to convince me that I was fortunate enough to have found true love, something so rare in our day. She said that she'd never met anyone as stubborn as I and once asked me angrily, "Are you really that blind, Lida? What are you waiting for? This affair could end in suicide."

It was February 1945 and Alexeyev was in a bad way. He told me that he had lost ten kilos in weight, was neglecting his work and his life was in turmoil. "I can no longer live with this uncertainty," he told me. "I need a final answer: Will you or will you not marry me?" I replied, "My conscience is clear, Alexeyev. I have never led you on or promised you anything; I've always told you that I want only to be alone." But he still could not bear to part from me permanently and, suffering, he lost control and started to run amok like a wounded animal, shouting, "It's too late, too late for us to break up." Then he raised his hands, looked at the heavens as if he were praying and asked over and over, "Why? Why do we have to part?" It is this picture of him that has remained engraved in my memory.

One day ten years later, when I was living in Izhevsk in the Urals, I was summoned unexpectedly to the MGB for a difficult, exhausting interrogation. Apparently certain people, who had never known Alexeyev or me personally, had been telling tall tales about us, and the MGB men began searching for Alexeyev. The search had taken a long time, until they finally found him. It was then that I discovered that Alexeyev still talked about me and praised me. My interrogators wanted to know why I had rejected such a wonderful man. They said that if Jews were such logical people, why would I do something so illogical? Then they offered to arrange for me to meet Alexeyev briefly. But I declined politely. By now we had both created new lives for ourselves and there was no point in reopening old wounds.

Now, as an old woman, I feel able to talk about my dreams. For years I had dreams in which I saw Alexeyev; he was holding me close to him and I was aware of what was happening in his life. I have accumulated enough material for a whole book on my dreams and the following are a few of them.

After the MGB interrogation, I dreamt that Alexeyev was in Tiraspol visiting places in which I had lived and worked during the occupation. I heard conversations he held with people I had known, such as my former landlord, Semionov, who had robbed and cheated me. I then saw that Alexeyev had managed to find Bogacheva in her new home and the two discussed me.

Following Israel's 1967 Six Day War I dreamt that Alexeyev visited Egypt as part of a delegation and met a fair-haired young officer who appeared very alarmed. He was spokesman for all the other army personnel standing to the side. I heard everything they said at their meeting. Alexeyev smiled at me and said that everything would be all right.

On one occasion I saw Alexeyev flying a plane. He gave me a piercing look, withdrew into deep thought and stopped flying the plane. I begged him not to endanger himself and he, at the last moment, pulled himself together and returned briskly to action. Although the plane was destroyed, Alexeyev emerged unhurt.

Sometimes in my dreams I can see the smallest details in the unfolding events; it is as if I'm looking at reality. I believe it was in 1969 that Alexeyev appeared in a dream and told me about something in the military. He was very anxious that something would happen to him and spent a long time wandering through the streets. He then took me to his home. I still remember what the quiet suburb, which was a short distance from the city, looked like. I was with Alexeyev at the trial, but simultaneously saw what was happening elsewhere. My dream took me to a place full of greenery, and I stood beside a smallish, two-story detached house. At the front of the house, near the main entrance, there were several steps. One side of the house was red brick, while the other was made of wooden logs.

Suddenly, the wooden wall parted, like a curtain, to reveal a large room that housed military headquarters. On the second floor, a distinguished army officer was pacing the floor nervously. In the right corner of the first floor, a fair-haired, energetic young soldier operated a telephone switchboard although he, too, appeared tense. After a short phone conversation the soldier jumped up and ran upstairs to the second floor to inform his commander that Alexeyev had been indicted and would soon be brought to them. I thought that the important officer was Alexeyev's brother. In my dream I even visited the long, multi-story prison with metal gratings on the windows. I walked along the length of the building until the end, where, on the first floor, I entered a room in which Alexeyev was lying on a metal bed in the middle of the room.

After a while, I saw in my dream that Alexeyev had recovered and was sailing alone in a small boat on the high seas, when suddenly a large wave began engulfing him. He struggled for his life and was released from prison. He hurried to his remote home. In my dream he brought me to an impressive apartment. Later, he brought me to a ship's cabin; he was bitter and distressed and wanted to be left alone. I asked him what a combat pilot was doing on a ship and he led me to the deck where many planes were lined up. From there I could see everything that was happening in the entire region, especially the different boats. After retiring from his job Alexeyev took care of three-year-old twin girls.

I think it was the end of January 1979. In my dream I saw Alexeyev enter my bedroom through the closed shutters. I was surprised to see that he was in another world and I didn't know why. I knew he was beside me, but couldn't see him. Suddenly, I realized that he was behind my head and for some reason he wanted me to remember the date. No words were spoken; afterwards he asked only one thing, "Why?" There was something heartrending in his voice, a kind of rebuke and accusation, as if I had murdered him. I replied, "The circumstances." Then he came very close and showed me what had happened to him. His head and neck were bandaged. Alexeyev said that the time had come for him to leave; but he continued to linger beside me. Not understanding what all this was about, I said I was going with him and then he disappeared. I ran after him and saw him wrapped in shrouds as he slowly ascended to the heavens. I was surprised that the heavens resembled terrace-like, multi-levelled buildings. I accompanied Alexeyev to the seventh level and then fell like a stone on my bed and awoke.

It might appear illogical to describe these silly dreams, but I can no longer ignore the strange occurrences that I've experienced all my life. What I see are visions and I have no control over them. In my dreams I often saw Alexeyev, but

I never saw my own murdered brother Efi, or my sisters, Nina, Raya, Liuba and Batya. It hurt me so much, because those children were an inseparable part of my life and my very being, and they have always remained in my thoughts. I did dream often of my mother and insisted that she show me the children, but she informed me repeatedly that they did not need my help and I shouldn't worry about them.

Since the Holocaust, I have shared a spiritual connection with several relatives in the next world. They visit me under special circumstances and appear to me through the wall or under the ground. Their faces and stature are of normal height but the heads and bodies are covered with black cloaks, like monks. My father, may he rest in peace, only visited me three times in fifty years. Mother once told me that Father objects to my visits and they have banished me, although Mother herself still visits me alone on difficult occasions.

My beloved maternal grandmother, with whom I lived for a while as a child, wanted no connection with me and always chased me away, while she watched from afar. Sometime around 1985, I tried to approach her again; this time she looked at me compassionately and asked me to wait for her to make room for me next to her. I wanted to return the same way I came, but Grandmother pointed me in a different direction, which led to stairs down a tunnel. Despite the twists and turns, I managed to count the steps and arrived at a dead end—a grave.

I don't know if there really is a paradise, but in one of my dreams I saw people coming up from hell. I discovered that the dead are very concerned with what people say about them in the world of the living. Does this sound silly? Yes, it does and it is completely incompatible with my logical, rational worldview; but it is what I saw.

There were times when I vehemently blamed my mother for not allowing me to see my beloved brother and sisters. Eventually, she told me that they were in Jerusalem, before

adding as usual that they didn't need my help. In that dream
I wondered how they had found their way to Jerusalem and
promised myself angrily that I would find them myself. And
then I awoke.

I had another dream some time later, in which I was walking
along a wide path, between tall mountains. Everything was
a light brown color, like pebbles or rock. At a spot where a
mountain ridge began, I tried to look around me to study
my surroundings, but was unable to do so. It was a sunny
summer's day. Before reaching the peak, I noticed to the
right, between the mountains, there stretched a flat field. In
the middle of the field appeared a translucent, exquisitely
colored pillar of fire. I was mesmerized by the vision that
imbued me with the spiritual tranquility and inner calm that
I had searched for all my life. On the other side of the field,
beyond the pillar of fire, there was a partition created by the
mountains. A small number of men and women of various
ages stood in straight rows at some distance from the fire, on
its remaining three sides, as if separated by an invisible fence.
The people appeared awestruck at the sight of the magical
flame and it seemed at first as if they would remain there
forever, but then they gradually began to leave the site as
other people came to replace them. I don't understand its
significance but ever since I dreamt this dream I have felt
calmer and more tranquil and I have stopped pestering my
mother to allow me to see the children.

Another of my dreams placed me in a narrow alleyway;
I could see no more than my immediate surroundings.
A ramshackle hut stood on the left side of the alley's entrance
with my mother standing inside it, secretly observing me.
With a start, I realized that my little sisters had emerged from
the hut and were crossing the road to the other side of the
alleyway. Yes, my sisters who had been murdered in 1942.
But little Efi was not with them. The girls wore light gray
summery dressing gowns. The kerchiefs they wore on their

heads were pretty. The tallest of the girls was eating a large red apple. I was spellbound; it had been fifty-four years since I had last seen them and I scrutinized them carefully, trying to make sure they really were my sisters. I awoke and felt that my mother was trying to soothe the pain within me (in another dream. Mother had advised me in detail exactly how to relieve my suffering). After much deliberation I concluded that my sisters had probably been reincarnated in Jerusalem.

By 1944, I knew for sure that all my relatives had been killed in the Holocaust and that I was alone in the world. Circumstances forced me to continue using my false identity card. I had no contact with people I had known before the Holocaust until suddenly I received a letter from my mother's younger brother, Michael Weiner. I had not seen him for years and was sure he had been murdered along with all the others. I was overjoyed to discover that he had managed to slip away from the Germans and save himself. He wrote that he had grabbed the first available opportunity to volunteer for service in the Red Army in order to avenge himself on the Germans who annihilated all that was dear to him. Michael wrote that he was happy at the chance to finally fight with weapons, as a proper soldier, and proudly described his triumphs in battle. In his letter, Michael showered me with love and concern and promised that he would assume responsibility for me like a father and take the place of my murdered parents. He promised to treat me as if I were one of his own children.

I had always loved this dear man; he was special in many ways, but in 1944, I pinned all my hopes on him. I was terrified of losing him again. We both yearned to talk about the terrible tragedy of our family and looked forward to being reunited as soon as circumstances allowed. Michael was still in the army, so we continued to correspond as we waited impatiently for a chance to meet. Finally, Konigsberg was liberated and I knew Michael and I would soon be able to see each other again. But it was not to be and, yet again, my hopes were dashed.

One day, a letter arrived from a doctor in a military hospital informing me that Michael Weiner had died as a result of wounds incurred in battle.

The doctor wrote that Michael had been an outstanding soldier and fought as courageously as a lion. He had been badly wounded in his last skirmish and had lost a lot of blood. He was brought to the field hospital in critical condition and his infected leg had to be amputated, but the infection had spread and resulted in his death. Michael Weiner was buried in Konigsberg in a mass grave, alongside his brothers in arms.

At around the same time, I received a letter from someone connected to Michael's military unit, who had nothing but praise for my uncle's bravery. This letter said that Michael was a daring and fearless warrior, who had taken care of his fellow fighters more than himself. Michael was even mentioned in the press and to this day I cherish an article from 1944. The original was written in verse.

Hero of the Battle for Konigsberg
One Warrior Against An Entire Company Of Germans
Michael Weiner liquidated seven Nazis and captured 67.

A street in the city of Konigsberg. Access is extremely difficult. Shots are being fired out of windows in the stone houses, and all around, the Germans are in hiding. Large numbers of soldiers shoot at them incessantly. Only the soldier, Michael Weiner is not shooting.

The young soldier, Weiner, crawls surreptitiously toward one of the houses, getting ever closer to the enemy's den. And now he stands and in a flash runs to the front door.

The lighter, Weiner, hurls an anti-tank grenade at the door; a loud explosion ensues, and the front door is torn off its hinges. Weiner advances with his machine gun, shooting as he bursts into the house. To his left two doors lead to the large living room. Weiner hurls a second grenade while shooting his machine gun into the living room.

The Nazis run outside in panic, trying to pursue the fearless warrior, but Weiner's shots take them all down, one by one. Weiner hurls three more grenades into the living room and bursts inside.

He continues firing, while shouting forcefully, "Hands up, *Hände Hoch*!"

The Nazis raised their hands and surrendered.

Weiner's courage led him to victory and glory. In this skirmish, he eliminated seven and took 67 enemy prisoners. Thus, he opened the way for the other Russian soldiers to advance towards victory.

One courageous and wise soldier was stronger than 74 German Nazis.

Kudos and accolades to our hero, Michael Weiner, in the Konigsberg battle.

What I know is that Michael Weiner participated in a cruel and grueling battle that took place at a port in Konigsberg. When the battle was over, Michael stepped out waving a white flag, unarmed, to appeal to the German soldiers to surrender. Michael's commanding officer, aware of this soldier's value to the army, had filled in all the forms necessary for Michael to attend a military academy but at the last minute someone decided to postpone Michael's studies. Michael continued to go around with his white flag and engage the Germans in negotiations, until one day the Germans shot and seriously injured him. Michael's comrades were unable to reach him and, when they finally found him in the basement of a house, he had lost too much blood and was in critical condition.

Unfortunately, decades have passed since Michael's death and I no longer remember all the names and dates connected to the event, which denies the story its just significance. I believe that the missing documents must be languishing in military archives in the city of Podolsk near Moscow.

The knowledge that Michael had fought like a lion and risked his life to protect his fellow soldiers came as no surprise. I remembered from my early childhood the way my uncle was—always helping others with their problems, devotedly caring for orphaned relatives, being there for friends who had fallen on hard times; even casual acquaintances were often on the receiving end of his generosity. To this day I can still remember clearly the awful dream I had as a young child in Korzec, which involved the Holocaust and my beloved uncle. Unfortunately, the entire dream came horribly true.

Michael was a tall, upstanding young man, who never knew the meaning of fear. In his short life, he was loved by all who knew him and had empathy and compassion for everyone. Before the war, he had been active in workers' rights organizations; in fact, his greatest wish had been to make the world right for all who lived in it. Michael Weiner was a proud Jew who supported the establishment of a sovereign state for his people; this, he felt, was the only way to save the Jewish nation.

How tragic it is that so many Jews such as Michael Weiner were not fortunate enough to witness and be part of the establishment of the State of Israel.

CHAPTER 16

Rootless

With the liberation of Gliwice in Poland our field hospital was transferred once again. Having lived in the Polish town of Korzec and attended a Polish school before the war, I felt perfectly at home and, like any Polish citizen, I knew the language and history well. I enjoyed the outings arranged by the hospital to various parts of liberated Gliwice; and I also joined my colleagues on trips to nearby sites during our free time. In fact, there was a frequent trolley car service between Gliwice and Katowice, which I visited with the other girls whenever I could. There were many young women in Katowice from different countries and I was offered the opportunity to emigrate illegally from Russia to the United States. True, I would have had to organize an illegal trip, but it could have been arranged. How many problems could have been averted if I'd seized the opportunity to leave Europe at that time: all that poverty, illness and suffering. The problem was that I yearned to visit Korzec, the city of my birth, the place where my family was buried. I knew that this was illogical: there was nothing there for me to return to. Yet, I was determined to discover what had happened to my family after I left them in the ghetto and was resolute in my desire to return eventually.

Every day, German women came to the hospital with clothes and shoes to sell. Since I knew the language and many of the other workers didn't, they would ask me to accompany them and translate for them when they wanted to buy something. Even though I never forgot what the Germans did to us (and who was to say if those shoes and clothes had not been stolen from Jews), I agreed to translate. I had no desire for revenge against these people. One day, I found myself translating for someone in the home of a German woman of around forty-three years old, who took an immediate liking to me and wanted to show me the pictures of her dead husband and only son. Both of the men in her life had been officers in the German armed forces and had been killed in occupied Russia. For a minute, I thought I would lose control of the storm that raged within me. It was an inconceivable situation, in which I, a Jewish girl from the ghetto who did not have the right to exist in the German world, was considered by them to be worthy of no more than annihilation as a subhuman species, was now being looked upon as an appropriate match for racist Germans. These same Germans had murdered my little sisters who, in many ways, were even more beautiful and talented than I.

The Germans complained that Poles had descended on Gliwice from far and wide, to prey on the *Volkdeutsche*[4] who had been living there for generations. It was said that the Poles robbed the Germans, beat them and abused them. I myself knew Polish families who broke into German-owned apartments, took over the property and food without giving so much as a crumb to the real owners. The Germans had no one to appeal to. I read an order received by the Germans from the Polish government according to which they were to leave their property on a certain date and return to Germany. The transfer took place very quickly. I wonder if humankind ever learns from experience...

On May 9, 1945, the war was officially over and I received an award of excellence for my part in the struggle against fascism.

---

4   *Volksdeutsche*—a Nazi term, literally meaning "German-folk," used to refer to ethnic Germans living outside Germany.

Some time earlier, I was supposed to have been awarded a citation for my nursing work. I burned all the documents connected with this event, together with all the other important documents in my possession about two years later, in a fit of pique.

One day, a new director arrived at the hospital together with his young wife. To my surprise, the director summoned me to his office. Apparently, this man already knew a lot about me, had decided that his wife needed a friend like me and had a plan for us. I soon discovered that he and his wife had written to the University of Foreign Languages in Moscow and were sent a detailed prospectus of the correspondence courses offered by that institution. The new director decided to enroll me in the university and gave me the necessary forms to fill in. "As quickly as you can," he urged. "There is no time to waste." We had to prepare the relevant documentation together with a sum of money to cover the cost of books that the university supplied its students. I was very impressed. This man, who was a former army major, promised me support and enormous encouragement and I felt very privileged. It all looked very promising and I started to study English together with my new friend.

In 1946 the hospital began moving from place to place, according to need. We spent the winter and spring of 1946 in Chernivtsi. In the summer of that year the hospital relocated to Vinnitsa and I continued my correspondence course from there. For the first time in many years I felt a measure of optimism for my future.

And then, just as I thought there might be some light at the end of the tunnel, just when I began to think I could acquire a profession and ensure my future, I was hit by another bombshell.

I awoke one morning feeling sick. It had happened to me several times before when I worked in the hospital. The difference was that this time the doctors were finally able to give me a definite diagnosis. I had tuberculosis.

It came as a terrible shock. I was a very strong person and a hard worker, and came from a family that enjoyed longevity; my father's grandmother had lived to be 117. Father used to tell us proudly that his grandmother had worked in the fields and on the farm to her last day. In fact, on both sides, my large extended family was healthy and lived long lives. Who knows what age my parents would have reached if the Germans hadn't murdered them before the age of forty.

I had outlived the German occupation, but it seemed that my survival bore a steep price tag. My health had been destroyed back then, in 1942, when I underwent periods of starvation, exposure and intense stress. My genetic background evidently enabled me to recover from several bouts of the disease in the years that followed my escape from the ghetto, but for a long time, none of the doctors was really able to provide the correct diagnosis for my mysterious eruptions of bad health.

I stopped my correspondence course after receiving the diagnosis. There seemed no point in continuing with it.

One day, when the hospital was located in Vinnitsa, a large delegation of important people paid us a visit and asked to examine the background of all the workers. According to rumors, one of the members of the delegation was a senior commander, responsible for all the Air Force hospitals. It did not take long to realize that I was under more scrutiny than the other employees and, indeed, I was duly summoned by the commander to the delegation's headquarters, where I was required to answer all kinds of questions about myself, including my motives for becoming a nurse and details about my family.

I was pained by the fact that someone was trying to open my wounds; it was almost unbearable. On the other hand, I was sick of living a lie; I looked him straight in the eye and told him the whole truth.

He listened and appeared to be deep in thought, his gaze focused somewhere beyond me. After a while he said he understood me perfectly because he had two sons my age.

He said his wife could help me and that I had no need for concern. From then on, everything would be all right, because he would be placing me in the hands of a good woman. He gave me his home address and told me his whole family would be happy to meet me very soon.

I have forgotten his name and address, but to this day I am sorry that I did not go to this family; I was ashamed and didn't want anyone to pity me. I couldn't change my personality and I paid heavily for it.

The war was over and work in the hospital was winding down. The people I worked with were being released from the army and making their way back to their families. I had no family to return to, I had nothing and nowhere to go. As I was familiar with the city and able to help reorganize the hospital, I decided to remain in Vinnitsa. Our senior doctors also tarried in the city for a while and helped transfer the hospital departments in an orderly fashion. They also had to wait in order to organize appropriate shipping for their personal belongings. It was very sad for me to say goodbye to these wonderful people who had taken me under their wings from my first day in the hospital. The two senior doctors, Dr. Turkov and Dr. Dimitrov, gave me excellent references. Unfortunately, nothing came of those references but I still have the picture that was taken of me, together with Dr. Turkov.

Meanwhile, new doctors started to arrive with their families at the reorganized hospital. Formerly, they had lived far from the battlefield; now we all lived together in one large room. We each kept our personal effects in our own corner, but it was an uncomfortable situation.

Summer 1946 and I wandered bitterly around Vinnitsa and did some serious mental stocktaking. When I ran into some female acquaintances from the military department and explained why I'd had to leave my job, the girls laughed and offered advice. One of them, Zinaida Saenko, urged me to come with her to ask her commanding officer for a job.

Thus, I started working as manager of a hotel that housed mainly Air Force personnel. My commanding officer was pleased with my work and promised that building would soon begin on a new hotel and my salary would rise. My photograph of Zinaida Saenko has stayed with me all my life.

I found lodgings with a lady I had met on my first day in Vinnitsa. She lived alone and used to invite me to visit her when I was working in the hospital. I needed a place to stay and she urged me to move in with her although the rent I paid her was higher than I had been asked for elsewhere. The lady was very happy with the deal. I didn't cook or do laundry, but I helped with many other chores.

As usual, I worked hard at my new job and was always willing to do overtime when necessary; anyway, there was nowhere for me to rush off to.

In a job like this one there was no need for a matchmaker and I soon discovered that there were plenty of men looking for a prospective bride and there was always someone waiting to escort me home after work; but I never invited anyone into the house.

Something happened in early 1947 that I will never forget. As usual it was late—after nine—by the time I finished my work for the day, and I was putting on my coat before stepping outside into the cold, carrying a basket full of coal, glumly resigning myself to heaving the heavy load through the snowy streets. An officer was pacing around the yard, trying to keep warm and I remembered having seen him leave the building a long time before; yet here he still was. I couldn't understand why he was hanging around, pacing back and forth in the cold so late at night. He lived in the hotel, but I had learned from the secretary that he also kept a rented apartment in town. When I turned to go down the steps, the man raced over to me quickly and took the coal basket, saying, "Allow me." Before I had a chance to respond, he grabbed my arm and started to walk with me, as if the whole thing had been planned. My new escort was tall, broad-shouldered and radiating self-satisfaction. I had the distinct impression that had he only dared, he would have whisked me away somewhere, coal and all. I tried to shake him off politely but he insisted on escorting me home and said he knew where I lived.

That night, I couldn't fall asleep, troubled by an important piece of news I had received only recently—that my younger brother Leon was not dead and that he had gone together with other survivors to live in Poland.

In my heart of hearts, I had to face the fear that my little brother would never forgive me for deserting him when he left his hiding place. As the oldest sister and our family's sole survivor, it was my responsibility to travel to Poland and look for my brother who had suffered for so many years. But I was simply unable to find a way to obtain an immigration permit to Poland. In order to obtain the necessary documentation I needed to live and work in the vicinity of Korzec, the city of my birth, and wait to receive official permission to emigrate from the Soviet Union to Poland. The trouble was that I couldn't bear the thought of spending even a single night in Korzec.

I awoke in the morning feeling dizzy and sick, but I was determined not to give in and dragged myself to my office, where I soon encountered the officer who had escorted me the previous evening. He was in a wonderful mood and said he needed an opportunity to discuss what he described as an important topic with me. The impression was of utter sincerity, until he said that he wanted to marry me.

His name was Colonel Alexander Shaposhnikov and he was a pilot. He had been born in the area of Sverdlovsk and married before the war; he and his wife had one son. But his wife had been forced to escape with the Germans because, like many others, she had become involved in various disgraceful and unforgivable affairs. Shaposhnikov had been very upset and furious by the betrayal and he'd considered killing his wife. His son, seven-year-old Nikolai, who stayed with him, attended military school in Moscow. Shaposhnikov had been cited Second Hero of the Soviet Union, and in 1942 he was awarded a Gold Star, the highest honor bestowed by the Soviet Union for military excellence. This star glittered above the many campaign medals he wore on his chest.

Shaposhnikov had been among the first to enter Berlin after the liberation and used the planes under his command to smuggle valuables out of the city. He rented a house in Kiev, where he stored his booty and installed his very conscientious aide-de-camp to take good care of it. However, when it was later discovered that Colonel Shaposhnikov had appropriated large quantities of aviation fuel for his personal use, he was arrested and court-martialed. As a war hero, Shaposhnikov manipulated the system and managed to exonerate himself and frame the chief engineer, who was then sentenced to ten years in prison. Nevertheless, Shaposhnikov was unable to completely rid himself of blame and was forced to serve on the Air Force base in Sakhalin. For him this was the worst kind of chastisement and Shaposhnikov talked bitterly about it. I thought he'd been very lucky, but he didn't see it that way.

After his return from Sakhalin, Shaposhnikov was still able to achieve promotion and according to his subordinates all the high-ranking officers in the air force were good friends of his. The man, who knew nothing about me, promised me the life of a fairy-tale princess. He wanted me to go to Moscow with him; I'd receive a new appointment and get to know his son. But he simply did not understand how I could be indifferent to his offer and wanted to know if there was another man in my life. Without thinking, I said, "Yes." Shaposhnikov jumped up in anger, demanding to be told why I was poor and alone if I had a boyfriend. What kind of a man would leave me on my own?

I was unable to tell him about myself without having to mention the German occupation. My suffering had turned into a huge, painful wound that could not be touched. No circumstances could force me to discuss the genocide of my city's Jews, although it would remain forever engraved on my memory. Even if I agreed to participate in a party or holiday,

I was never able to ignore or repress the awful visions from my past. There was no reprieve from the horrors that filled my soul; let alone tell a stranger that every day I see the terrified, naked, exhausted and starving Jews awaiting their deaths on the edge of those open pits; victims who were no longer even capable of weeping. And when they entered the pits, they were forced to lie on top of the previous layer of corpses in a specific order, like sardines in a tin, so as to make room for them all. And then they were shot. These were my little sisters and brothers, my still young parents and all the many other relatives I loved. How easily I, too, could have been one of those corpses.

Is it possible for someone like me to dress up in furs and jewels and have a good time as if nothing has happened? Yes, I always tried to maintain an attractive appearance, as part of holding on to my humanity and also because other people's attitude to me was based on my appearance. But inside, I could not fool myself. Even when deep in sleep, my eyes are wide open; when I awaken, my eyes are full of tears and I weep uncontrollably. The first thing I see when I awake in the morning are those familiar faces demanding vengeance. Their scream still accompanies me every day of my life, wherever I go. When I eat, I see my dead relatives on my plate; when I try on new clothes I feel I'm betraying my family and I hate myself. Something always comes up that causes me unbearable torment. They murdered my soul, and I have no need for enjoyment. I feel foreign in this world.

Yet, at the same time, there were moments when I thought in my heart that a high ranking officer such as Shaposhnikov could provide me with powerful support and if I accepted his offer, I could perhaps achieve a measure of rest and recovery. On the other hand, I was afraid of failure and I couldn't disappoint this man who loved life and wanted to enjoy all it could give him.

I decided to leave my job in Vinnitsa and return to Korzec, to look for ways to reach my little brother Leon. By that time,

I had learned that he had immigrated to Israel; probably when I was working as a nurse in the mobile field hospital.

More than five years had passed since the Germans had destroyed everything I held dear. During that time I had matured and become a woman; also, I had reconciled myself with my assumed name. It had been hard work to obtain the important documents that helped me secure a new identity, obtain work and earn my livelihood. In my wanderings, I had met many good people who had become my friends. Still, the war had ended and I knew it was time to relinquish everything I had achieved during the past five years and return to my real name. To me this seemed unbearable. I didn't have the strength to start afresh.

One way or the other, I decided to spend a few days in Moscow, to visit the Polish embassy and other places and to examine the possibility of emigration. In those days, ordinary people were forced to use random means of transport when necessary because it was impossible to obtain a ticket for an intercity bus.

I arrived in Moscow in early summer, 1947. Although it was my first visit there, I did not feel foreign. My funds were very limited and I had to be very careful with my spending. I was worried that I might not have enough money to pay for my accommodation but fortunately a doctor friend from the hospital sent a letter and a straw basket full of onions and garlic with me for her Moscow relatives. I don't know what she wrote in the letter but when I found the family in one of the town's side streets, they insisted that I stay with them while I was in town. For four whole days, I ran from one government office to another. I visited every possible ministry that had any bearing on immigration, yet each time I hit a brick wall. I was very disappointed and decided to leave Moscow soon after, before my money ran out.

Now I had to find transportation and was alarmed to find this to be virtually impossible. People who were more experienced than I advised me to exploit every opportunity to find a ride, even for short distances. So I went to the freight trains, but all the cars were full of Russian soldiers. The war had been over for two years, so I wondered to where all these men, who were aged between 30 and 40, were on the way. I scrutinized them and noticed that their military uniforms were devoid of any insignia, neither rank nor medal. Moreover, they carried no weapons; anyone would have thought they were prisoners.

Usually itinerant travelers waited near freight trains for the right moment to hop quickly onto the roof or any other available surface and hold on tight so as not to fall under the wheels. But here I was, the only itinerant in sight. I soon found an answer to this. Right after the war, the Soviet government accused many soldiers of treason. Large numbers of these unfortunates were still in jail, while the ones I now saw were on their way to Siberia.

After a long and arduous journey, one that I shall never forget, I finally arrived in Zhitomir. On the way to Rowne, my final destination, I decided to visit the Grigorevich family with whom I still felt a strong connection. I had visited them in the past, on my way to Vinnitsa. Then, like now, I bought each of them an expensive present. They also visited me and we had exchanged photographs, which I still have and treasure, as if those girls were my sisters. On the backs of the pictures the girls had all written affectionate messages, emphasizing how important I was to them. In this visit, I gave them almost everything I owned because I knew I would not be seeing them again. I heard all about their financial difficulties and couldn't help but compare their present standard of living with that during the German occupation. But I loved them still, just as they were. If I could, I would have happily helped them again.

I arrived in Rowne and decided that the time had come to use my new identity card. I had received it recently, based on testimony provided by acquaintances and it bore my name as it had been before the Holocaust—Anna Rubinstein.

In my search for lodgings and a job I met a young local man who had recently been released from his military unit, where he had been given the documentation necessary to immigrate to British Mandate Palestine. It was difficult to believe that in 1947 such a possibility even existed. I was told that a further fifteen Jewish soldiers from special units had received a similar license to immigrate. Out of curiosity, I agreed to meet all these ex-servicemen in the large public park. It transpired that none of them had a single surviving relative; they had all been killed in the Holocaust. My new friends told me that after the war ended in 1945 they had been transferred from Germany to the Japanese border, where they fought against the Japanese. Many Jewish soldiers from the Volhynia region had been killed and there was no one to mourn them, because all their relatives had perished at the hands of the Germans.

To my surprise, these Russian ex-servicemen expressed a warm patriotism towards their historic homeland in the Land of Israel and were well versed in current events; moreover, they were impatient to go and join the battles there to liberate their homeland. The young men were very kind and helpful toward me, offering advice and tips on how to obtain a coveted emigration permit. They were obviously keen for me to travel with them but, unfortunately, nothing came of it.

One of the group was a handsome, talented young man of around twenty two, called Igor Stepanski, who offered to postpone his departure and to wait for an opportunity to leave with me. I rejected his offer firmly, not wishing to be beholden to him. He ignored my signals and moved heaven and earth in order to find another solution for me. One day, he told me that he would pay for me to buy forged documents and a passport so that I could leave with him. Although it seemed a very attractive offer, I was afraid of being caught at the border and remembered all too clearly how I had suffered with my previous forged papers. I simply could not survive any further interrogation.

Moreover, I was desperate to see my brother; I hadn't seen Leon since 1942 when he was five years old, but neither did I want to die in prison. Years later, I learned that a Russian girl from Odessa had bought the forged documents meant for me and had managed to get to Palestine safely. The man who had sold the documents was a high-ranking Russian officer.

Various circumstances caused my new friends to delay their journey by two months and allowed me to continue meeting them. I learned that Stepansky and his family had also endured the occupation and had been through all that hell. In 1942, the Germans and their Ukrainian henchmen led a large group of Jewish men to forced labor; Igor and his father among them. The group was led to an open field, where they were forced to dig pits. The Germans wasted no time and buried the Jews alive in the pits they had dug. Igor's father was one of the first to die and Igor was the only one to escape, although he was injured.

Igor had nowhere to return to because the Germans had killed many of Rowne's Jews that day, including his own family. He endured horrendous hardships before reaching and enlisting in the Soviet army. He was an outstanding soldier and after the war he was offered the chance to study foreign languages at the University of Moscow, at the army's expense. Alone and penniless, Igor was thankful for help in planning his future, until he discovered that a group of survivors was trying to make its way to British Mandate Palestine to liberate the ancient Jewish homeland. Igor decided to abandon his original plans and join the Zionist cause: independence and freedom for the Jewish nation, so that his own children would never be dependent on other nations. He was released from the army and at the end of December 1947 Igor and the other fifteen ex-servicemen left Rowne for the shores of Palestine, where they immediately enlisted in the Palmach Jewish military units and, as experienced soldiers, proudly contributed to the national revival of the Jewish homeland.

One day, I was waiting at the train station in Rowne, surrounded by hordes of unfamiliar people, when a young man approached me suddenly, apologized and said that he had known a girl before the war who resembled me. I suspected him of trying to pick me up but my curiosity was piqued, so I stayed to listen. Apparently his family had once lived near my grandfather and as children we had played together. He, too, had been a child when the German occupation began and had escaped with his family to Tashkent, where they had hidden throughout the war. We were talking as if we were old friends when he suddenly pointed out a young couple standing nearby and told me the woman was my cousin. But they did not appear familiar to me and they didn't seem to understand why I was staring at them. As it happened, however, the young man was right; the woman was my cousin Bella and we didn't recognize each other because we hadn't met in over ten years. Bella had married a rich cousin of ours when she was sixteen and I can still remember their lavish wedding. They had owned large areas of land, forests and huge wheat fields. They also owned a large cattle farm and much real estate. At the beginning of the occupation they had three children. The Germans killed them all, except for Bella, who had managed to escape and join the partisans. There, in the forest, Bella met a young man, Mikhail Ivanovich Anikin, who had been sent with a group of others from Moscow to help the partisans in the western Ukraine. Mikhail married Bella and in 1945 they had a little girl. After the war, Mikhail worked as a district court judge.

At our first meeting, Mikhail told me that as his wife's relative, he would treat me as if I were his sister and invited me to live with them. I did not want to take advantage of his generosity, choosing instead to stay with Valia, a new acquaintance, who had invited me to lodge with her and her mother. Although their house had several rooms, I slept in a bed in one of them, while the mother and daughter shared a second bed in the same room. It seemed odd, but I asked no questions. I paid regular visits to Bella and Mikhail Anikin's home.

The Anikins introduced me to influential people in the Rowne municipality and elsewhere. Bella was a housewife and a wonderful hostess and their home was a meeting place for old friends and former partisans who now held important positions. They all kept close contact with each other and the Anikin home was a wonderful place in which to spend my spare time, especially as it was frequently visited by Anikin's many lawyer friends.

After arriving in Rowne in 1947, I began investigating the liquidation of the Korzec ghetto. The final *Aktion* had taken place in fall 1942, after I had already left the ghetto. Mitka Zavirukha, chief of the Ukrainian police, was happy and proud of himself. He had a respectable and lucrative job. Still, something continued to eat at him like a worm in a rotten apple—how dare that Jew, Wolf Rubinstein, refuse to work for him and insolently humiliate him in public, in the presence of the local population and his police underlings. Mitka's pride was deeply wounded. My father had nothing to lose and spoke out against Mitka, exposing him for the criminal he was. Mitka decided it was not time to kill the courageous Jew and told Father that he would settle accounts with him later, in the police dungeon. We all knew that Father would die a torturous death and that his punishment was inevitable.

When the ghetto was liquidated Father was nowhere to be found. Mitka issued a command that the Jew must be found and caught, at all costs. He was found eventually and thrown into the infamous dungeon run by the Ukrainian police together with the Gestapo. On the brink of death, having been forced to undergo horrific torture, Father was taken to Kozak Forest, which was where the corpses of most of Korzec's Jews had been thrown. There, my beloved father was thrown onto the local garbage dump. During one of my visits to Korzec, I went to Kozak Forest and the pits that constituted the mass Jewish grave. I spread-eagled myself on that mass grave and wept bitter tears for the devastation of my family. Suddenly,

I noticed someone standing nearby. I looked up and saw a face that was familiar; it was the local agronomist. He sat down and explained that a small number of Jews had survived the final liquidation of the ghetto and had gone into hiding in the nearby fields and forests. However, continued survival was impossible in the midst of a hostile population and, eventually, even they were caught, brought to the garbage dump, and murdered. My mother and sisters had fled to Kostopol Forest and managed to stay alive for some time until they were finally caught. The agronomist told me that he himself had witnessed the death of my mother, Idit Rubinstein, and her children—my twelve-year-old sister Nina, my three-year-old sister Liuba and baby Batya. I have never been able to verify all these details regarding the fate of my family after I left the Korzec ghetto.

I heard many descriptions of the abuse the Jews were subjected to during the liquidation of the Korzec ghetto. The Germans and their murderous henchmen did their best to ensure that no Jew remained alive in any hiding place. They threw noxious substances down chimneys and other openings, which caused a thick smoke and an excruciating death by suffocation to anyone inside.

There were many eyewitnesses to the final liquidation of the ghetto and the tragedy that took place there. The German murderers used the same cruel methods in our town as in all the other mass exterminations they carried out. Police Chief Mitka Zavirukha was overjoyed to help the Germans in ridding the town of its Jews, and went out of his way to carry out the perfect murder. Just as in the great *Aktion* of June 1942, Mitka abused children and babies for his own perverted pleasure. He was a monstrous sadist, thirsty for Jewish blood, with an excellent opportunity to use children for target practice, then throw bodies of dead Jews onto the wounded children. Among those children was eleven-year-old Shmuel Widro, who was badly wounded by Mitka; Shmuel survived and eventually moved to Israel, which he made his home. How can anyone live with such memories? After liberation, the Russians arrested Mitka Zavirukha and imprisoned him for war crimes.

One afternoon I went to buy some fruit in the large, well-organized market in the center of Rowne. Many of the town's inhabitants had taken to selling off surplus Jewish possessions and, ironically, some of the buyers were Jewish Holocaust survivors who had been robbed of all their property. In the market, I noticed a woman holding up and displaying large velvet bedspreads. The beautiful colors on a red background caught my eye from afar and I was shocked to recall that there had been something similar to them in our home in Korzec. My mind traveled back in time and I remembered how, after Father had bought our house, we started receiving gifts from abroad. One of the packages sent by relatives or friends had contained three large sections of a bedspread together with a beautifully patterned tablecloth. Once, when I was folding the bedspread, a corner caught on a nail and the material tore. I was upset and worried about what my parents would say; I would have to find a way to repair the damage. Luckily, I was a talented seamstress, because it was not an easy job and one that required numerous different colored threads to reconstruct the pattern. Carefully and in secret I sewed the torn corner and succeeded in doing a good job. Those bedspreads stayed with us for quite some time; when I left our home in the ghetto, they were still hidden away under the floorboards. And now, here in Rowne, more than 60 kilometers away from Korzec, I was looking at those velvet bedspreads that had once belonged to my family.

I forgot my hunger and approached the woman with the market stall. I recognized her immediately as the hypocritical Russian who had taken advantage of my parents, pretending to be their friend. She had been the first to walk into our home with her son and rob us shamelessly in broad daylight and in front of our astonished eyes. Feverishly I examined the corner of the spread, and there it was; my small repair in the fabric. I managed to pull myself together and asked her casually why she was trying to sell such expensive goods at such a late hour; she answered that she lived and worked in Kostopol and could only get to Rowne in the late afternoon. She obviously didn't recognize me, because she had last seen me about five years before and I had grown up since then. She clearly believed that none of my family had survived because she told me she had never been to Korzec in her life. Then I called her by name and asked her when she had moved away. An inquisitive crowd gathered around us and it was then that I fainted. When I came round I was wet, dirty and weak and the woman had escaped with her stolen goods; no doubt helped by the onlookers. I never understood how or when that awful woman had managed to get to my parents a second time.

One day, the Anikins hosted some close friends in their home. One of the guests had been the commander of their partisan company and the others waited impatiently for his arrival. This guest, a tall broad-shouldered man in his mid-thirties, in an MGB uniform with a high-ranking insignia, behaved differently from the others. He was courteous and polite and addressed all our questions pleasantly but, unlike the other guests, this man clearly tried to maintain a low profile. The other guests were all familiar with his family; even his grandfather had fought with the partisans at some point. Someone mentioned having searched for him in the MGB offices in Rowne, Kiev and Moscow, but no one knew where he'd disappeared to. The guest explained that he had had important work abroad and any time he was able to pay a visit to his homeland he was so busy with work that there was little time left over to spend with friends. For some reason, I thought this man had all the characteristics of a professional spy and I wouldn't have been surprised to learn that he was employed in international espionage. I was keen to hear this interesting man's every word, sure that he had fascinating stories to share. But he was not at all talkative and did not utter an unnecessary word. Finally, I told myself to stop being silly. I thought, "Why are you so concerned with this guest, he isn't even looking at you. What does it matter what they are celebrating? All that matters is that you are invited to their table. You should be pleased at the chance to spend a few carefree hours with the Anikins."

The guests talked about their lives as partisans; they were all proud of having participated in battles against the German occupation. Everyone became drunk, except for the important guest who appeared to have taken no alcohol at all. The guest then filled his glass with vodka and raised it, gesturing to the others to follow suit. Suddenly, Anikin stopped everyone and said, "We're all so used to bragging about our past exploits and considering ourselves big heroes, but so much showing off makes us blind to real valor. We have here a shy, retiring young woman who went through hell at a tender age. After the Germans killed her entire family, she continued to struggle for her life and even worked for the Germans, although they searched high and low for Jews. Can you imagine how this girl must have felt, all alone in the lion's den? And now, here she is with nothing to say. She can teach us all a lesson in humility."

The important guest did not appear to be listening to Anikin. Without saying a word, he placed his vodka glass on the table, walked over to the window and gazed outside. The rest of the guests scrutinized me as if I'd come from another planet. I was annoyed at Anikin for placing me in an uncomfortable position, although he himself knew nothing about me. So I looked for an excuse to make a quick exit before I became the center of attention.

In 1947 there was a large building in Rowne that housed a municipal bank on its ground floor and a regional bank on its top floor. Across the road was a restaurant famous for its extreme cleanliness. Most of its customers were lawyers and during court recesses the restaurant became very crowded. I used to visit that restaurant about once a week and two days after the party at the Anikins I was there with a group of female friends. We chose the largest table and took our places around it. Suddenly, who should approach me, but the distinguished officer I had met at the Anikin home. He said he had been trying to find me because he had something important to discuss with me.

At his request, we stepped outside, where he said in a persuasive voice, "You have been through a great deal of suffering and you need peace and quiet in order to your enjoy life; as a Jew, your life has not been easy, but still you don't understand the difficulties that lurk everywhere you go as a Jew." According to him, I should continue to live under the assumed name I had used during the war, and to try to live somewhere where people had known me during that period. This stranger, who didn't know me at all, was offering me all the necessary help in accomplishing this. He was a high-ranking Russian officer, but, once again, I did nothing with his generous offer. Here was a savior, a kind of angel with whose help I could obtain the emigration permit I so wanted, to join my only brother Leon in the Land of Israel. But recently my world had overturned yet again. I had tuberculosis and I needed special medical treatment. I was in turmoil, because the kind of help this officer was offering was no longer suitable. My condition was so complicated that I saw no way of getting out of the abyss into which I had fallen. Once I'd learned everything about this awful illness, the prospect of immigration had lost all its significance.

I therefore decided to waive the immigration option and with it any possible reunion with my brother. I wanted to spare him any further hardship. My brother and I had been separated when he was a child of five, completely alone, forced to make his own way in a cruel and hostile world. The boy's wounds had certainly not healed and I didn't wish to be a burden on him.

I had to give the officer my answer, if only out of politeness; after all he was not responsible for my problems. But I was confused and could not find the right words to thank him for his concern. The words were stuck in my throat. The man beside me tried to persuade me that his intentions were good and that he had the means to improve my quality of life. When he saw that I was unable to speak, he calmly wrote down his address and several phone numbers. As he handed me the note, he reiterated that he would be happy to help me in any way necessary.

Not everyone likes spending time with people who are sick and pathetic; some try to elegantly avoid such people. Thus, I made a point of concealing from my friends that I paid regular visits to the Lung Disease Clinic. Not only did I suffer from my disease, I was also acutely ashamed of it. Who would have believed that someone as seemingly invincible as I could be a victim of a disease that haunts me to this very day?

Tuberculosis is a dangerous disease and settles in one's body for a long time, and the sufferer needs special conditions as well as the help and support of his or her family. I, personally, had none of these. Instead, I lived with strangers who expected to exploit my ability to run errands for them. My landlady was the first to notice that my cough was getting worse and started to ask my acquaintances why I was preparing medicines from cactus plants; she always had questions about that. At work, too, I was careful to hide my condition; otherwise I could have lost my job. I didn't dare ask for sick leave because people in management might use this as an excuse to replace me with one of their relatives. My job as a bookkeeper was indeed a good one and many people had their eye on it. Almost every day I was required to visit the banks in order to settle work matters. On the way, I often took the opportunity to do some personal things and sometimes I was able to find a bargain or two.

My condition deteriorated and my doctor, who was an expert in tuberculosis, insisted I take sick leave and move to a convalescent home to recuperate. Unfortunately, I couldn't afford such an expensive luxury. At that time there was a professional association in Russia that could have helped me, but I had no connections or pull there.

I was also forced to cope with living conditions that weren't compatible with the restrictions caused by my health. All the municipal and public institutions, including factories and other businesses, had been ordered to send workers out for three hours every day, after work, to clear away the rocks and other debris left in the city after the war and the work was carried out under tight supervision, even in the pouring rain; there were no exceptions or exemptions. For me this forced labor was catastrophic, because the thick clouds of dust irritated my lungs and exacerbated my coughing. As a TB patient, suffering from chronic exhaustion and lack of appetite, I was forced to do this backbreaking work for a long time. In the end the ruins were transformed into lovely public parks; but my health had suffered severely.

My doctor asked me routine questions about my life and my medical history and was appalled to hear my shocking history. She took the tone of a stern mother and told me to take myself in hand, to start a family, so long as I still could. In response, I was silent as usual and then she shouted at me that she had felt for a long time that I had a death wish. "But it's not as easy as all that," she said, "as you can see because death from TB is long and drawn-out and is accompanied by much physical and mental suffering." She wanted to prove her point and invited me to visit the hospital, to see with my own eyes the TB patients' agonizingly slow decline; unable to die. At that time, where I lived, there was no medicine capable of curing tuberculosis. The doctor insisted that I fight and take advantage of everything possible in order to survive. She advised me to get married and to try to move to an arid region where the dry climate suited my disease; since the humid climate in Rowne affected me adversely.

I lay in bed, as still as a log, totally oblivious to everything around me. Outside it was damp and chilly. Valia's mother saw me and decided to heat the apartment a little. But this woman had never used coal in her life, and didn't see any obstacle in her inexperience. She pushed a large quantity of coal into the heater and worked hard to ignite it; then she closed the flue, believing that the heat would escape during the night if she left it open. The heater was in the room in which all three of us slept, Valia and her mother in one bed and I in the other.

I felt very sick that night, but couldn't move so much as a muscle to call for help. My hearing was impaired and there was ringing in my ears. It was as if I was hearing desperate cries for help from very far away, followed by a knocking sound that became a loud boom. I couldn't open my eyes to see where I was or what was happening. However much I tried, I simply could not get up. Deep inside I knew I didn't have long to live and that I had to do something before it was too late. I braced myself and stumbled weakly and dizzily out of bed. I noticed Valia and her mother in the other bed, looking as if they were dead, but some instinct of self-preservation finally drove me to save my own life and get out of that room. I don't understand how I managed to get to the door and open it; I couldn't even see properly; everything was black. I crawled to the house opposite and, with my last strength grabbed the handle of the first door I encountered. Then I lost consciousness and my body fell heavily against the door.

I was told later that an NKVD (the People's Commissariat for International Affairs) officer lived in the house opposite and that was the reason for our yard being closed; so as to prevent entrance to the NKVD living quarters. The man who found me was appalled at the sight of my near-lifeless body and quickly called an ambulance belonging to the organization he worked for. Doctors soon arrived and decided that Valia, her mother and I had absorbed near fatal quantities of noxious gases and that our condition was so bad that we had to be laid outside, in the rain.

CHAPTER 17

Happiness that Defies Feeling

On that black day, when my body was weak and racked with
constant vomiting, an unexpected guest visited me. I had first
met Aharon Podgajecki three years earlier on one of my visits
to mutual friends in Rowne.

One day when he called my office to ask after me, someone
had told him I was sick and he was happy for an excuse to
visit. Almost three years had passed since our first meeting
and now, here he suddenly was, at the most critical point in
my illness, when I didn't even have a decent bed in which to
lie comfortably.

It was impossible to hide my miserable situation from my
guest. Aharon thought for a while then told me authoritatively
that I must spend a few days with his family, where I could rest
and recuperate properly. I knew them well and was confident
of a warm welcome in their home. Still, I hesitated. In the end,
however, I knew I had no choice and that I should be grateful
to anyone who was willing to help.

Thus, an extraordinary situation developed in which
Aharon Podgajecki was able to wash my feet, polish my shoes,
make my bed and do anything else for me that helped with
my illness. Moreover, he promised to create the necessary
conditions that would cure me of my tuberculosis. Indeed, he
insisted that he would care for me for the rest of my life and
bring me breakfast in bed. Quite honestly, I wasn't impressed
by these promises; as a fiercely independent person, I am not

afraid of hard work and supporting myself. Since the Germans had murdered my family, I felt no need for a life of luxury. What I did want, though, was a husband who was able to adjust himself to my standards, over which I was not willing to compromise. I believed I had a foolproof recipe for a life that was respectable and suitable to us both; as it turned out, I was wrong. I desperately needed someone to support and care for me; for a while at least. I therefore agreed to marry Aharon, albeit reluctantly. I had no choice but to adapt to the new circumstances of my life.

Our fist decision was to move to the Ural Mountains where the cold, dry climate was far better for my health. I began to prepare myself for an unknown future. It was between 1950 and 1951, a time in which Jews were leaving Russia, which had been a refuge for them during the Holocaust, and were trying to enter Western countries. I was fighting for my life, as the tuberculosis had struck again, and searching for ways to cure my chronic disease. It was for this reason that I decided we would move to that remote region in Russia.

We had no money or other resources when we arrived in the cold, foreign city of Izhevsk in the Urals. Physically, I was in a bad way and unable to work. In those years, the stores in Izhevsk were empty and, in order to acquire basic commodities, you had to learn how to 'play the system.' One day, for example, I stood in a short queue for one kilo of flour I needed for some baking. But because of the 'system' I stayed in the same place for two days. When I finally reached the head of the queue it was night and there was no flour left. I cried bitterly and swore to myself that as soon as I was healthy, I would find the kind of work that would allow me to obtain food without having to queue.

I experienced all sorts of strange changes in my body during the first few months of our lives in Izhevsk, as if my limbs were constantly being turned around. But soon, I began to feel the miraculous effects of the climate in the Ural Mountains.

Somehow, I recovered from the disease I had suffered from for so long. I was so happy to be able to function normally that I thought I had beaten the disease completely. Later, experience taught me what a cruel disease TB is, always lurking in wait for an opportunity to strike again when its victim is physically or emotionally weakened. But for the meantime, I felt much better.

A year after recovering from that bout of TB, I started to lead a normal life. I needed friends so I invited people to the house and I also visited people. I went to parties and my circle of friends expanded to include members of the local intelligentsia. I felt reborn. It was only natural for me to run our home as my parents had run theirs. I was popular and many people were attracted to me. It was a wonderful period in my life.

But then I had another relapse, from which I barely survived. My health deteriorated by the minute and I had extreme difficulty breathing. My body ached all over and, if that wasn't enough, I was pregnant and suffering from all kinds of pregnancy-related symptoms. The doctor who examined me decided to hospitalize me as quickly as possible because my life was in danger. But in the overcrowded emergency room the doctor refused to admit me because he claimed I was dying anyway, so there was no point treating me. According to one nurse, so few beds were available that they should be reserved for patients with a better chance of living. I was in critical condition, lying in a corner and waiting for the end. My husband was panic-stricken, seeing me dying unattended in the hospital, with no one willing to treat me, so he appealed to some influential acquaintances and asked for their help. Someone called the hospital director and, although it was the middle of the night, the distinguished professor rushed to the hospital and issued instructions for my treatment. I was hospitalized immediately and placed on a large leather couch in the professor's office. He personally provided me with round-the-clock care, including a personal nurse.

This was the second time my husband saved my life; but still I believed my marriage to be a failure. I wanted to be free of him again, but this was no simple matter. My husband told me many times that so long as he was alive I would never be rid of him. He would rather give up a part of his body, than me.

I really wanted to change things, but simply couldn't; I continued to be haunted by the Holocaust and what else could I have done? Even my marriage did not improve my financial situation. I worked overtime to pay for the high cost of living in the town center. I was destined to stay under the same roof with my husband for the rest of my life. Outwardly we were the perfect couple and some people even envied us.

Aharon was a native of Rowne, and his large family had been murdered in the Holocaust. Of his eight brothers and sisters, only he survived. Aharon had made his living as a self-employed bookkeeper and was an outstanding soccer player, playing against the Polish team. Aharon was a man who would not budge so much as an inch from the law. All his life, he was a God-fearing, honest and decent man, who preferred to be unemployed than to work at anything even remotely shady or questionable. In those days, however, this was a real problem.

He was forever volunteering to help others; he loved the streets and the poor unfortunates who lived there and needed help. There was a time when we lived in Izhevsk, when Jews who held responsible positions were singled out at random and sent to prison. People feared being in contact with those unfortunates, but my husband was the only one to visit them and try to help. Usually it was our family that paid the price of this generous involvement in other people's problems. I felt as if I were the man of the house; I took care of everything, I even did renovations single-handedly, since there was no one to help me. More than anything else, however, I needed a shoulder to cry on.

Since 1941 I had not had a single happy day in my life, in which I could relax and think and act without being burdened with tension and sadness. After losing my entire family, I was sure I would never marry and have children. It was a decision I took, like an oath. For years, I imposed on myself a life of absolute isolation. But my circumstances changed my decision and I married against my will; and then I started bringing children into the world.

It was painful for me to see other mothers; how full of vitality they were, chatting happily about their forthcoming births, all joy and anticipation. They discussed their plans for a future without worries, surrounded by the love and concern of their families, who waited impatiently for the new arrivals. Unlike them, I felt I was on a different planet and had nothing to say. After giving birth I suffered from a high fever that lasted a long time and prevented me from nursing my baby. I suspect that my doctor was worried I'd sue for medical negligence because he released me from the hospital despite my high fever; he actually said my recovery would be quicker at home within a family environment, where my relatives could be there to help and pamper me. It was the middle of winter and I was handed the baby wrapped only in a diaper; I was given a half-liter of donated breast milk and sent home. As someone who endured hell in this world, I was not capable of standing up for my rights and needs. Someone like me needs the comfort and support of a guardian. I never had anyone like that. So when I gave birth I did not even mention my sad family situation and miserable economic circumstances.

Unable to get his hand on a winter carriage and horses during the day, my husband, with the aid of a friend, brought me home after midnight. That trip was a nightmare I will never forget. Next to our house the snow had accumulated to a height of two meters, so we could not open the front door. Aharon and his friend ran to the neighbors to ask for help. The newborn baby was wet and hungry and didn't stop crying, but I was unable to tend to him in the middle of the street. I waited a long time in the cold until they had finished shoveling aside all the snow.

Our apartment, which belonged to my husband's employers, was also freezing when we finally entered it because the heating system had not worked in years. Only now did he set about trying to ignite the wet heater, which I had finished building just before I went into labor. I felt terrible; my fever rose to almost forty degrees and I almost blacked out. I was sick, miserable and apathetic but still I forced myself to care for my poor baby. I started searching among my possessions for something that could serve as a diaper for the baby, because I had not prepared anything for him. I laid him on a large pillow, so he wouldn't freeze to death. But as my health continued to deteriorate I was simply incapable of tending to my poor infant. My breath was labored and painful; I could barely function. How long can anyone fight for survival? Nor was I always able to obtain milk for the baby.

A person's life is short and even the most wretched situations pass at a greater pace than it seemed at the beginning. The years went by; little Vladimir, my son, grew and developed and started visiting the homes of other children. In these homes he often encountered his friends' maternal and paternal grandparents and the numerous uncles, aunts and cousins who came to visit, bearing gifts and toys. He learned that other children had extended families, people laughed and played with them and pampered them. But my innocent child, who knew nothing about the world, stood by astonished and compared our life with theirs. He wanted to know where his grandparents lived; he had many questions and wanted clear answers, because the matter had become very critical to him. Sadly, I was too immersed in my own thoughts about the past and didn't notice the void that opened in my own child's life, a void that so needed to be filled. When I heard his questions, I realized that I needed to deal with a new problem; I had to raise my child in a way that would spare him the sadness and suffering I was subject too. I would shield him from all knowledge of the Holocaust, because I knew the whole subject would be too painful for such a sensitive, gentle child, a child who had never even seen a movie, who knew nothing of wars or fighting. How could I tell him that 'they' had killed his own parents' mothers and fathers?

I did a lot to prevent my child from learning about the Holocaust and kept secret the tragedy of our own families. Nonetheless, and despite all my efforts, Vladimir became a partner to my terrible destruction and knew the bitterness of life from the day he was born. It is no pleasure to be born to Holocaust survivors, such as we were. Our home knew no *joie de vivre*: I continued to mourn and light memorial candles. Thus, our child bore the burden of the Holocaust, even though neither his father nor I ever told him so much as a word about it.

In the fall of 1954 I noticed that I was being followed by a man of about thirty; but I ignored him. I had done nothing wrong—not violated any state laws or breached any security regulations, so why should I be afraid? I paid no attention to my stalker for about six months, when his surveillance became more and more blatant; everywhere I went, I noticed a man following and staring at me wordlessly. He seemed to be waiting for some response on my part and I, naturally, did not like this state of affairs but I had strong nerves and simply continued with my daily routine. I saw no reason to mention it to anyone, for the time being, anyway.

This continued until one Sunday in the summer of 1955. It was on Sundays, when people didn't work, that I made a habit of inviting friends to visit. After lunch we decided to take a walk, during which we ran into mutual friends. We continued our walk together and stopped and chatted for a while outside the home of another friend. Suddenly, a strange man appeared, clearly masquerading as a drunk and listening intently to our conversation. Our friends included two highly-placed engineers and the behavior of this pseudo-drunk troubled them considerably. We all agreed that there were too many cases of innocent people being victimized and accused of crimes they did not commit. The question was, which of us was the target this time? I knew someone had been following me for months and became very worried; only now did I begin to make a connection. My heart fell; I had no stomach for new problems. "How had I sinned?" I asked myself.

In those days, it was unwise for Jews to stand in a group talking on a street corner; it could draw suspicion and provide a reason for surveillance. My friends were confused, but still decided to ascertain, once and for all, which of us was being followed. We walked towards my house, and the pseudo-drunk followed us. The weather was glorious and we stood near my house for a while. Usually I am a gracious hostess, but this time I was not in the mood to invite everyone in for tea and cake.

When our friends dispersed, the pseudo-drunk remained near our house. It was now clear that we were the objects of the investigation. And it was not long before all our friends distanced themselves from us, as if we were lepers.

Soon afterwards, an MGB officer visited my office flashing his ID card and ordering me to go with him. The company I worked for was large and I encountered many of my colleagues on the stairs; they looked at me with undisguised shock and curiosity. None of these people knew about my Holocaust background.

The officer drove me in a jeep to the MGB office in the town center, where I was cross-examined for two days. The interrogation process was stressful and the atmosphere tense. I had two investigators and when I needed the bathroom a woman accompanied me and did not leave me alone for a moment. Anyone would have thought I was a dangerous criminal with plans to escape up the chimney.

It was two days before I discovered that somebody had accused me of being a spy and then I understood why it had taken them so long to accumulate the necessary material about me. They had a copy of a letter I received from a girlfriend of mine who had moved to Israel and wrote to me from there in 1949, when I was living in Rowne.

The false charges against me were based on the fact that I had neglected to mention, when filling in the necessary forms when I first went to work in Rowne, that during the war I had borne the name of the Christian Lida Nowakowska. To the MGB this was enough evidence to accuse me of espionage.

The MGB interrogators demanded the names of people who had known my family and me before the war, and who could testify to my family's fate under the Nazi occupation. I had no choice; in order to save my life, I was forced to give them names and addresses of members of the Jewish intelligentsia in Rowne. These people had known me as a child and I had become reacquainted with them in 1947 when I moved to Rowne. They had taken me under their wing and treated me like one of their family and now I was tormented by the thought of their being interrogated on my account; they'd be required to go to the MGB offices in Rowne to discuss my family. Would they suspect me and never want to see me again? And the truth was that although I shared a common history with the Jewish survivors in Rowne, I had never actually confided in them about the way I had survived the occupation; it was something I never told anyone about.

I remembered the cruel interrogations in Tiraspol in Moldavia and that the MGB had a file on me in Zhitomir and sought me out because I'd worked for the Germans. It seemed the MGB had a file on me in Rowne, too, and had asked my acquaintances about my family and me, as if I were a dangerous war criminal. And now they also had one against me in Izhevsk, this time with the far more serious charge of espionage. All these interrogators dug cruelly into my still-open wounds, none of them caring about the damage they inflicted on my friends. We lost all our friends and I suffered at work, too, as soon as it became clear that the MGB had its eye on me.

My interrogators also took a copy of a picture of my father, suspecting that he was still alive. It was the only photograph I had of him, and I have none of the rest of my family. This picture was sent to me in 1947 from pre-state Israel; it was from an anonymous photographer in Korzec who used to chase after my father to photograph him for his store's display window. In it my father is a handsome young man, in an elegant suit with the athletic body of a model. Later, I lost this picture, but a copy of it remained in the MGB file in Izhevsk.

In general, my life in Izhevsk had been relatively good and I'd even felt that my physical and emotional wounds were beginning to heal. Now this hit me like a bolt from the blue and my fragile health deteriorated once again. My nerves could no longer cope with the stress and tension. I could neither sleep nor eat, and it is under such circumstances that the tuberculosis strikes again, and the old holes opened in my lungs. Only a tuberculosis sufferer knows how cruel this disease really is. My lungs were very bad and I spent a long time in the TB sanatorium in Izhevsk in the Urals. The physician, who treated me, warned me that I needed a complicated surgical procedure.

In those difficult days I dreamt that my mother and her younger sister (my beloved aunt) rushed to my bedside and placed something under my pillow. I begged them to take me away and when they didn't respond I grasped them with all my might. They ran away and I ran after them, but they disappeared into a forest and I lost sight of them. I opened my eyes and understood immediately the significance of that forest. It was the infamous Kozak Forest, where they had all been murdered.

In other dreams I used to see my beloved aunt from a distance, gesturing to me to stay away from her. This aunt had cared for me tenderly when I was a baby and in my early childhood. When, as a child, I lived with my grandparents, my mother's younger sister had been unmarried and had cared for me like a mother.

They transferred me to an isolation room and began preparing me for complex lung surgery. The two lung specialists who examined me both confirmed that only surgery could save my life. I wanted to die; the worst that could happen was that I would be unable to take care of myself. At home, before I was hospitalized, my four-year-old son, Vladimir, had cared for me during outbreaks of the disease. Vladimir, an angelic child, immediately caught tuberculosis from me. It was disastrous and I felt that I had become a burden on others and lived at their expense; this was not the kind of life I wanted. But nor did I want my son to become an orphan at a tender age, something I had experienced. My heart was torn.

On the night before the procedure, when I had sunk deep into tragic thoughts of parting from this world, the nurse came to tell me that the head surgeon wanted to see me. I was surprised; I thought I already knew all the medical staff. The nurse led me into a large, well-furnished office. A man in the uniform of a colonel, who was also the hospital director, sat behind a wide desk and scrutinized me with great interest. He wanted to know everything about me before delivering the news that I was not strong enough for the difficult surgery. However, he was so appalled by everything I told him that he promised to help me in another way. Some time later, he prepared a detailed treatment plan for me, including a visit to a specialist in Moscow, although I had to remain in Izhevsk until I was strong enough to make the trip. Years later, I discovered that in the West antibiotics had already become available for tuberculosis patients; but they were still unknown where I lived.

Then my husband contracted pneumonia and we were forced to place our son in temporary care. The four-year-old boy cried day and night and begged to see his parents. His suffering was so great that he became weak and contracted chicken pox accompanied by high fever. When I learned of my son's suffering, I was beside myself with guilt and sorrow. I knew that my condition prevented me from leaving the sanatorium for even an hour, but I yearned to see Vladimir. There was no one I could turn to, no one to help me. In the end, I mustered my last strength, slipped out of the hospital and took a trolley to the care home. I wanted to visit my child as he slept, but my heart could not contain my suffering. I shivered and trembled like a leaf, before collapsing there, next to my sick son's crib. At that time, I had given birth to another baby, who had died in the hospital. There was no one to arrange the funeral and we didn't have the money to cover burial expenses. I realized that they were going to use his tiny body in scientific experiments and I could do nothing to prevent it. Thus, my dead baby stayed in the hospital, far from where I was hospitalized. The burden of these tragedies weighed so heavily on me that I barely had the strength to cry. I became apathetic and oblivious to my surroundings, half dead. But I am certain that all this would not have happened had the Germans not murdered my and my husband's families.

Decades have passed since my newborn baby died in that hospital, but the pain is as fresh as ever. Sometimes I lose control over the pain and slam my head against a wall until the blood flows. He was my own flesh and blood, a very special child; yet for years, he never appeared in my dreams. Then, in 1995, I suddenly saw him in a dream that was very strange indeed. I awoke crying bitterly, as the dream became part of my tragic reality. What kind of a mother was I, who could not bury her own son? Who can justify such a thing? To this day my conscience continues to torment me and I hate myself for it.

Finally, I was well enough to be released from the sanatorium. I made my way to the orphanage to collect Vladimir and bring him home; I was tense and very emotional in anticipation of the big reunion. Day and night I had waited for the opportunity to take him out of the care home and hoped and prayed for the ability to compensate for all the suffering I had caused him. We met on the street because my husband had already gone on ahead to release Vladimir from the care home. No words can describe that meeting. As soon as Vladimir saw me, he jumped up all at once and ran towards me with an expression of emotion that cannot be described. Joy and grief mingled as he wept and laughed; he stroked my clothes, hugged my legs and kissed me all over my face. Once again, I was forced to acknowledge the tremendous responsibility involved in bringing a child into the world and I knew for sure what significance my life had for as long as this child needed me and remained under my protection.

On my release from hospital, I was issued documents according to which I was disabled and no longer fit for work. According to law I was entitled to a monthly disability benefit. However, since I lacked a full year of employment, I was not eligible for the benefit. I tried to explain that I had been in employment from an early age and that I had done forced labor under the Germans; but the authorities refused to count this as official employment. And now, this benefit, to which I was entitled in every sense of the word, and was of such vital importance to us, was denied me and I had nowhere to turn. Again, I was being punished for having committed no crime.

After losing my baby son, I thought I would lose my mind, but it was my first born, Vladimir, who made me resolve to cope and not give up. He, too, had contracted tuberculosis and it was my duty to take care of him. It seemed that I always needed to suffer physical pain in order to ease my emotional pain. In 1955, I had reached a low point in every respect—health, finances, family life and loneliness. I decided to leave my husband in Izhevsk and take my son to Rowne. My husband had an older brother in Rowne, also a Holocaust survivor, and I thought that I might ask him for a loan to cover the cost of a trip to the TB sanatorium.

My brother-in-law had lost his entire family in the Holocaust and had married a fellow survivor after the war. They were broken, sick and helpless people; in fact, they were themselves in need of help. And it was these unfortunates that I wanted to ask for help; I had hoped to leave my sick son with them while I went to the sanatorium. But I simply saw no other solution.

Parting from my sick son was heart breaking and I felt miserable throughout the trip to the sanatorium. All I could think of was that I had left Vladimir with people who were incapable of caring for a sick child and that it was selfish of me to be concerned with my own health at the expense of my child. My heart ached with longing and I was so depressed that I didn't even notice where we were going. So it was a shock to see that I had arrived in Stalingrad and to hear a radio announcer describing the city's terrible, but heroic battle against the Germans. My thoughts shifted from my own problems to the scarred, war-torn city before me and I listened to the announcer naming the heroes who fell in its defense.

After six weeks in the sanatorium, my health began to improve. Unfortunately, just as I was feeling encouraged, my husband wrote from Izhevsk, telling me that he was sick and needed help. Worse still, we had to vacate our apartment in Izhevsk, because the landlords had to sell it to pay off debts. I was forced to leave the sanatorium and go home.

My finances were very low and people advised me that the cheapest way to Izhevsk was by boat. I embarked on a lengthy, completely unplanned journey that began on a ship from Stalingrad on the River Volga. At the city of Kazan I had to transfer to a ship that sailed to the Urals, but I was notified that I would have to wait all day for the ship to sail late at night. I was pleased at the opportunity to tour the capital city, with its ancient historical buildings, and joined an organized tour, although I knew I mustn't exert myself. In the evening, when I returned to the harbor, I was tired and sick but content. Next, I embarked a ship that sailed via the Kama River to the port city of Sarapul; from there I took a freight train to Izhevsk. On the way, I picked up my son from my husband's family.

Due to the changed circumstances, I was unable to undergo lung surgery in Kiev.

CHAPTER 18

My Brother

This is the story of my brother Leon. In 1942 my parents had entrusted five-year-old Leon to a Ukrainian family who promised to save him, in return for a very large payment.

After the Germans liquidated the ghetto, my parents and siblings managed to go into hiding, finding shelter in garbage dumps, forests and other uninhabited places. It was fall 1942 and the weather was already very cold. My family escaped the ghetto with nothing; they had neither food nor clothing and no roof over their heads. My parents knew the end was near and they could not survive for much longer under those inhuman conditions, surrounded by a hostile population. During those critical days, hounded by death, my father tried hard to find where Leon, who was now five and a half years old, was hiding. He needed to know, before he died, if his son had any chance of survival and wanted to see Leon one last time, to talk to him and teach him some important facts of life before parting from him forever. It was a very challenging and risky objective at a time when 'they' were searching high and low for every single Jew.

Father managed to overcome all the obstacles and reached the village of the Ukrainian family that had promised to keep Leon safe. At night, Father crept into the shed where the family kept their work tools and there, asleep in the straw, he saw Leon. Father described the hopeless circumstances of the family following the liquidation of the ghetto. "You are no longer a baby, Leon, you understand the situation," he whispered. "The end is near; we can't hold onto life under these conditions. But someone must survive from a large family such as ours, in order to remember and tell the world what the Germans did. Leon, I am ordering you to be strong and to fight for your life." He then asked Leon for forgiveness for bringing him into such a hostile, dangerous world and encouraged the boy to survive at all costs, that he had nothing to lose. "And if by some miracle you and Anna both survive this hell," Father continued, "you must find each other after the war and always remember what happened to your family." Father returned to Korzec, where he met his death shortly afterward.

The Ukrainian family needed working hands for their farm and exploited the boy whose life depended on them. Leon's main job consisted of taking the cattle out to graze in the fields. It was not long before the other villagers realized that the small cowherd was a Jew. Representatives of the village then told the Ukrainian family that the boy must be killed. The mistress of the house said she would drive him out of the village and into German hands and let them do what they wanted. She picked up a long pole and started chasing after Leon, shouting and threatening, through the village streets, to prove to everyone that, just like them, she, too, hated the Jews. As soon as the woman stopped running after him, Leon fell to the ground in an exhausted heap outside the village. He was sorry he had left his parents and wished he were still with them. When he eventually regained consciousness he realized he was in an open space; in the morning he would be found and that would be the end of him.

However, as a cowherd, Leon had become familiar with the topography of the area and remembered the frightening old pit outside the village that people made a point of avoiding. So, under darkness he crawled silently towards the pit. It took him all night to find what he was looking for and, luckily, he was undetected. He entered the pit before daybreak and quietly suffered there all day. Only at night did he dare leave his hiding place in search of food. He knew there was a pigsty in the vicinity and that the locals brought food for the pigs every day. Leon learned to steal food from the pigs, although there was not always enough left for him in the pig trough. At night he would sit outside, next to the pit, and tell the moon and stars about his life. When there were no stars or moon in the sky, it was very dark. There was a lot of rain in that area, even torrential rains with strong winds, the kind that adults in the comfort of their warm homes are afraid of, not to mention a young child alone beside an exposed pit. The winters in that area were bitterly cold and the locals carefully prepared themselves and their domestic animals well in advance. Here was this poor child, alone and stripped of his humanity, banished outside to the freezing cold, chased away with only the meagre clothes on his back.

How can anyone who has never been in such a situation understand what Leon went through all those months, both physically and psychologically? How can a child exist in an open grave for two years, lacking all contact with the outside world?

In that region of the Ukraine, not even the most courageous of Jews had a chance of survival because the local population hated Jews and collaborated with the Nazis. Even when the Nazis retreated and Russia liberated the Ukraine, local criminals formed anti-Soviet underground resistance groups known as the Benderovtsy. These gangs, who were wanted by the Soviet authorities, were extremely violent and prolific murderers. The situation became so intolerable that the Soviet authorities were forced to intervene to restore law and order.

After the liberation of the Ukraine, a full six months passed before Leon learned of the change of regime and defeat of the Germans. It so happened that he was hiding in an area rife with violent gangs, where no stranger dared to step. If any of the gangs had known about Leon's existence, they would have killed him outright.

Some gang members fell into the hands of Russian military units and were interrogated; they soon began talking and giving away secrets about their underground resistance network. They named their leader, who turned out to be none other than the man who translated for the Ukrainian mayor. A devout Nazi, he indoctrinated the local youth with Nazi propaganda; also, he was the same man who had sworn to my father that he would save Leon's life and it was his mother who had chased Leon out of her house with a broomstick. And now the Day of Judgment had arrived and Russian soldiers scoured the area for the gang leader. When they finally found him in a cemetery, they killed him on the spot.

Eventually, these same Russian soldiers came across the pit in which Leon was hiding and pulled him out. He was naked and barely alive; his clothes had long since rotted off his body. The sight of that poor emaciated child was one that even those war-weary soldiers could barely believe and many of them wept openly. Their young officer ordered them to rush the boy to hospital as quickly as possible; and Leon, whose healthy, robust genes had served him well, miraculously survived and soon, he even managed to stand on his two feet. The soldiers who had rescued Leon could not stop talking about it: a child who had lived for two and a half years in a grave, and survived.

One day, Leon went for a walk with one of the soldiers to get some fresh air and happened to pass by the home of the Ukrainian family that had promised him shelter from the Germans. The soldiers were getting ready to burn the house with all the family's possessions inside and to kill the mistress of the house. Leon fell on the officer's knees and kissed his boots, begging him not to harm this family. The soldiers exchanged astonished looks, and Leon said, "You have already killed the gang leader, isn't that enough punishment for the family?" The officer told the others to do as Leon asked so as to spare him additional suffering, and that's how that evil family was saved. The soldiers told the story repeatedly;

unable to understand how this Jewish child was capable of forgiving enemies who tried to murder him.

Leon had nowhere to go so he remained in the army camp with the soldiers who had saved his life. They taught him how to use firearms, and he became one of them. The commanding officer, a young man from the Moscow area, became very attached to Leon and assumed responsibility for him. He told Leon that his excellent connections in high places could help the child get into a military academy. The officer was very busy but kept a constant eye on his young protégé. He managed to acquire a military uniform in Leon's size, and gave him a machine gun that was bigger than he was. Locals and passers-by would stop and laugh at the strange little soldier, but Leon didn't pay any attention. Instead, the soldiers taught him all about military life and the art of warfare, and Leon insisted on accompanying them on their missions despite the dangers involved. It's difficult to know what would have ultimately become of Leon, had the officer not been killed in action. The loss of his hero came as a huge blow to the young boy, who had come to rely on and trust the officer, and he was inconsolable.

Leon decided to immigrate to Poland. At that time people who had survived the Holocaust were able to return to their places of birth in Poland and Leon joined other orphans, wandering around together, seeking food and basic commodities. At the end of 1945 Leon finally arrived in Lodz, where he joined a group of youth (known as a *kibbutz*) of the Poalei Zion Dror movement; he subsequently transferred to another group called Laipis. In 1946 the orphans set sail on an illegal immigrant ship to the Land of Israel. Along with many other young Holocaust survivors Leon was taken to Kibbutz Yagur, where he was taught to use firearms. Having participated in these kinds of military exercises when he lived with the Russian soldiers, he felt experienced. He didn't know his exact age, and although he was obviously very young he was taken into the Haganah military forces, where he tried to be as useful as possible.

Leon's childhood had been unconventional and had forced him to be emotionally and intellectually mature beyond his age. On the surface he was a brave and daring young man but inside he longed for a parent figure or mentor to support him psychologically and financially. But the reality of his times was cruel and everyone was busy with his or her own needs, and Leon remained alone.

Numerous orphans of the Holocaust fell in the battle for the establishment of the State of Israel. Leon was greatly affected by these losses, which drained him emotionally. Nonetheless, he was not indifferent to the Jewish nation's need for a sovereign state of its own; now more than ever. Leon was one of the first to liberate the town of Eilat on the Red Sea. In the Palmach, the military arm of the Haganah, he volunteered for the most dangerous missions, such as dismantling land mines under fire or rescuing the wounded from inaccessible locations. One night he drove through a minefield in order to rescue a comrade, and a mine exploded right under the wheels of his car. He sustained multiple injuries but, miraculously, he survived.

Due to the special circumstances of his life, Leon married at a young age. He took evening classes to compensate for his lack of schooling and eventually graduated from university. But his health had suffered under the occupation and since being rescued from the pit, he suffered from several chronic ailments that required constant medical treatment and frequent surgery.

CHAPTER 19

Israel

In 1957, when we were still living in Izhevsk, I opened the newspaper one day and saw something that immediately caught my attention. I read that people who had been born under the Polish regime were permitted to emigrate from the USSR to Poland. This was very good news as our ultimate objective had always been to immigrate to Israel and Poland was the first step in that direction. So we started to make the necessary preparations and in 1958 we moved to Poland.

It was not easy in those days to emigrate from Poland to Israel and the process required a large sum of money. We, of course, had no resources so were obliged to wait patiently in Poland. Two years later, we succeeded in obtaining the necessary funding and traveled from Poland to Italy, where we met *shlichim* (Jewish Agency emissaries) from Israel and, finally, on September 2, 1960, we reached the port of Haifa in Israel.

From Haifa in the north we were taken to Kiryat Gat in the south, and there I collapsed. The home we were allocated was tiny and still under construction. It provided no protection from the sweltering heat and we suffered terribly. Having lived for years in the Ural area we were accustomed to a very cold, dry climate. The change was extreme.

We also had financial problems. Although he had old friends living in Israel with good jobs and connections, my husband refused to ask for help in finding suitable employment. Aharon was a very stubborn man and insisted that if anyone really wanted to help, they would step forward on their own initiative. So it took a long time for him to set himself up as a self-employed bookkeeper. For a while he worked in Tel Aviv, but we continued to live in remote Kiryat Gat. I remember him setting out on foot in the morning, hoping to hitch a ride with someone on the way to Tel Aviv. In those days, there was no proper public transport.

In his youth my husband had been an outstanding soccer player and was a member of the team in Rowne. Even when he got older he continued to run twenty kilometers a day without floundering. Aharon remained as quick and nimble as a young man and enjoyed boundless energy. Since he could find nothing at home to occupy himself with, he established a voluntary pension society for retirees of his place of work. He worked tirelessly to develop the society and was chosen by its committee to represent them on the Makefet Pension Fund. But this wasn't enough for him; he also organized wonderful annual gifts for the members, sightseeing trips all over the country and lavish parties for the holidays. My husband was an expert on cultural affairs and we often visited museums and flower shows and went to see movies and plays.

The 1991 Gulf War was terribly traumatic for me, as it stirred up awful memories from the German occupation. I had already seen what blind hatred leads to. This time, an Iraqi Scud rocket fired during the war fell very near our home. We heard an ear-splitting explosion and thought our end was imminent as the bomb fell literally under our window. Before we had managed to gather our wits, people were running to see if there were any casualties. They were amazed that Aharon and I had survived the blast intact.

In those terrible moments after the blast, I looked around and saw the drastic change our apartment had undergone in those few seconds. It was appalling; the windows were shattered and hanging wide open, as was the front door; the shutters had come off their hinges and had been hurled into the yard. It was January, the middle of winter; it was raining and cold winds swept through the apartment. On top of it all, the entire area had no electricity.

I was badly affected by the Scud both physically and psychologically; the fear that gripped me literally rendered me paralyzed. There was no one to comfort me because my husband had his own problems and was in terrible pain from severe spinal problems. He needed complicated surgery but now was not the time to spend in hospital; we were exhausted, broken and badly in need of a rest. I went from room to room with a candle in my hand, looking for a place to lie down, but the apartment was full of broken glass; even the beds and other pieces of furniture were under a layer of debris. I was confused and didn't know where to begin. My self-confidence had gone and it was hard to believe I'd ever cope on my own with this devastation.

CHAPTER 20

Back to Korzec

In Israel I joined a Korzec Holocaust survivors organization that provides a forum for people like me to meet each other throughout the year, to discuss issues that relate to us all. Every year, on the eve of the *Shavuot* holiday, the anniversary of the big 1942 *Aktion* in which most of Korzec's Jews were murdered in Kozak Forest, we conduct a memorial service for our families and loved ones at the Volhynia Jewish community hall in the Givatayim branch of the International School for Holocaust Studies. We also hold memorial services in the Givatayim cemetery where we erected a monument in memory of the Korzec victims. During one of these gatherings, several fellow survivors mentioned their visits to our Ukrainian birthplace. Apparently, the area had changed completely and the mass graves in Kozak Forest had been desecrated. Kozak Forest, eight kilometers from the city of Korzec, is the burial place of my murdered family: my father. Wolf Rubinstein; my mother Idit; my sisters Nina, Raya, Liuba and Batya; my brother Efi; together with uncles, aunts, cousins and friends. I learned that members of my immediate family were killed on different dates and are therefore buried in different mass graves. Thus, the bones of my family are scattered throughout Kozak Forest.

After World War II, some of the locals who lived near the forest started to use this sacred site as a place on which to breed cattle and they allowed the animals to graze freely over the graves. Later, the area was used for growing vegetables and even wheat. Holocaust survivors whose relatives are buried in the forest appealed to those locals who desecrated the graves to relinquish the land soaked with Jewish blood. Finally, survivors living in the US, Canada and Israel raised a large sum of money to pay for the forest to be fenced in. The area was cleaned and large, beautiful headstones were erected.

In August 1995 our group organized a trip to the Ukraine to visit the site and see the renovations with our own eyes. My husband was in the hospital at the time and I had a rare opportunity to leave him for a few days in the care of the hospital staff and join the group. We were a very large group at the memorial in Kozak Forest and we invited local residents to join us. The Korzec mayor attended together with other high-level municipal staff. In addition, local officials from Rowne arrived, bringing with them a TV crew and a journalist. The forest was so crowded there was barely room to move, but no one left. This was a good opportunity to ask all those present to respect the sanctity of the cemetery by refraining from desecrating the monuments. Some of our members read their meticulously prepared speeches. Then, all together, we said *Kaddish*, the Jewish prayer for the dead. Someone played a tape recording of the Israeli national anthem, *Hatikva* and the group sang along, full of pride and pain; tears flowed like water. We placed flowers on the headstones and lit memorial candles.

However, when the group returned to the forest early the following morning, to be alone with our memories and to hold a religious memorial service for our families, we found none of the candles and flowers we had placed there just the day before.

The sugar factory still exists in Korzec, only a few kilometers from Szytna Forest in which the Germans and their Ukrainian henchman murdered 550 young Jewish males in 1941. The organization's committee erected large gravestones there as well. Our group conducted a memorial and candle-lighting service there and visited graves of other relatives who had been killed in that area. Aharon's Rowne family had been murdered by the Germans in Sosenki Forest, outside the city. The site, which we visited twice, is now clean and well-tended. On the site are one large and several smaller monuments in honor of the victims. But human bones are still scattered throughout and when I was there, a woman in the group who was born in Rowne was shocked to discover a baby's skull just beneath her feet. I joined her and we quickly collected a large pile of children's bones that we buried in a pit, while we cried bitter tears.

Many of Rowne's Jews were murdered alongside two large mass graves in dense forestry in the Kostopol area. The site is remote and difficult to find, yet the Rowne committee erected two large monuments on it. They told us that Holocaust survivors come to that site from all over the world to pay their respects. Bones are scattered throughout that forest and we saw many under the leaves of the trees.

After visiting the graves of the Jews I made my way to Korzec. I wanted to see with my own eyes where I had spent my youth. The city has changed beyond recognition. The town center where my father's store had stood, and which used to be the focus of action, no longer exists. Instead, there was a young, green tree and grass planted by the municipality. Our house was also gone. A park has replaced my grandmother's house.

Epilogue

My writing and the way I write is completely different from that of other writers. Usually a writer will choose his or her words carefully, select expressions and sayings, delete and polish the written draft, perhaps change the order. Whereas I go through hell in order to extract something of my terrible memories from the depths of my soul. The wounds have not healed; some of the lesions cannot be touched, let alone scratched. I am an old, abandoned mine that that must not be disturbed. The pain and suffering continues to exist inside, preventing me from using my memories, as I would wish. But I want the whole world to hear my screams, the shrieks of pain and terror of my brother and sisters, my parents, grandparents and the rest of my innocent relatives. I want the world to hear it with all its intensity, all its details and minutiae, without censoring my words. At the same time, however, I know I must not dig endlessly into the atrocity, because digging too deeply is likely to bring on additional calamity. Therefore, I will content myself with what I have succeeded in putting on paper. **The primary purpose of my writing was to create a monument for my family.**

Millions of Jews were trapped in the Nazi inferno, including me, my family and everyone dear to me. I am a living witness to the terrible period of despicable murder; I cannot explain how I managed to escape the inferno. True, I remained alive, but at what cost? Decades have passed since the Germans murdered my family and I still feel buried under the weight of the destruction. Memories of the Holocaust still haunt me like excruciatingly heavy boulders that I cannot escape. For three years I waged a cruel battle for my wretched life, yet in effect I continue the struggle to this very day. The mass murder of the Jews was not one event with a clearly defined ending; it was not like a single bomb that makes a loud boom and then the heavens clear afterwards. The passing years prove that the consequences and results of the Holocaust are ongoing occurrences that hold specific ramifications for me.

I am wounded in body and soul. I have remained totally alone, orphaned and bereaved. My heart is broken, as is my spirit. From my youth to my old age, I have remained penniless and very ill.

I have had the opportunity to hear people ask questions about the Holocaust of the Jewish people. People sometimes wonder what really happened between the lines; some ask, how can such deep hatred erupt for no reason; was this really blind hatred? How does everyone turn suddenly into antisemites? People who did not live under the Nazis are not capable of understanding how ordinary people collaborated so enthusiastically with the Nazis and abused the Jews to such an extent. I personally can testify that I know of no reason for the accumulation of such hatred towards the Jews, a hatred of a kind that did not exist before the occupation. All our troubles began when the world abandoned us, when were deemed subhuman and sent to our death, when our property became that of everyone but ourselves.

People fell on us like vultures on carrion, to build their wealth and happiness on our destruction. I suggest to anyone who is still skeptical, to view the movie about the trial of the Polish priest, Jerzy Popieluszko.[5] What connection can there

---

5   Jerzy Popieluszko was a Roman Catholic priest from Poland, associated with the Solidarity Union. He was murdered by three agents of the Polish Communist internal intelligence agency, Security Service of the Ministry of Internal Affairs.

be, you ask, between the abduction and murder of a Polish priest, and the genocide of the Jewish nation? The answer is simple: human nature does not change and there are always people who strive to exploit all circumstances in order to benefit personally, even resorting to the murder of their fellow man.

Annihilation of the Jews, in the scope with which it was carried out during the Holocaust, could not happen to a nation with its own state. The Holocaust could not have happened had the State of Israel existed then. Yes, a country can lose a war and suffer casualties, but nothing is equivalent to the genocide of the Jewish nation that had no homeland.

Most of the 'enlightened' world preferred to watch the unfolding of the Jewish tragedy with apathy and indifference. All my life I have been sensitive to the suffering of the persecuted without regard to race, nationality or religion. My compassion extends to all victims everywhere, despite the fact that no one cared when my people were led to death. It is a fact that none of us (the entire human race) was asked to be born and none of us can anticipate our fate and fortune in this world.

Yet, I personally can say that I chose my nation and people, the Jewish nation. The circumstances of my life were such that I could have decided to live out my life under my assumed identity, the identity that allowed me to survive the war years and not have to endure the anti-Semitism that continues to dance over the dead bodies of Jews. But I chose otherwise; I chose to return to my roots and re-adopt my Jewish identity out of my identification with the persecuted, all those who suffered only because of theirs. If there really is a God, as people believe, then He is the only one who is capable of judging genocide. There is no lack of testimony to the crimes committed by the Germans and their henchmen against the Jews, and their attempts to wipe us off the face of the earth. Yet, despite all the evidence, few of them were brought to judgment to suffer the consequences of their deeds. Moreover, recent years have seen the public emergence of Holocaust deniers, who attempt to trivialize the crime and even erase the enormous stain of blood left by the Jews in such a large part of the world. I hope they don't succeed.

I sit and write this beside my sick husband's bed; Aharon is in terrible pain. His entire family was murdered by the Germans in the Holocaust so I am the only one left to care for him. It pains me that I was in this world, but did not see it. I hope that it will be better for me in my next incarnation.

It is clear that with my sisters at my side, or my husband's large family, our lives would have been very different. In difficult moments human beings need support and help from devoted relatives who really care.

Someone gave me the poem below when my husband was dying. I don't know the author.

Give us health.
Give us a healthy throat to shout in pain,
A healthy heart to be heartsick.
Healthy eyes to see how dark it is.
And healthy teeth, to fall out.
Give us health.
Give us health to cry over what we lack,
Health to envy, health to complain,
A little bit of health for fears, for loneliness,
And even for despair—give us a little health.
Give us abundant health to be properly sick,
And another drop of health for the suffering,
And give us health to understand the simple fact
That we lived in vain and will also die in vain.
Give us health.

In May 1996 my husband died in hospital after being in a coma for a week. I did not post death announcements, but still he had a very large funeral. Many friends and acquaintances came from all over the country.

Now, for the first time in my life, I have time for myself. The problem is that there is no way to protect myself from the memories that attack me and take my thoughts back to events from which I run away, as from fire. There is not even a corner of my memories to hold on to without pain. The exaggerated, irrational altruism that has remained in me my entire life has caused me only pain and suffering. This cannot be changed; it is too deeply embedded in my personality.

For decades I have been carrying inside me the heavy baggage of the Holocaust that left me wounded in body and soul. I have struggled and made powerful but unsuccessful efforts to leave the destruction behind, to distance myself from my great tragedy. How sad it is to live in a wonderful world without the ability to enjoy it. The destruction was too great for me to build a new life and I have failed in everything I undertook.